robbiekeane
the biography

robbiekeane
the biography

andrew sleight

JOHN BLAKE

Published by John Blake Publishing Ltd,
3 Bramber Court, 2 Bramber Road,
London W14 9PB, England

www.blake.co.uk

First published in hardback in 2007

ISBN: 978-1-84454-332-8

British Library Cataloguing-in-Publication Data:

A catalogue record for this book is available from the British Library.

Design by www.envydesign.co.uk

Printed and bound in Great Britain by William Clowes Ltd, Beccles, Suffolk

1 3 5 7 9 10 8 6 4 2

Papers used by John Blake Publishing are natural, recyclable products made
from wood grown in sustainable forests. The manufacturing processes conform
to the environmental regulations of the country of origin.

Photographs © Getty Images P1,5,6,7,8,9,10,11,12,13,14
and Sportsfile P2,3,4,15,16

Prologue

'He spent years standing on the terraces. He is a genuine supporter who had a boyhood dream. A lot of people have that dream, but not many get to fulfil it. He has. This is the classic story of the fan who becomes a star. It is a remarkable story, but then, he is a remarkable young man.'

Mick McCarthy, 1999

B efore he reached 26, Robbie Keane had been awarded the Republic of Ireland's captaincy and also broken his country's goal-scoring record – not bad for a player that Sir Alex Ferguson apparently valued at just £500,000.

Now Keane has established himself as a supremely gifted footballer, bringing his unique brand of artistry to both the Premiership and the international stage. Not only is he worshipped in his native Ireland, but he is also adored wherever his spontaneous brilliance has taken him – from his two-goal debut for Wolves to his 22nd goal for his country in only his 55th senior international. Both unpredictable and committed out on the pitch, Keane is a free-spirited entertainer who has already left an indelible mark on the game he so clearly loves.

But it hasn't all been plain sailing for Keane. A lucrative move to Italian giants Inter Milan didn't work out and the subsequent switch to Leeds United left him frustrated and unable to do what he does best – score goals and entertain people. At times, his spell at Tottenham has also tested his unshakeable self-belief. Heralded on his arrival as the next Spurs great, Keane has had to fight to retain his place in the starting line-up, but he soon became Tottenham's vice-captain and chief attacking threat.

His famous cartwheel celebration has electrified crowds across the globe and Robbie Keane is now a fully fledged Premiership star. This is the story of how a remarkable footballer from Tallaght somersaulted his way into the hearts of millions of fans and made all his dreams come true.

Acknowledgements

I would like to acknowledge the support of everybody who has contributed to the book, including my parents, brothers and friends.

I would also like to express my gratitude to Robbie Keane's former managers, coaches and team-mates who very generously shared their memories and experiences of working with such a unique character and phenomenal talent.

Thanks also to the following people who helped to piece together Keane's fascinating career: Dan Clifford, Gabriele Marcotti and Tim White.

Thanks are also due to Nick Callow for providing me with such a rewarding project, and to Lucian Randall as well as the team at John Blake Publishing for their help and professionalism.

I also have to thank all like-minded souls who were in the Inn on the Green that memorable summer day in 2002 to watch the Republic of Ireland take on Germany – hopefully, their hangovers weren't nearly as bad as mine.

Finally, thanks to Robbie Keane himself. He is one footballer whose breathtaking genius makes the hugely inflated ticket prices in the Premiership worth every single penny. Hopefully, he has gained as much enjoyment from playing football as everyone has had watching him play. This is his story so far.

Contents

Prologue   **v**

Acknowledgements   **vi**

The Talent from Tallaght   **1**

A New Star in Old Gold   **17**

Glory in Green   **47**

Sky Blue Heaven   **67**

Baby Irish's Italian Adventure   **93**

To Elland Back   **117**

The Saviour of Seoul   **147**

Keane Earns his Spurs   **181**

The Entertainer   **211**

The Perfect Ten   **235**

Epilogue   **259**

chapter **one**

The Talent From Tallaght

'We had to fight for everything we had in the part of Dublin where we lived. Tallaght, it's called. But we had a strong family, a good family. I've never been shy. I've always enjoyed having a *craic* with the lads in the dressing room. In many ways I'm a typical Dubliner.'

Robbie Keane, 2006

Described as having the population of a city but the status of a village, Tallaght is a unique place in today's Republic of Ireland. Located on the south-west fringe of Dublin City, Tallaght was a tiny village, but, as Dublin's population swelled in the 1960s, the authorities decided to build more and more houses there. Soon Tallaght outgrew both Galway and Limerick in terms of population.

A solidly working-class area, Tallaght suffered greatly during the years of recession, the 1980s. High unemployment combined with poor transport links to leave an entire generation with very limited prospects. Fortunately, the area has improved significantly over the past decade, but the stigma of having so many social problems has stuck. It's tried to smarten up its act and improve both its amenities and reputation. But what the place really needed was a champion, a standard bearer for civic pride to put Tallaght

1

on the map for all the right reasons, so it's lucky that a charismatic footballer by the name of Robbie Keane came along at just the right time.

Robert David Keane was born on 8 July 1980 in Tallaght Hospital. He was the third of four children born to Robbie Snr and Ann. Both his parents had grown up in nearby Crumlin, then moved out further south to Tallaght once they were married, setting up home in Glenshane Grove in the Jobstown area.

Robbie was brought up in a happy and honest household with his sister Natasha (eight years older), brother Graham (four years older) and sister Amy (three years younger). The family home was always filled with music, often produced by his father who was a born entertainer and a popular figure in the local community. The front man of a band called Renegade, Robbie Snr was a regular on the pub circuit and well known locally for his singing – his tastes ranging from Bruce Springsteen and the Beatles to traditional Irish folk music.

Watching his father performing in front of crowds with effortless showmanship struck a chord with Robbie Jnr, although he wasn't always allowed to watch him sing. As he later told the *Irish Times*, 'If he was playing locally, maybe I'd have gone to see him, but when you're a kid you can't get into the pubs. Anyway you'd be sick of hearing him in the house!'

Young Robbie developed his own love for music and learned to play the guitar, a skill which earned him the nickname BB Keane from the Irish press while on tour with the Republic of Ireland Under-18s. As a kid he sang for his own enjoyment, but his great love affair was with a football. As a passionate Liverpool fan, he worshipped the likes of Ian

The Talent From Tallaght

Rush and John Aldridge, dreaming that one day he would follow in their footsteps by playing in England.

Keane revealed his boyhood love for the Reds of Anfield to the *Independent*: 'I wasn't just a fan, more a fanatic. I had posters all over the walls, bedsheets, everything.'

His maternal grandfather, Thomas Nolan, had been a talented footballer in his day with St Agnes in Crumlin and made an eerily accurate observation about Robbie Jnr's soccer skills – even though his grandson was barely a toddler at the time.

Robbie's mother told the *Daily Mirror*, 'Dad was a brilliant footballer and he played until he was 50. Robbie walked at nine months and was playing with a football when he was one. I remember my father saying to me, "If God spares me, that young fella is going to be a brilliant footballer." I remember asking him why and he told me, "He kicks with both feet."

'Ever since Robbie could walk he's been playing with a ball. He was always mad about football. My dad went to see all Robbie's matches. He used to cycle around to them. He would have travelled the length and breadth of the world to see him. He worked in CIE [an Irish travel group] and had a travel pass for the boats when he retired, so he would have always been over and back. My father died when Robbie was 14, so he never got to see him playing in England.'

But Thomas Nolan's sporting genes were passed down and two of his grandsons later went on to represent the national team – namely Robbie and Jason Byrne.

Fortunately for Robbie's burgeoning talent, there were hundreds of like-minded souls on his estate who lived and breathed football, too, and would join him for a kick-about as often as possible. Tallaght was a hotbed of young Irish talent, all of whom had honed their skills in the parks and streets of the area. The loosely arranged matches weren't leisurely strolls designed to kill time by neighbourhood kids. They were the be-all and end-all of many young lives.

A scrap of wasteground would suddenly be transformed into Lansdowne Road as the youngsters tried out new skills and re-enacted the feats of their heroes – particularly in the summers when the 1990 and 1994 World Cup were being played and everyone was swept away on a tidal wave of football fever. When David O'Leary struck the decisive penalty in the Republic of Ireland's shoot-out win over Romania in Genoa, Robbie was being babysat by his brother. Overcome with excitement, they raced out into the street to celebrate. It was a turning point in his life. During the tournament, Robbie fell head over heels in love with football and found a new use for his pocket money.

He recalled, 'I first remember following the Irish team coming up to the 1990 World Cup when me and my brother used to collect the stickers in the Italia 90 album. Mick McCarthy and Packie Bonner were two of the biggest names.'

Two streets away, a burly young lad called Richie Dunne was taking his first steps towards making the grade, while on the same estate his school friend, Jason Gavin, was also making waves on the football field. To underline the quality of footballer coming out of the area back then, when the Republic of Ireland won the UEFA Under-18 championships in Cyprus in 1998, eight of the 18-man squad came from either Tallaght or Crumlin.

The place was teeming with gifted players and the backstreets and fields of south-west Dublin turned into a production line for the next generation of Irish talent. But, in a sea of up-and-coming football talent, everybody was starting to sit up and take notice of a small skinny boy with phenomenal ability and eye-catching balance: the legend of 'Whacker' – Keane's childhood nickname – was born.

When he wasn't spending hours with a ball at his feet, Robbie attended St Aidan's Community School, but he has since openly admitted that he wasn't a particularly attentive student during his time there. Keane confessed in an interview with the *Irish Times*, 'I wasn't interested in school, [I was] always just there for the football and the Gaelic, played everything just to get half days. I never concentrated in school. I could never concentrate; I was always getting other people to help me out. I'd come home and then I'd be out playing football on the street. That's how I grew up.'

St Aidan's Vice Principal Frank Moran tells a slightly different version of his famous ex-pupil's time at the school. 'He was a tremendous young lad and not a bad student. He stayed with us until his Junior Certs and by then the soccer scouts were already queuing up for his signature. His talent shone through from an early age – he was small but had lightning pace and was a wizard with the ball. His goals for the school team won us the Leinster Schools' Championship – he could do things with the ball to make your jaw drop.

'We are intensely proud, as is St Aidan's Primary, who have an annual sports achievement award in his honour. One thing I will say about Robbie is that you can't fault his loyalty to his friends, to his area and to his school. He has visited us countless times but the kids never get sick of seeing him – he is a real inspiration. And he is a modest lad who keeps himself to himself. When he visits his parents Robbie and Anne, he likes a quiet drink in Molly's Bar – he is a real hero.'

Robbie Keane

But homework always took a back seat as Robbie developed his own preferred form of education – mastery of a football. For hours, 'Whacker' would practise his skills, perfecting the art of turning past an opponent – the bigger the defender, the bigger the thrill when he succeeded. If he had no one else to play with, then he would revert to one of his first loves – juggling the ball. He soon realised that his own natural knack for keeping the ball up, which stemmed from his phenomenal combination of balance and co-ordination, was a special gift.

But he worked hard to polish all his skills and, as a self-confessed perfectionist, he never stopped practising until he was satisfied he had mastered a particular trick or exercise. Keane told the *Independent* about his hunger for football as a child. 'When I came home from school, it was bag straight down, uniform still on and out until I got a call for me dinner. Then it would be straight back out again until it was time to go to bed. I love football, you know. It's a joy to play.'

While his peers struggled to keep hold of the ball during lunchtime games on the playground, Keane would hang on to it until he became exhausted, or one of the bigger lads shoved him off balance. Like his father, Robbie Snr, Keane loved being centre stage, doing something he really enjoyed and receiving praise for it. In Robbie's mind, there was no bigger buzz than that and he intended making use of his bag of tricks to take him as far as possible.

Keane later explained that he taught himself to play on the fields of Tallaght and, more than a decade later, he felt he had stayed true to his own natural game. He said, 'Football is my life. I play football as I played in the park back home. Of course it's different now, but I like to express myself and enjoy my football. I've always done that since I was a kid. The way I play hasn't really changed. That's the way I am.'

Robbie was confident that he could eventually make a living from the game, but some teenagers from the area ended up going off the rails. 'It was a very tough area and you had to be able to look after yourself. I was a tough little kid and had a few fights,' Robbie said. 'There was a lot of car stealing and crime, but my upbringing made me a strong person. It was difficult to keep out of that way of life because it was all around, but, although I was not that clever at school, I was very streetwise and never fell in with the wrong crowd. I had a strong family behind me. I've been lucky enough to be given a chance to do something I love and get well paid for it. Because of that, I've looked after my family well and bought them houses, including my brother and sister.

'My parents did so much for me. They always tried to get the best football boots even though they didn't have a lot of money. It was hard for them because sometimes they couldn't afford what I wanted, but they tried and that meant a lot.'

Robbie started playing organised football when he was nine, joining the local youth-club team, Fettercairn. Despite later becoming the greatest striker in the history of the Republic of Ireland, Keane was slight and tiny for his age and was picked to play at right-back – he still ended up being the team's top scorer. But once his uncle Noel Byrne, father of future Shelbourne and Republic of Ireland international striker Jason, took over coaching the team, there was only one position for young Robbie – up front in attack.

Robbie Keane

Byrne was a football man through and through. He had married the sister of Robbie's mum, Ann, and immediately recognised that his nephew was something special when in possession of a football – nobody could take it off him. Robbie responded with a bucket-load of goals. In fact, his form spearheading Fettercairn's attack was so impressive that, after two goal-laden seasons, he was forced into his first career move when he transferred to Crumlin United.

Crumlin United's home ground was a few miles from the Glenshane estate, but Robbie realised that it was the logical step for him if he wanted to be watched by scouts from the big English clubs. His worst fear was that, if he stayed on at Fettercairn, then he would be left on the shelf and his dream of playing in the English top flight would be shattered.

'I played there for three years and went to play for Crumlin when I was 12,' he told the *Irish Times*. 'I wanted to play for a bigger team; no disrespect, but no scouts were going to watch me playing for Fettercairn. Ma and Da's family are from Crumlin, so there was some mini-leagues going on and me mam knew some of the people.'

In fact, Crumlin was far from unfamiliar territory for young Robbie because he had plenty of aunts, uncles and cousins in the area. United was a home from home. The club, which formed in 1967, was famous for producing players who went on to carve out successful careers 'across the water'. It was also the place where a certain Brian Kerr began his coaching career a year later, in 1968, as an eager 15-year-old. Kerr was actually a founder member of the club and he knew Tallaght well. He understood why so many talented players emerged from the area during the mid-1990s – they took in football with their mother's milk.

Kerr said, 'Tallaght is a strong working-class area. The

fathers of those lads would have moved out from areas like Inchicore, Drimnagh, Crumlin and Walkinstown. They would have been working-class soccer people who were involved in football themselves. There wasn't much else for the kids to do apart from play street football. It is unusual that so many players came from the same area at the same time, but they had a real hunger and passion for the game. All around the world, the top players come from areas like that.

'Teams became organised and then players, who started off with small local teams like St Marks, Fettercairn, Newtown Rangers and St Maelruans moved on and were spotted. The likes of Robbie and Jason Gavin played locally and then went to Crumlin, while Richard Dunne went to Home Farm. As in most places, soccer was the street game and most of those lads would have played full time on the street and then gone on to better things.'

In the age group two years above Robbie at Crumlin United were defender Alan Mahon, who went on to pick up two caps at senior level, and striker Michael Cummins. Both were offered apprenticeships by English clubs and that was all the motivation the ambitious young Keane needed. His elder brother Graham and cousin Jason – who both later turned out for St Colmcille's – also joined Crumlin, while his neighbour and school friend from Glenshane, Jason Gavin, four months older than Robbie, joined the same team on the recommendation of his tiny pal.

In 2006, Jason recalled, 'I've known Robbie since the age of 11 or 12 and we have always been good mates. Originally his family were from Crumlin and I met him at school and he invited me down to play for the team.'

Jason was a stylish central defender who was courted by

scouts from Newcastle, Everton and Middlesbrough. He opted to join the Teesside club because they had a sizeable Irish contingent and eventually went on to play first-team football at the Riverside. Several childhood friends from the neighbourhood – including Richie Dunne – would later reunite in the green shirt of the Republic of Ireland's revered Under-18 side which made history in the Cyprus sunshine in 1998. But it was at Crumlin where Robbie first earned money from the game he loved – he was paid 50p for every goal he scored. The financial gains were immaterial, though. All he wanted was to play football and match the lofty standards he set himself for every game he took part in.

In 2000, Crumlin United coach Martin Loughran told the *Daily Mirror* about the junior club's greatest ever signing. 'He signed for us as an Under-11 player. Larry Fox and Jimmy Loughran were in charge of the team at the time, and it was a good side. Robbie was good, but nobody thought he was going to be that good.'

Robbie and Jason Gavin weren't the only rising stars in the team, however – it was crammed with future professionals who would go on to represent the Republic of Ireland at youth level. In goal was Dean Delaney, who won the FA Youth Cup with Everton and played for Port Vale before joining Shelbourne, while defender Brian McGovern represented Arsenal, QPR and Norwich prior to ending up at Bray Wanderers. There was also Sean Mannion, who spent two years at Stockport County. Loughran added, 'That side went on to win two All-Irelands, two Leagues and two League Cups before Robbie left at Under-16 level.'

Even then, Robbie stood out as an outstanding prospect and his knack of scoring goals regularly soon became legend in Dublin football circles. Loughran remembered, 'In the

The Talent From Tallaght

Under-16 Premier Division he scored 60 goals and the team won the league that season – it really was a phenomenal total at that standard. Everywhere he went, he was expected to score goals. All he wanted to do was play with the ball and that was fine because at that age that's what we encourage them to do. The physical side of things is brought in gradually.'

But his small build and lack of inches suggested he might miss the boat when the English clubs spread their nets in search of fresh Irish talent. Loughran said, 'Back then, he might have been seen as too slight to play at the top because he didn't make the Kennedy Cup squad, and he didn't represent Ireland at Under-15 level. Actually, he only made his debut at Under-16 level due to a stroke of luck. Thirty-two players were named in a provisional squad for a trip to Austria and, when it was reduced to the final panel of 22, Robbie was left out. They were flying out on a Sunday, but on the previous Wednesday one of the selected strikers pulled out with an injury. Robbie was called up and scored on his debut against Austria.'

Around this time, Robbie began to despair, as he later told the *Independent*: 'When I was younger, before I was 15, I got overlooked. A lot of people – scouts, people from the Irish team – said I was too small, too weak. I never played for the Irish team until I went to the Under-16 tournament in Austria. It was my first call-up and it was only because someone got injured. Every week I was playing for Crumlin United and I was top scorer in the whole league – and I still never got picked.'

Whoever had decided on that incentive of 50p-a-goal was left horribly out of pocket as Robbie plundered a phenomenal number of goals, prompting concrete interest from three famous English clubs – West Ham United, Nottingham Forest and Wolverhampton Wanderers.

Keane told the *Irish Examiner*, 'West Ham United were the first club on to me when I was 14 and I went for a week's trial. Then Nottingham Forest and Wolves came calling. I went over to all three, but, when I did not hear anything back from West Ham, that narrowed it down to two clubs. I couldn't believe that a club like Wolves who were outside the Premiership could have such a massive stadium as Molineux. I must admit that I felt I had a better chance of making it at a club like Wolves, though, and they really made me feel at home.'

Five years earlier, Nottingham Forest had signed another promising young Irishman with the surname Keane for £10,000 from Cobh Ramblers. Roy Keane went on to become their best player, before joining Manchester United for a record British transfer fee of £3.75 million. Forest's scouting network in Ireland was then ordered to find the next great talent on the Irish football scene and Forest swiftly earmarked Robbie Keane as just that. But, in between, the scout that had recommended Roy to Forest, Noel McCabe, had let Robbie's beloved Liverpool know about the lively young striker with an eye for goal, and so the schoolboy left Tallaght to see what his favourite team could offer.

As Keane later told the *Sunday Mirror*, 'I was over at Anfield for a week and got to meet all the players I had worshipped on the telly, people like Ian Rush and Robbie Fowler. Everybody at the club was nice to me, but I still didn't accept when they asked me to sign. Somehow, I had this feeling that it would be better to build my career elsewhere. That's not to say that I wouldn't go back to

The Talent From Tallaght

Liverpool at some point in the future if I got the chance, but Anfield just wasn't for me at that particular time. My dad told me that just because I supported Liverpool didn't mean that I had to sign for them – and he was right.'

Despite their Premiership status and reputation for bringing through young Irish talent, Forest were gazumped in the race to sign Robbie by a club that was often described as a 'sleeping giant' – Wolverhampton Wanderers. Four decades earlier, Wolves had been the dominant force in British football, before almost sliding into oblivion after a catastrophic period in the 1980s. Wolves had climbed back out of the doldrums with fans' favourite Steve Bull contributing most of the goals, and the club were now in English soccer's second tier, threatening to get back into the big time. The club's ambitious nature and huge potential appealed to young Robbie Keane and the seeds were sown for a brief but memorable association.

Eddie Corcoran, who later became the logistical co-ordinator for the Republic of Ireland senior squad, had first spotted the schoolboy Robbie Keane when he was 14 and recommended him to Wolves. The experienced scout later admitted that he had stumbled across Robbie purely by chance and initially thought the striker might not be big enough to make the grade.

Eddie explained, 'It didn't happen all at once. Jack Bermingham, who is with me at Coventry, and myself were just down watching the Crumlin Under-13s. It was a routine visit. Crumlin were a successful side at that level and there were plenty of good players in the team, like Robbie and Jason Gavin. Robbie was quick off the mark, but he certainly wasn't big. I remember thinking that, if he started growing a bit, he might have a chance of making it. But we continued to monitor his progress and, by the time he was playing in the Under-14s, everyone was watching him and the team. Jack and myself kept going down to have a look.'

When Nottingham Forest, Everton, Liverpool and West Ham started to show an interest in the slightly built boy wonder, Corcoran told Wolves they could not afford to miss out on such a promising talent. 'To look at, there didn't seem to be anything extraordinary about him,' said Corcoran, 'but he did have a good football brain and I thought he would do well if he got stronger. But I would say that most of the clubs probably did have a look at him and decided he wasn't strong enough, or whatever.'

That was when Robbie first came into contact with a man who would later play a huge role in shaping his career – Wolves youth-team coach Chris Evans. An articulate Welshman, Evans was passionate about identifying potential in young players and then helping them to fulfil their promise.

Evans, now Wanderers' Academy director, recalled, 'Robbie Keane was picked out by our scouting network in the Republic of Ireland. Robbie came and visited us as a schoolboy when he was 14 years of age. He came over during school holidays to train with us. In his Under-16 year, when he was close to leaving school, his profile in Ireland rose as he scored more goals. Several other clubs came in for him. In particular, he was courted by Nottingham Forest, who offered him an apprenticeship. But I had built up a particularly good relationship with Robbie and his parents. I was very keen that he joined us at Wolverhampton Wanderers.

'I flew out to his home in Tallaght and persuaded him to sign. He had turned down many other clubs – Liverpool,

The Talent From Tallaght

Everton, Nottingham Forest and Newcastle. He was regarded by some as being too small, but we thought that his football brain more than made up for that. We sold him the club based on the fact that, as I told his mother and father, he would be given a greater opportunity to play in our first team early. I also made a pledge to his mother and father that, if he did come into my care, I would always look after him and not let him down. Likewise, I wanted his parents to share in his development which they did.'

Robbie had a gut feeling that the offer from Wolves was right for him, but he still stalled over making a final decision as he weighed up the pros and cons. The 15-year-old had taken a day off school to discuss the move with Wolves' officials and was hanging around the house, while his mother, Ann, fervently cleaned and polished everything in sight as the family waited for the men from Molineux.

Robbie recalled, 'Eddie came to the house with Rob Kelly and Chris Evans. They arrived in a big black car. Me mother is looking out, and next thing she's in a panic. Is the place clean enough? They asked me to sign. I knew it was definitely Wolves for me, but I said to them that I'd think about it. "Just give me a few weeks to think about it." I could have signed for Liverpool, but Mam said, "Don't sign for Liverpool just because you followed them," and it was good advice. When they came, I knew it was Wolves, but I didn't want to rush into it and regret it later. I signed a couple of weeks later and went over just before I turned 16 on 4 July, Independence Day. I turned 16 on 8 July.'

Evans later said that Wolves feared they would lose Keane to Forest – that was after spotting the Tallaght schoolboy at the City Ground on television. 'We were really keen to snap him up, but then we saw him – during a televised game –

standing in the tunnel at a Nottingham Forest game, talking to all their players.

'So we flew over to Robbie's home that September day, met up with his parents – Robbie Snr and Ann – and promised them we would take good care of Robbie. In return, he pledged his future to us and he was as good as his word, signing a contract the following July on his 16th birthday.'

After a handshake, Robbie Keane signed for Wolverhampton Wanderers, taking a giant step on the path towards greatness.

chapter two

A New Star in Old Gold

'Robbie always stood out and I think the difference between a good player and a great player is incredible self-belief. Robbie always had that. I played with Ossie Ardiles and Glenn Hoddle at Tottenham and they both had it. I think that is the difference. You have to have the ability to back it up, but all of those players had it without being bolshie and using it the wrong way.'

Ex-Wolves manager Colin Lee in 2006

As he waited on the plane for the short flight over to England from Dublin, Robbie felt both anxious and excited ahead of a journey that would determine whether or not he could live out his lifelong dream of playing professional football. He flew over with two other Dublin teenagers, Alan Dixon and Stephen Hackett, the latter also hailing from Tallaght, with only one thing on his mind – to make an impact at the club and not get sent home.

To begin with, Robbie felt homesick, missing the Irish way of life and longing to see his large extended family back in Crumlin and Tallaght. His mum Ann is part of a big family and Robbie was used to seeing familiar faces all around him. In Wolverhampton, everything seemed 'foreign', but he was level-headed enough to know he would have to make sacrifices to fulfil his ambitions.

Chris Evans immediately pulled out all the stops to make

Robbie Keane

Robbie feel at home. Robbie and Stephen were well looked after in Josie Edwards's digs in Willenhall not far from Wolverhampton, so they were able to concentrate on developing their game and enjoying their football. Robbie enjoyed life in his digs so much that he stayed on after becoming an established first-team player. That was before he moved to a house in Priorslee, near Telford.

He said, 'I'll not be tempted to live away, not yet anyway. I know there's nothing better than a friendly family for me. Josie's a brilliant cook and friend, and I love the way she does chicken.'

Two other Irish lads, Keith Andrews and Seamus Crowe, joined him at the club the following week and Robbie was helped to settle in by another Dubliner, Glenn Crowe, who was two years older and from Whitechapel, Clonsilla, on the west side of the city. Even with so many other Irish lads at the club, Robbie still felt strong pangs of homesickness, but eventually learned to overcome this and enjoy his new life in England.

In the summer of 1998, Keane told the *Irish Examiner*, 'I did feel a little homesick at the start and I still have my bad days over there, but the gaffer let me home six times last season and that's not a bad return.'

Wolves did everything imaginable to make Robbie feel valued, emphasising their belief in the skinny striker by offering him two improved deals in his first two seasons as a professional. 'I got a good contract when I went to Wolves. I got a four-year contract. Next year, that was ripped up and they gave me another. I signed four contracts in two years at Wolves. I was quite clued in as a young fella, needed a bit of advice, but knew what I was doing.'

One former Wolves youth-team player who remembered

the immediate impression the Irish teenager made at the club was defender Robert Sawyers, who was a year older. 'I remember when he first came over we played Nottingham Forest youth team,' he said. 'He was only a little lad with a small build. He came on as substitute at half-time and he was absolutely amazing. His first touch was unbelievable. Everyone left the ground talking about him, but at that point we weren't sure whether it was a one-off. Then, when he came to the club on a full-time basis and training every day, some of the things he did were unbelievable. I knew that he would make his debut before his YTS had finished and he did the year after I left the club. He was so talented – he was brilliant.'

Despite standing head and shoulders above the rest of the youth team in terms of ability, Robert remembers Robbie as a young man who left his extrovert streak on the pitch, remaining quiet and modest off it. Robert said, 'He did struggle a little bit to begin with and maybe he was homesick. But there were a few other Irish lads about as well which helped him settle in quite quickly. To be fair, everyone at Wolves was sound and did everything they could to make you feel comfortable. To speak to him, he was a sound lad and, even though he was loved at Wolves, he was never big-headed.'

Keane's emergence as such an outstanding prospect had a knock-on effect for fellow Dubliner Glenn Crowe's stay at Molineux – it led to the striker being released. Fortunately, Crowe managed to rebuild his career after the disappointment of leaving Wolves and, after forming a forward partnership with Keane's cousin Jason Byrne at Shelbourne, he was later called up into the Republic of Ireland squad.

Robbie Keane

Robert said, 'I was good mates with Glenn Crowe as well and I was gutted that Glenn went. But it turned out the club let him go because they had Robbie coming through. For his age, what Robbie was doing was out of this world and Wolves wanted to push him through.'

After training, Robbie and the other YTS lads would meet up around Wolverhampton or go to each other's digs – Robbie would do anything to relax and keep his mind off what he could be missing out on back in Tallaght.

Robert remembered what the teenagers used to get up to at the end of the training sessions. 'We'd often meet up in the evenings and play pool or go to the cinema. We'd often just go over to each other's digs and play football on the computer. Wolves made sure that every young player settled in quickly.'

Keane immediately set himself ambitious targets and he was given an added incentive by one of the senior strikers on the club's books, Don Goodman. As Keane later told the *Irish Times*, 'I remember Don Goodman took me and another chap, Mark Jones, the other striker, aside and said, "50 quid for the top goal-scorer." Well, when you're that age, 50 quid is big. It's still a good bit of money. I scored 38, managed to beat him by about 12.'

When he returned to Wolves for the start of the pre-season ahead of the 1997/98 campaign, Keane had just turned 17 and felt sharper than ever. More importantly, he now felt settled at the club and, as a result, his confidence began to grow. At that point, first-team football still seemed a long way off. Robbie had only started two reserve games the previous year, so he was willing to bide his time and wait for his chance to shine. But Wolves boss, Mark McGhee, wasn't that patient when it came to fast-tracking his brightest young talent – although the fact he had a ready-made superstar at his disposal came as a surprise. McGhee recalled, 'As a manager, you wander over and have a look at the youth team, and in the first few days they were back for pre-season I did just that. Robbie looked a different class to the players he was with, so I said we'd take him in the first team's training session and again he just looked a different class – he was the best player. So we then decided we were going to take him to Scotland and we gave him bits of games and again he looked our best player.'

Robbie was given the call-up and travelled north of the border with the first-team squad up to Scotland and not only did the slightly built youngster hit the ground running in senior football, but he stole the show.

Keane later told the *Irish Times*, 'Then I got taken and put into the first team. They seemed to like me. I went to Scotland on pre-season and played against Dundee United and Stirling. An hour against Dundee, then Stirling, and I think I scored in both and got given the nod to play against Norwich.'

McGhee believes he had no choice but to give Keane a chance. 'The thing that stood out was his ability to keep possession. Seasoned defenders were unable to get near him because he moved the ball too quickly; he could see things early and he could finish. By the time we got to the Norwich game, it seemed the obvious thing to do – even though he was only 17, we had to play him.'

But Keane felt indebted to his first boss in senior football and later told the *Daily Mirror*, 'It was such a huge bonus when Mark McGhee told me that I was in the first team for a pre-season game. After that, I was on my way and things just kept happening. He's been great for me and I owe him everything. He took a chance on me in the first place and I'd like to think I didn't let him down.'

The whole coaching staff were hugely impressed by Keane's ability to retain possession and improvise in tight situations, most notably Wolves assistant manager, Colin Lee. Lee remembers the big dilemma concerning Keane was where exactly to play the impish teenager.

Lee said, 'We established a role for him on a pre-season tour of Scotland when we felt he wasn't quite strong enough yet to play up front and yet he wasn't athletic enough, in terms of his development, to play in midfield. So we found him a role just behind the striker and that is where we played him initially. He wasn't a wide player and he wasn't quite ready to play up front. At one stage, we thought of playing him in an advanced midfield role, but in the end we decided to play him in between.

'Robbie has the intelligence to do that and, if you watch him play now, he still drifts back into that area and is able to play as a midfield player as well. He is able to create opportunities for others and still get into the box himself. I think it was the right decision. If we had stuck him up front initially, I think it would have been too much for him at that stage in his development.'

For the curtain-raiser of Wolves' Division One season, Keane was given the nod to start in a role just behind the strikers and he was buzzing with excitement at the prospect of playing against Norwich at Carrow Road. Chris Evans was thrilled, too, at Keane's rapid promotion into the starting line-up and he pulled out all the stops to ensure that Robbie Snr and Ann Keane were there to see their son make his first-team debut.

Evans recalled, 'It was unheard of that happening to a

youth-team player. I asked Mark McGhee whether it would be OK if I secretly flew in his mother and father. He said it would be all right just as long as nobody got hold of it because he didn't want Norwich to know who he was going to play. So Robbie's parents were flown into London and chauffeured to the match where they saw him score two goals on his debut. His mother and father, who were sat next to Mark McGhee's wife in the directors' box, were delighted and I recall, when Robbie scored his goals, Robbie Snr shouted out, "That's my boy!" It really was *Roy of the Rovers* stuff. Robbie Keane's career had well and truly started.'

Keane played without fear and ran the show with two outstanding goals – a dipping volley followed by a smart finish after a spellbinding run. In the process, Keane wrote himself into the club's record books as the first player to score two on his Wolves debut since Ted Farmer in 1960. But Keane didn't celebrate too loudly after his groundbreaking beginning. As he later told the *Irish Times*, 'Wolves flew the family across and I was lucky enough to score two goals in my first professional game. We went back to me mam's hotel afterwards, but that was it. Just went to bed early.'

McGhee had unleashed his secret weapon and the expectation level soared among Wolves fans – could the club that dominated the old First Division of the 1950s return to the top flight again? Playing in 'the hole' behind the experienced forward pairing of Steve Bull and Don Goodman, Keane flourished with so much freedom to roam and McGhee told him to express himself out on the pitch. Robbie was never cut out to play a conventional role within a rigid team structure and he took his season's tally to four with two more in a comfortable 4–2 win against Bury.

Another Wolves striker scored a double in that match,

fans' favourite Steve Bull, who was a mere 15 years older than his fellow goal-scorer. Bull – nicknamed the 'Tipton Skinhead' – had been at Wolves for over a decade and provided hundreds of goals to take the club from the brink of relegation into the Conference to the verge of gaining promotion to the Premiership. Worshipped by the club's supporters, Bull was the undisputed 'King of Molineux', but now there was a fresh-faced contender for his crown, Robbie Keane. Then 32 years old, Bull had featured in England's successful 1990 World Cup campaign and thought he had seen it all in an eventful career – until an excited teenager from Tallaght turned up alongside him in Wolves' first team.

Bull recalled, 'He was different class, a young up-and-coming player and he was a bit cheeky, to be fair. He had to have the odd squeeze every now and again to bring him back down. But I think he proved to everybody at Wolves that he was worth the money he went for in the end.'

But Robbie's unpredictable approach play and individual trickery at first left Bull, even with his grade-two shaven head, pulling his hair out. 'My first impression of Robbie was that he left me feeling frustrated. He was one of these tricky players who does 10 skills, but only one comes off. So I'd be in the box for the other nine and the ball would never reach me. Then, the one time the ball did get there, I wouldn't be there to score, so it was a frustrating time.'

When this continued to happen, Bull, the top dog at Wolves, gave his junior colleague a rollicking on the pitch to try to make the Irish kid mend his ways. But this ploy didn't work because Robbie struggled to understand Bull's strong Black Country accent. 'I used to have a go at him to begin with, but he couldn't understand me,' remembered

Bull. 'But, as the games went on, we got to know each other and I knew where he was and where he'd put the ball. That was it – we just clicked.'

There were several other big names in a star-studded Wolves team, including Mark Atkins, who had won the Premier League title with Blackburn, former England internationals Tony Daley and Keith Curle and also Steve Sedgley, who had won the FA Cup with Tottenham. Sedgley had played alongside the legendary Paul Gascoigne during his time at White Hart Lane, so he knew talent when he saw it and he instantly admired Keane's unique repertoire of tricks.

Sedgley recalled, 'Obviously they were different types of players, but I would say they are both match-winners in their own right. I knew Robbie was a special talent straight away – he had everything. He was quick, had unbelievable ability and an eye for goal. Robbie had the full range in his bag of tricks, but it wasn't just about that. Like Gazza, it was his attitude towards training that always stood out – he just loved his football. You always had to drag him off the training pitch because he was always looking to learn. That is the sign of a good player.'

Robbie then went off to represent the Republic of Ireland youth side, before returning to Wolves to face promotion favourites Middlesbrough at Molineux. In front of a bumper crowd of 26,896, Keane faced a Boro side that contained the likes of former Republic of Ireland captain Andy Townsend, Paul Merson and Emerson, but Robbie upstaged them all by scoring the winner.

He conjured up a precise lob to beat Boro keeper Mark Schwarzer to keep Wolves' play-off hopes alive in the November chill. Robbie then followed that goal up with another well-taken finish against Ipswich in a 1–1 draw, so by Christmas 1997 the teenager had clocked up six goals in his first four months of professional football – an ideal present for under-fire boss Mark McGhee.

After New Year, Robbie began to find playing week-in, week-out physically exhausting. As a result, he was rested by McGhee because nobody wanted to see the team's best individual talent burn out before he had turned 18 – least of all his manager.

McGhee recalled, 'Towards the end of his first season Robbie had started to run out of energy simply because we had asked so much of him. Perhaps we had asked too much really because he was practically carrying the team. Physically he got tired, but mentally there were never any problems for him.'

Robbie continued to haunt Norwich, though, and he scored the opening goal in the return fixture against the Norfolk club – a 5–0 mauling at Molineux. His goal tally in January extended to two after he popped up with a smart finish in a 3–1 win at Bury, showing sharpness and composure against physical opposition. At this point, opposing teams' managers were trying to suss out how to nullify the attacking threat of Keane because not only was he lethal in front of the target, but he was also creating lots of chances for his team-mates. Operating in that deep-lying forward role meant that Keane was difficult to pick up – until opponents assigned players specifically to mark him all over the pitch.

Colin Lee remembers how the coaching staff tried to aid Robbie's development as a footballer and also how they attempted to protect him from over-exposure. Lee recalled, 'Like all young players, Robbie went through periods of good form and poor form. Getting the balance right was very important – when to play him, when to leave him out. We had to do that carefully because all the supporters wanted Robbie Keane to play every game. But we realised that a young player like him couldn't play every game. Unfortunately, when you haven't got enough players within a squad, it takes a strong manager to make those decisions because they've got to do what is best for the team. But with a highly talented individual, you've got to know how to develop that player and we had to do that with Robbie.'

With his impish style of play, Robbie rapidly became the darling of the Molineux crowd. Always happy to throw caution to the wind, Keane played without fear and brought the crowd to its feet.

In February, Robbie was called up into the Republic of Ireland's B side for a friendly match against Northern Ireland. Alongside a young Damien Duff, the team lost 1–0, but this led to Robbie being considered for the next full international squad. Robbie refused to get carried away with the heady heights of playing on the international stage because he knew he had a job to do – scoring goals for Wolves.

Later that month, Robbie got his first taste of playing against Premiership opposition when Wolves faced Wimbledon in an FA Cup fifth-round replay. He had missed the first game at Selhurst Park, but Mark McGhee had no hesitation in throwing him back into the starting line-up for the high-profile match. Wolves progressed through to the last eight of the competition with a late Dougie Freedman goal securing a 2–1 win, but Keane didn't exactly cover himself in glory. Frustration boiled over and Keane saw his name scribbled in referee Uriah Rennie's notebook – only the second caution of his senior career.

Robbie Keane

Nevertheless, Wolves had made it through to the quarter-final stage where they faced red-hot favourites Leeds United at Elland Road. The romance of the FA Cup appealed to Robbie, but he had to make do with a place on the bench as Wolves took on high-flying Leeds. Robbie was introduced into the white-hot atmosphere with only 12 minutes remaining and had an almost immediate impact when, four minutes later, Don Goodman turned his marker, Robert Molenaar, and scored a dramatic goal.

An upset was in the offing. Mark McGhee hollered from the touchline to get plenty of Old Gold shirts behind the ball in order to close the game down and book a semi-final spot. Robbie was listening and moved back into defence to help keep Leeds out, but his inexperience was exploited by the know-how of Jimmy Floyd Hasselbaink. A mistimed tackle from Keane may have produced minimal contact with Hasselbaink inside the area, but referee Paul Durkin gave over 30,000 Leeds fans something to cheer about by awarding an 88th-minute penalty to the home side. Hasselbaink took the resultant kick, but Wolves keeper, Hans Segers, guessed correctly and expertly palmed away his Dutch compatriot's spot-kick to send Wolves into the last four of the world's most famous domestic cup competition.

Giving away a penalty in such high-profile circumstances would test anyone's confidence, but Robbie's unshakeable self-belief was still intact as he made amends for his error with the winning goal against Crewe seven days later.

In March, Robbie again wrote himself into the record books when he became the second-youngest player ever to represent the Republic of Ireland in a senior international. Boss Mick McCarthy couldn't ignore the effervescent young star with the burgeoning reputation and brought him on just after half-time in a 2–1 friendly defeat at the hands of the Czech Republic in Olomouc.

Robbie was riding the crest of the wave – it looked like the sky was the limit. But then he was brought back down to earth when he was rested for the following league match against Portsmouth and only brought on as a late substitute in a goalless draw with QPR.

Next on the fixture list was a short trip across the Midlands to Villa Park, Birmingham as Wolves' fairytale FA Cup run had taken them just one step away from Wembley. Robbie had grown up watching FA Cup Finals and he was champing at the bit to get the chance to help his club make it all the way to the Twin Towers. The only obstacle in the way was Premiership leaders Arsenal, a celebrated side who were on course to lift the Double for only the second time in their history.

Arsenal's Christopher Wreh had given the Gunners an early lead and it was always going to be a tall order for Robbie to change the outcome – especially as he was warming the bench. Robbie eventually came on with seven minutes of the contest remaining, but found the Arsenal defence of Tony Adams, Steve Bould, Nigel Winterburn and Gilles Grimandi impenetrable and Wolves crashed out of the FA Cup.

In that semi-final exit at Villa Park, Robbie got his first taste of football's big time and was duly awarded with a place in the Republic of Ireland's starting line-up for the pre-World Cup friendly against Argentina at Lansdowne Road. A Wolves contingent of Chris Evans, Mark McGhee and Colin Lee travelled over to Dublin to see how Robbie would fare against some of the best players in the world. Instead of just holding his own, Keane produced arguably the most accomplished home debut Lansdowne Road had ever seen. In a 2–0 home defeat, Keane was universally recognised as being the stand-out performer – he had arrived on the international stage.

Chris Evans reminisced about the game: 'Robbie was Man of the Match that day and had 38,000 fans chanting his name.'

Three days later, Robbie was back in action at Molineux and struck two goals in a 4–3 defeat by Stockport County before Wolves were held to a 1–1 draw at Middlesbrough.

Wolves' season ended on a disappointing note as the side underperformed on the Wirral, losing 2–1 to Tranmere Rovers and finishing ninth – just outside the play-off spots. From Robbie's perspective, it had been a hugely productive rookie season. He ended the campaign as the club's leading goal-scorer in the League with 11 and he played in 38 of Wolves' 46 Division One fixtures. On top of that, he was given a huge seal of approval by his fellow professionals when, after what was his debut season in the senior game, he was voted into the PFA's [Professional Footballers' Association] Nationwide League Division One team of the year and heralded as the 'find of the season'.

The full side was: Alan Miller (West Bromwich Albion), Kieron Dyer (Ipswich Town), Mauricio Taricco (Ipswich Town), Nigel Pearson (Middlesbrough), Colin Cooper (Nottingham Forest), Lee Clark (Sunderland), Georgiou Kinkladze (Manchester City), John Robinson (Charlton Athletic), Robbie Keane (Wolverhampton Wanderers), Pierre Van Hooijdonk (Nottingham Forest) and Paul Merson (Middlesbrough).

It was high time for a summer of rest and recuperation for the most talked-about teenage footballer in northern Europe – apart perhaps from England's Michael Owen, who had won the PFA's Young Player of the Year award. But Keane didn't stop and picked up his third cap in a goalless friendly versus Mexico at Lansdowne Road at the end of May. He then trained for three weeks, before playing a pivotal role in helping his country win the UEFA Under-18 championships in Cyprus.

After a brief holiday back in Tallaght, Keane reappeared for the start of the 1998/99 season and calls for tickets from Premiership scouts for games at Molineux rose to a crescendo. Mark McGhee suddenly became aware that the Wolves wunderkind was on the radar screens of several clubs. McGhee revealed, 'Everywhere I went people sounded me out about his ability. In boardrooms and at games that I went to watch, people wanted to know about this boy, Robbie Keane.'

McGhee's Wolves were one of the bookies' favourites to go into the top flight after a 14-year absence but the Scot knew he was running out of time and money to achieve his goal – he had to deliver promotion this time around. McGhee told the *Irish Examiner* about Keane's role in the side: 'We have a lot of hope in him. He's matured physically and mentally and he'll be a lot more capable of playing a lot of games this season. Clubs have star players and Robbie is our star. We worried about overburdening him last year and we'll still nurture him – but, as opposed to last season, when we hoped, this season we expect.'

Despite missing the club's pre-season tour of Austria, Keane was still excited ahead of his second season and said, 'Last season was a good season for me and I enjoyed every minute of it. Mark McGhee has said he's going to build the team around me and that's a compliment. I'm delighted he's said that and, though a lot of people have been saying there's a lot of pressure on me, I don't feel that. All I can do is my best and see what happens. There's a bit of pressure on me, but I don't let it get to me.'

Keane was well aware of his responsibility to the team and was relishing the prospect of helping Wolves back into English soccer's top tier for the first time since 1984. 'It's time we got into the Premier League,' he said. 'We did well against the Premiership sides in the FA Cup, beating Wimbledon and Leeds, but we didn't do as well as we could in the League. Two years ago, we had a good season, but got knocked out by Crystal Palace in the play-offs. But Wolves should be a Premier League club. We have the fans, a great stadium and everything else. There's a lot of young lads coming through and, if they can keep producing these, hopefully Wolves will become one of the top teams in the next few years.'

To begin with, it all went according to plan for both Keane and Wolves with an opening-day victory over Tranmere. It took Keane, who had turned 18 the previous month, just 19 minutes to open his account for the season, with Keith Curle adding a late penalty to secure maximum points. But then the cracks began to show in the McGhee team following a shock 2–1 loss in the first leg of Wolves' Worthington Cup first-round tie against Division Three minnows Barnet.

Keane, too, had an off day at Underhill and was marked out of the game by a familiar face – his former youth-team colleague Robert Sawyers. 'I was overjoyed just to play against them and especially against Robbie,' said Sawyers. 'In training, I loved coming up against Robbie because he was so tricky and skilful. I think the fact I knew him helped me to mark him in that game. I knew what he was capable of and that, given the chance, he had the ability to make me look silly.'

The watching Arsene Wenger was far from impressed and Keane's general performance belied the tabloid rumours that Arsenal were preparing a £6 million bid to sign him. But Keane made amends with a spellbinding performance in the return leg a week later at Molineux where he was Barnet's chief tormentor, contributing two goals in a 5–0 win.

One of his efforts defied belief and illustrated the gulf in class between Keane and his opponents – he didn't break stride before drilling a shot past Barnet keeper Lee Harrison from an acute angle. Sawyers, who had been named among the Barnet substitutes, recalled that, even in the heat of battle, Keane had time to share an on-field joke with his old friend.

Sawyers said, 'I'll never forget it because, after the first game, I was giving him stick, saying that he was in my pocket because I'd marked him so well. But I was sat on the bench and, as he scored his second goal, he came running over and looked at me. He then put his hand in his pocket and winked at me as if to say, "You're now in my pocket." I just started laughing and that sums up what type of character he is. I can't speak highly enough of Robbie and he was well liked by all of the YTS lads at Wolves.'

Steve Bull had returned from injury for the second leg against Barnet and his partnership with Keane really started to take shape that night, with 'Bully' scoring a hat-trick. As their understanding improved, so did Wolves' results and Keane won the decisive penalty, scored by Curle, in the team's 1–0 win against Swindon.

A 2–0 win at Watford quickly followed, with Bull and Keane clocking up a goal apiece – proving that the old master and the impish youngster could work together up front. It was goal number 305 for Bull in Old Gold and it proved to be the penultimate strike in his celebrated Wolves career. His forthcoming retirement signalled the end of an era at the club. Wolves had an ageing side, with nine players over the age of 30 and one of the biggest wage bills in the division. The team may have had experience and quality, but they lacked energy and kept on conceding expensive late goals.

A below-par performance in the 2–2 home draw against Stockport led to a morale-sapping 2–1 defeat at Port Vale – even though Keane struck a second-half goal in the Potteries. The pressure on McGhee was starting to mount and the weight of expectation – particularly at Molineux – was starting to take its toll on the team.

Title favourites Sunderland were the next visitors to Waterloo Road and, despite Keane showing wonderful awareness to give Wolves the lead with 22 minutes left, the away side equalised in stoppage time through future England international Kevin Phillips. Wolves were crying out for a win to kick-start their season and hoped that the Worthington Cup tie against Bournemouth would bring welcome relief away from their Division One woes.

But, after a 1–1 draw in the first leg at Dean Court, Wolves crashed out of the competition with a surprise 2–1 defeat in the return leg at Molineux. Once again, Keane got on the score-sheet with a well-taken strike, but two goals from Bournemouth's Mark Stein compounded McGhee's misery.

Those two disappointing results were sandwiched around a disastrous 2–1 defeat at Huddersfield. Keane's stoppage-time goal proved to be nothing but a consolation effort as Wolves began to slide down the Division One table. Steve Bull stopped the rot temporarily with the only goal in a much-needed win over Bury before Wolves collapsed at home and McGhee's men were on the wrong end of a 2–1 scoreline against Queen's Park Rangers. On-field matters went from bad to worse when influential striker Steve Bull pulled his hamstring in a goalless draw at Crewe and Keane picked up the first serious injury of his career while on international duty with the Republic of Ireland. After featuring at Gresty Road, Keane flew over to Dublin to win his fourth cap in a European Championship qualifier against Croatia which Mick McCarthy's side won 2–0.

Disaster struck as Keane was relaxing away from football and his bad luck left McGhee without his key forward for a crucial run of games that would determine his fate as manager of Wolverhampton Wanderers. McGhee explained how Keane picked up his injury to the *Express & Star*, 'Robbie was kneeling down and put weight on his leg as he reached for the TV remote control. It sounds strange but that is the way it happened. It could not really have come at a worse time for the club.'

The teenager threw more light on the story to the *Sunday Mercury*: 'It didn't happen like that – it's a problem I've had since I was young, but the physio team at Wolves have done a great job in getting me back so quickly. But it has been frustrating for me. It's the first major injury problem I've had, so it's been the worst month I've had in the game so far.'

Keane underwent an operation on his knee and missed seven first-team games as he recovered, but by the time he returned in November, McGhee had been relieved of his duties. Wolves' chairman Sir Jack Hayward felt that he had backed his manager as much as he could, but the team was not progressing at a satisfactory rate. In a results-driven business such as football, a manager is judged on his team's form and, unfortunately, McGhee's plans had been jolted by a number of injuries to important players during his time in charge.

Wolves' bid for promotion had ground to a halt and a run of just two victories in 12 League games led to Hayward terminating McGhee's contract, but Keane would forever be thankful to the former Aberdeen and Celtic striker for giving him a stage to perform on. Keane was upset and disappointed with the decision, but understood that managerial changes are part of professional football. He vowed to prove Wolves' doubters wrong with a stronger second half of the season.

Before Keane's injury setback, Tottenham had been rumoured to be charting the teenager's progress, although Spurs director of football David Pleat insisted that a swoop for Keane was not on his agenda. 'There is nothing happening with Keane,' he said, 'but we are aware of his abilities.'

McGhee's assistant Colin Lee was placed temporarily in the post of caretaker boss and the players responded immediately with a 6–1 win at Bristol City, followed by another win over Sheffield United. Keane returned to action at one of his favourite hunting grounds – Norwich City. But he couldn't find the net on this occasion after replacing Guy Whittingham as a second-half substitute at Carrow Road.

Whittingham, who days earlier had celebrated his 34th birthday, was a former soldier who once scored 48 goals in a single season for Portsmouth before joining Aston Villa and Sheffield Wednesday, then moving to Wolves on a month's loan. Even though he only worked with Keane for a handful of weeks, Whittingham was impressed with Keane's ability – both on the pitch and the training field.

Whittingham recalled, 'He was very enthusiastic because

he wanted to show everybody what he could do. He wanted to be on the ball all the time and a lot of people were tipping him to go further. He was always one of the first at training and the last to leave. He was always looking to work on things. He was also very keen to get involved in the small-sided games and, once he got the ball, it was hard to get it off him. He was a good lad.'

Whittingham made an observation about the teenage Keane that stuck in his mind. 'Back then, I think he was probably a scorer of great goals rather than a great goal-scorer. He would score memorable goals with great finishes and some outstanding individual work. As his career has gone on, I think he has become more and more of a team player. He was very keen to show people what he could do, but now he maybe scores more straightforward goals as well.'

Despite the next match being the West Midlands derby against near neighbours Birmingham at Molineux, Lee resisted the temptation to throw Keane back into the starting line-up. Lee didn't want his prize asset doing too much too soon after recovering from knee surgery, so, once again, Keane was named among the substitutes.

With Birmingham leading at half-time through a Paul Furlong goal, Lee reviewed his pre-match strategy and quickly realised that the only way Wolves could get back into the match was by introducing Keane. Five minutes after the break, Keane was brought on to a crescendo of cheers from the home crowd and his arrival sparked a memorable fightback with his close friend Carl Robinson contributing two goals in the last 10 minutes of a fine 3–1 win.

After the game, the club's board decided that Lee's 'caretaker' tag should be dropped and that he should manage the side on a permanent basis until the end of the season. Hayward's decision to keep Lee in charge pleased Keane because he had developed a great rapport with the Devonian and craved continuity behind the scenes.

Keane said to the *Sunday Mercury*, 'Now Colin is in and we want to keep the run going. It's the same group of players, though, so I don't know exactly what's different. There does seem to be a real spirit in the side, however. We've come back from behind three times in the last four matches to win – apparently, we hadn't done that in two years beforehand, so that shows you the sort of commitment we have at the moment.'

Unfortunately, the Black Country derby that followed at West Brom saw Wolves' mini-revival come to a close. Despite Keane's reinstatement in the starting line-up, Albion won 2–0 with Keane's international colleague Kevin Kilbane among the second-half goals.

Keane got back on the goal trail himself with two in the return match against Norwich at Molineux – scoring twice in the final six minutes to salvage a point. The following week he also found the net in a 2–1 defeat at Bradford City. Irrespective of the result, Keane was back to his best and looking sharper in every game.

Wolves' first game of 1999 saw Colin Lee's men make the potentially daunting trip north to face fellow promotion-chasers Bolton at the Reebok Stadium in the third round of the FA Cup. All eyes were on Keane and he responded with a magnificent display, contributing both goals in a hugely important 2–1 win in Lancashire – despite only recovering from a severe bout of flu days before the game. After his headline-grabbing performance, rumours linking Keane with Middlesbrough and Arsenal began to fill the back pages of the tabloids.

A New Star in Old Gold

The north London team's name was pulled out of the hat to face Wolves in the fourth round of the FA Cup – a rerun of the previous season's semi-final. Revelling in the spotlight that suddenly fell on Wolves, Keane found the net after just 39 seconds in front of the Sky TV cameras in an away win at Tranmere. As a result, the 14-goal teenager was feeling confident ahead of the home tie against the FA Cup-holders.

In a pre-match press conference, Keane said, 'I'm looking forward to it immensely. It's going to be a tough game, but it's a great occasion for the club and myself. I was obviously disappointed to play only the last few minutes of the semi-final against Arsenal at Villa Park last season. All players want to test themselves against the best sides.'

Former England boss Graham Taylor was quick to praise the young striker. Despite being the club's first-team manager when Keane signed YTS forms at Wolves, Taylor played no active role in luring the Dubliner to Molineux – that had been down to the efforts of Chris Evans, Eddie Corcoran and Rob Kelly. Nevertheless, Taylor was a huge fan of Keane and pointed out, 'Robbie has very quick feet and is extremely dangerous around the penalty area. You have to be very careful how you challenge him in the goalmouth.'

Before the FA Cup clash, Wolves confirmed publicly that the club had received an approach for Keane from Middlesbrough several weeks beforehand. But the club's managing director John Richards stressed that the approach had been rebuffed and that Keane was not available for transfer. Richards said, 'If Robbie was available, we would expect the whole of the Premiership to be in the queue for him.'

Keane played down the speculation suggesting he could

soon be plying his trade in the Premiership with Arsenal or any other top-flight club. 'It's flattering to have my name mentioned in connection with other clubs,' he said, 'but I don't read the newspapers and I don't know if any of it is true. I'm just concentrating on my football and letting everything else take care of itself. My ambition is to play for Wolves in the Premiership because I think the club deserve to be up there. The job in hand is all that matters to me.'

Lee laughed off suggestions that Wolves were ready to sell Keane to Middlesbrough for just £5 million. 'Talk of £5 million is a joke – that wouldn't even buy one of his arms, and it's his legs which are supposed to be valuable. For £5 million, I'd buy him myself and double my money tomorrow. The stories are rubbish. Bryan Robson is supposed to have spoken to me about him yesterday, but I haven't spoken to Robson for ages. In fact, no one has phoned me about Robbie Keane, or spoken to me, or made an offer.'

But Lee understood that it was only a matter of time before Keane headed off for pastures new and hailed his young striker as one of the best in the business. He added, 'Perhaps people are still assessing the lad. But he will improve and mature into a fantastic player, possibly a world-class player because he has the character to go with his skill and ability. He is capable of going to the very top. That's because he has the greatest gift of all – the skill to put the ball in the back of the net. He has already regularly topped the goal charts season after season at every level even though he is only 18.'

Nine months previously, Wolves had been outgunned by Wenger's Arsenal and Keane was wary of the same outcome at Molineux. He predicted it would be the toughest test of his club career to date against the likes of Tony Adams and his legendary defence.

Keane admitted, 'Their defensive record over the last 10 years, in particular, speaks for itself. It could well prove to be a very tight game for us in which we only get one chance. If that's the case, we have to do all we can to take it. Hopefully, we'll have a good day and they'll have a bad one.'

In the end, it was an unfortunate case of deja vu for Wolves and, despite Havard Flo cancelling out an early Marc Overmars goal, Dennis Bergkamp struck the winner 21 minutes from time. Despite the FA Cup exit, Wolves were still on course to attain a play-off spot, but Keane was set to miss the run-in after being called up into the Republic of Ireland's squad for April's World Under-20 Championships in Nigeria.

Put in an awkward position, Keane said, 'I'm hoping someone else makes the decision for me. If I go to the tournament, I will be missing matches which could decide whether Wolves reach the play-offs or win promotion. If I don't go, I could be seen to be letting Ireland and its people down. I don't want to let anyone down.'

In February, Wolves lodged an official appeal to the FAI because it appeared Keane would miss a substantial part of the club's April programme – up to six Division One fixtures. Lee stressed, 'Robbie is a full international and we feel this should be taken into account, but we are aware that, if our appeal is turned down, there is nothing we can do as they are within their rights to call him up.'

But after scoring in successive home games – a draw against Oxford and a win over Port Vale – Keane was off to Africa as part of Brian Kerr's squad, missing five important League games in the process. When he returned, Keane was used as a second-half substitute in the derby against bitter rivals West Brom, but he looked visibly jaded when he came on to the pitch in a 1–1 draw.

But, rather than taking a chance to recharge his batteries, Keane then flew over to Dublin to represent the Republic of Ireland in a friendly against Sweden – just two days before Wolves' Friday-night showdown against Bolton. Keane was exhausted and Colin Lee desperately tried to persuade the Republic's boss Mick McCarthy to omit the teenager from the starting line-up at Lansdowne Road in order to rest him because 'Whacker' was 'whacked'.

Lee said, 'I hope that Ireland treat him as we have. Robbie's whacked and it would be crazy for him to play in a friendly when we are leaving him out of crucial games.'

With their play-off dream stuttering, Wolves could only draw at the Reebok. With five minutes remaining, Keane was replaced by Flo after failing to score and getting booked in the process. A goalless draw at Grimsby followed by a 3–2 home defeat at the hands of Bradford meant that Wolves' season ended on a sour note.

Wolves had missed out on a play-off place by a meagre three points, with surprise package Watford joining Bradford and champions Sunderland in the Premiership. Robbie finished the campaign with a healthy goal tally of 16, but the general consensus was that, had he not gone to Nigeria, it would have been far better. Robbie had to take a series of injections before flying out with the squad and it clearly affected his performances for Wolves in March. In fact, when he was withdrawn from the action against Barnsley, it was his sixth game without a goal – a barren spell previously unheard of in his career.

Once the season was over, Robbie Keane had the chance

to rest for three weeks after playing constantly for over a year. Then it was time to join up with the Republic of Ireland for a friendly against Northern Ireland in late May. Nine days later, Robbie was raring to go as the Republic of Ireland entertained Macedonia in a European Champion-ship qualifier and he admitted that he had benefited after a short break from football.

Keane explained to the *Irish Examiner*, 'I felt a little flat in that game against Northern Ireland and that was reflected in my play. But I've been on the go all season and travelling to Nigeria with the Under-20s in April took a lot out of me. Basically, we've taken things very easy this week which has suited me. Training has been light and the fact we had no international on Saturday was probably a blessing because it means I've had a longer break. I feel refreshed compared to a week ago and I think that will show on Wednesday night if the manager selects me.'

With the season over, though, the transfer rumour mill went into overdrive, with David O'Leary's Leeds United the latest club to be linked with a lucrative swoop for Keane's services. But Keane played down the speculation, insisting that a move to the Premiership was the last thing on his mind ahead of his ninth senior international. He insisted he was happy at Wolves.

He said, 'I've got three-and-a-half years on my contract at Wolves and ideally I would like to stay. I've a lot of respect for manager Colin Lee and believe the club is capable of winning promotion to the Premiership. All the speculation is just that as far as I'm concerned. There is nothing to it.'

But a week later, Keane's future at Molineux was once again under the microscope. This time, however, Wolves were making noises that suggested that, if the price was right, they would be willing to sell the hottest property outside the Premiership. 'Sooner or later, most players move on,' said managing director John Richards. 'In Robbie's case, it could well be sooner. There have been no firm bids yet, but, if someone offers us the kind of figure we are seeking, then we probably won't be in a position to refuse.'

With Arsenal, Newcastle, Leeds, Aston Villa and Middlesbrough all expressing an interest in Keane, Lee even went as far as to claim that he would need to sell Keane in order to bring in reinforcements. 'It would be better if Robbie went quickly. Otherwise, I don't have a single penny to spend in the transfer market, which makes it difficult to bring in the players I want.'

Wolves' coffers were bare and the Premiership's elite were circling around Molineux preparing to swoop, while Keane went off on a well-deserved holiday away from football.

The new season began with predictable glory for Keane as he produced a match-winning display in his opening League game – scoring the only goal at Manchester City – before finding the net against Portsmouth in a 1–1 draw. But, as his phenomenal form continued, so did the enquiries from Premiership clubs concerning Keane's availability and price tag. Aston Villa had lodged a £5.5 million offer in July, which was rejected by Wolves because it fell below the board's valuation of the player.

After that, Middlesbrough had a formal bid accepted and Keane travelled north to inspect his potential employers before making a final decision. It was a heartbreaking time for Lee and, seven years on, the decision to sell Robbie Keane remains the hardest moment of his managerial career.

A New Star in Old Gold

Lee explained, 'What happened was that it was a very difficult period for Wolves. Obviously, I was the manager and I was told that there was no money available. Plus, the team was struggling and we didn't really have a team that was going to be able to compete in the old Division One. So we had a board meeting and we had to look at our saleable assets and obviously Robbie was our most saleable asset.

'It was agreed at a board meeting that, if we received an offer of £6 million, then that offer would be accepted. The money would then be used to rebuild the whole team. Basically, he ended up going to Coventry and, at the time, it didn't seem like the right move for him. But it turned out OK because not long after that he was on his way to Inter Milan.'

Lee recalled just how difficult the process was: 'That was probably the biggest decision I ever made in football. But we either sat there at Wolves with an inferior team near the bottom of the table after having lost to Walsall. We had lost potentially our best player for £6 million and it was a very pressurised situation. But what people didn't know was the only way we could improve our team was by acquiring the finance to do that. There was no money coming in from the board of directors, so I had to make a major decision and sell Robbie.

'Thankfully, by using the money, we ended up seventh in the League and two points off the play-offs. So I think the decision was the right one at the time. But I wasn't very popular, put it that way!'

chapter three

Glory in Green

'I have not run out of cartwheels just yet, and it would be the icing on the cake for me
if I could get the match-winning goal against Germany. We are all enjoying playing in
the tournament, but football is my future and that's why I want to win this one so badly.'

Robbie Keane speaking to the Irish Examiner *ahead of the*
UEFA Under-18 Championships final, 1998

Republic of Ireland Under-20 boss Brian Kerr was confident ahead of the 1997 World Youth Championships in Malaysia, but wanted his team to be suitably prepared and arranged some high-intensity practice games before they flew out of Dublin. As a result, the former Crumlin coach handed a last-minute invitation to 16-year-old Robbie Keane to attend the final training sessions along with the rest of the squad.

Although it was too late for the Wolves striker to be considered for inclusion, Kerr thought it would give Keane an insight into what international youth football was all about. Keane's prolific form for Wolves youth team had not gone unnoticed back home and Kerr wanted to test his first-choice defenders – the likes of Dave Worrell and Robbie Ryan – against the best underage player in the country.

Robbie Keane

Keane met up with the rest of the squad and instantly felt relaxed among familiar faces – including Middlesbrough's Micky Cummins, who had played for Crumlin United, and Glen Crowe, who was two years above him at Wolves. Needless to say, Kerr was hugely impressed with his first glimpse of the unique talent that Keane possessed and recognised he had a very bright future.

Kerr later recalled, 'We had three days in Dublin before we flew out and I had just come into the job and decided I needed to know what was going on with the younger teams, so I rang round all the players and the clubs to ask if I could take them in for an afternoon. That team going to the World Cup was the Under-20s and Robbie was with the Under-16s at the time. He was one of the ones I got to come in. He came in on the Sunday and gave our defenders who were going to the World Cup a torrid time.

'He was a skinny fellow at the time, but he had already been making waves by scoring goals for the youth team. I had known about him in Crumlin because Crumlin was my original team. But I had not seen him until that day and I genuinely thought about taking him to the World Cup in Malaysia, but it was too late. We were taking Damien Duff, who was a year older, and we had the squad picked.'

Even in the absence of Keane, Kerr's boys in green progressed through to the semi-finals where they lost to eventual winners Argentina, who fielded the likes of Juan Roman Riquelme, Pablo Aimar and Esteban Cambiasso. But with the UEFA Under-18 Championships next on Kerr's agenda, the Republic of Ireland youth boss made a mental note not to ignore the 'skinny fellow' from Tallaght under any circumstances.

Accordingly, Keane was selected in late October 1997 to play in a double-header staged in Moldova, where the Republic of Ireland Under-18 side would face both the host nation and Azerbaijan within the space of two days. In Chisinau, Keane scored the final Irish goal in a 4–2 victory over Azerbaijan, with Luton's Liam George netting twice and Middlesbrough's Ronnie O'Brien also getting on the score-sheet.

A couple of days later at the same venue, Keane scored the only goal against Moldova to book the Republic's place in a two-legged play-off against Greece to determine who would qualify for the finals in Cyprus in the summer of 1998. Kerr later summed up the importance of Keane's match-winning effort: 'That was a crucial goal for us and played a big part in helping us qualify.'

The manager of the senior team, Mick McCarthy, was quickly notified about the emergence of Keane – he was already aware of the sophisticated talent of Blackburn's teenage winger Damien Duff. The future looked bright for the Republic of Ireland. With a growing collection of talented youngsters now reaching maturity, McCarthy arranged a B international against neighbours Northern Ireland for February 1998. He felt it would be a good way of measuring how close the teenagers were to making the step up to full international status. It was vital that McCarthy started fast-tracking young talent because the last remnants of the Jack Charlton era were beginning to fade away and he needed quality reinforcements.

When the game finally arrived, Keane was picked in a three-pronged forward line alongside Duff and Barnet striker Sean Devine, widely considered to be the most potent attacking force in the English lower leagues.

In front of a sell-out crowd at Tolka Park, Dublin, the starting line-up was as follows: Nick Colgan (Chelsea), Alan

Robbie Keane

Maybury (Leeds), David Worrell (Blackburn), Richard Dunne (Everton), Philip Hardy (Wrexham), Mark Kinsella (Charlton), Graham Kavanagh (Stoke), Gareth Farrelly (Everton), Sean Devine (Barnet), Robbie Keane (Wolves), Damien Duff (Blackburn).

McCarthy had spelled it out very clearly to the hopefuls that, if they performed well, then they would be considered for the senior squad for the friendly game against the Czech Republic the following month. McCarthy told the *Irish Examiner*, 'It should be a useful exercise with all the players in the squad out to stake their claims for places.'

In the end, the side lost 1–0 to Northern Ireland's B team, with George O'Boyle scoring the only goal, but the result was immaterial and Keane's immense promise shone through clearly on the night. Keane was subsequently selected in the senior squad for the trip to Olomouc and was named among the substitutes for the encounter with the Czech Republic. It was one of the youngest-ever squads to represent the Republic of Ireland, with fellow teenagers Duff and Maybury chosen to start the game. The whole country waited to see whether the kids could cut it on the international stage.

Keane was aware of the fact that, if he came off the bench, then he would become the second-youngest player ever to represent his country – behind fellow Dubliner Drimnagh-born Jimmy Holmes. Full-back Holmes picked up the first of his 30 senior caps in a European Championship qualifier against Austria at Dalymount Park in May 1971, aged just 17 years and 200 days. Keane was just 60 days older than Holmes when he made his senior bow – replacing 19-year-old Maybury at half-time – and, in freezing conditions, became a full international.

Glory is Green

In front of a crowd of 9,405, the Czech Republic won 2–1, but it was an encouraging performance and it signalled the dawning of a new era in Irish football. A satisfied Mick McCarthy told the *Irish Examiner* afterwards, 'They were better than us, I'm not going to suggest anything else, but I have to be pleased with the way our young lads handled themselves.'

Keane said, 'It was special. I was just delighted to be involved. To get 45 minutes was enough for me, I enjoyed every minute.'

While Keane was making headway in Olomouc, a first-half goal from Ronnie O'Brien handed the Under-18 side a priceless first-leg win in Veria over Greece – this was a major step towards securing qualification for the UEFA finals in Cyprus. Four weeks later, Keane was again handed a call-up into the senior squad for the friendly against Argentina at Lansdowne Road as the South American giants limbered up for the World Cup finals in France that summer.

Keane was a rising star and, in the month that followed his inaugural cap, he had already become a celebrity in the Republic of Ireland. Everyone wanted to see how he would fare against Gabriel Batistuta, and already comparisons between the lad from Tallaght and greats such as Liam Brady and John Giles were being made. The 17-year-old had been told he was scheduled to start the game in attack alongside Niall Quinn in a 4-4-2 formation and he was thrilled at the prospect of performing in front of his hometown crowd.

As Keane told the press, 'I suppose half of Tallaght will be there. It's brilliant for me to play for my country in Dublin against one of the best teams in the world. Hopefully, I can do the business. I think I will handle it OK. I played in front of 40,000 people in the First Division, so I don't see why

Lansdowne should be any different. Still, it was nice to get my first cap away from home, under less pressure.'

His partner up front, Niall Quinn, who had grown up in Crumlin, was immediately taken aback by Keane's sheer fearlessness and brash confidence. Quinn later recalled the teenager's first training session with the senior squad in *Niall Quinn: The Autobiography*: 'I remember Robbie Keane getting into this Irish team when he should have been learning to shave. He came out in the first five-a-side and treated us senior professionals like traffic cones laid out for him to dribble around. Every time he scored a goal he'd run around asking us: "So where's John Aldridge? Who was John Aldridge? Who was Stapo? Bring 'em on!" We loved him straight off, the crazy fox.'

Some two months before he turned 18, Keane proved he wasn't just a major football-talent-in-the-making – he was already an established phenomenon – as he won over the 38,500 crowd. In fact, the Irish supporters ended up booing when Argentina's Gabriel Batistuta was voted the sponsors' Man of the Match; they felt Keane deserved the honour. Argentina, who also fielded the likes of Ariel Ortega, may have won the game 2–0, but Keane was the star of the show and produced arguably the greatest-ever home debut by an Irish footballer.

Irish great John Giles said, 'I can't remember seeing a home debut quite like that one. You had to pinch yourself as a reminder that Robbie is so young. He tried things even a seasoned pro would be frightened to try against opposition like Argentina. He didn't seem to have a nervous bone in his body. He has practically everything else, though – pace, skill, great awareness and finishing ability. The only shame was that he did not get the goal he deserved.'

Glory is Green

Quinn didn't hold back on dishing out compliments, either, regarding the impact his new team-mate had made. 'You won't see many better home international debuts than that. Robbie was exceptional and he's got a great future ahead of him. It's great to see a performance like that. Irish football has been great in the last 10 years or so, but no one has come through to grab you by the throat like Robbie Keane did to everyone in the ground on Wednesday night.

'Even with five minutes to go, he was still full of running and bursting to get in on goal. I couldn't keep up with him. He never tired and he was a pleasure to play with because you knew every time the ball arrived in the box he was a genuine threat. They marked him very tightly and he ended up on the deck over and over again, but he just jumped up and got on with the job. Against world-class opposition, that's a fabulous compliment to him. He's a star in the making and he has a great future ahead of him at club and international level.'

In the middle of April, the Under-18 side faced the return match against Greece at Tolka Park without the injured Keane. The teenager had sustained an ankle knock in his previous match for Wolves and was forced to sit it out – much to Kerr's annoyance. Kerr also told the *Irish Examiner*, 'Robbie's ankle is just too sore and he couldn't train yesterday. I don't know whether he will make it for the Mexico match with the seniors or not. I am deeply disappointed that he can't play for us here in Dublin.'

In the event, Keane's non-appearance didn't prove too costly as the team breezed past Greece, with Alan Quinn scoring a late goal in a 2–0 win. Confidence was high as the FAI started looking at brochures for Cyprus – glory was approaching in the sunshine. After recovering from injury, Keane won his third senior cap in late May against Mexico at Lansdowne Road and he added further weight to his growing reputation as a world-class talent with another sparkling display.

Keane lined up alongside David Connolly up front in a side with an average age of just 23 and landed the Man of the Match award for his contribution in a 0–0 draw against the World Cup qualifiers. McCarthy hid his excitement about Keane's precocity by playing down the hype surrounding the teenager. He said, 'He is a very talented young man and he has got a big future in the game. But I also think that to put that weight of expectation on him – the way we all tend to do – is a bit unfair.

'I wouldn't want to affect his performances by putting extra pressure on him. Young players have to grow up very quickly as it is and he has come from school to the youth team to international football in double-quick time. Players don't get any education in handling that sort of pressure, from the media, agents and supporters. It is a very difficult transition for him and he will need the right assistance and advice from those around him.'

Stand-in captain and Drogheda native, Gary Kelly, joked to the *Daily Mirror*, 'Why should Robbie be worried about the Mexicans or Argentineans? Sure, isn't he from Tallaght? He doesn't give a damn about anyone.'

Fellow defender Gary Breen also shared his thoughts on Keane: 'Robbie has a total lack of fear. He is so unpredictable. He tries things other players don't. In that way, he reminds me of Darren Huckerby. Both can be frustrating for team-mates, simply because they take so much on themselves. But you just have to accept that this is what match-winners do – sometimes they will score great goals, sometimes they will give the ball away easily.'

Glory is Green

Birmingham-born Lee Carsley was also delighted with the way Keane was handling the spotlight, but was worried his young team-mate had picked up a Black Country twang. Carsley told the *Daily Mirror*, 'You don't see Robbie's name in the papers too much – certainly not on the front pages. The only effect football here has had on him is that he is developing a Wolverhampton accent – I'm not too impressed by that!'

In July, Keane flew over to Cyprus as part of Kerr's 18-man squad, but Damien Duff was a late withdrawal because of a groin injury, with Nottingham Forest's David Freeman taking his place in the travelling party. Two days after watching France become world champions with a shock win over red-hot favourites Brazil, the Republic of Ireland's Under-18 side were looking to cause a few surprises of their own.

The final squad that represented the country at the finals was as follows: Dean Delaney (Everton), Alex O'Reilly (West Ham), Thomas Heary (Huddersfield), Richard Dunne (Everton), Keith Doyle (St Patrick's Athletic), Gary Doherty (Luton), Jason Gavin (Middlesbrough), Gerard Crossley (Celtic), Barry Quinn (Coventry), Alan Quinn (Sheffield Wednesday), Paul Donnelly (Leeds), Stephen McPhail (Leeds), Ronnie O'Brien (Middlesbrough), Liam George (Luton), Richard Partridge (Liverpool), Ryan Casey (Swansea), Robbie Keane (Wolves) and David Freeman (Nottingham Forest).

In an eight-team tournament, the Republic of Ireland were grouped with Croatia, England and hosts Cyprus, while Spain, Germany, Portugal and Lithuania were all in the other group. To qualify for the following summer's Under-20 World Cup in Nigeria, the Irish had to finish in the top six and Kerr underlined the importance of that to anyone who would listen. Kerr told the *Irish Examiner*, 'The first priority is to qualify for the next World Cup finals in Nigeria. But, obviously, we are going out to Cyprus to try and win the tournament as well.'

The Irish were based in the Cypriot holiday resort of Agia Napa and the entire squad was looking forward to taking on Howard Wilkinson's England because, apart from League of Ireland player Keith Doyle and Celtic's Ger Crossley, that was where they all played their football. They got off to a flying start with a 5–2 thumping of Croatia. In humid heat, goals from Keane and Liam George put Ireland two up within eight minutes, but Croatia somehow clawed their way back to 2–2. Further goals from Stephen McPhail, Richie Partridge and a second from George sealed the win, though, and it had Kerr purring ahead of the next game against England.

Kerr said, 'It was madness out there at times tonight in the first half and at 2–2 I thought that might be the end of the scoring. But no, the goals just flowed and we might have won by even more if we had taken all the chances we created. The pace was lightning quick out there and it was a fabulous game. The first half-an-hour was incredible and I couldn't believe just how fast the time was going by. It was mad stuff at 2–2, but I think we deserved it in the end. It's important to win the first game. Confidence will be sky-high now for tomorrow night's crunch match with England.'

Meanwhile, England had defeated Cyprus 2–1 with a brace from Leeds United's Lee Matthews. Ahead of the game in Deryneia – close to the Turkish-Cypriot border – Ireland were undefeated in 10 games and the players felt capable of sending England out of the tournament. But after a late goal from Alan Smith, England edged a narrow 1–0 win in front of a crowd of over 500 Irish fans. In stifling heat, Ireland created a hatful of chances, but England, who fielded the likes of Seth Johnson, David Dunn and Matthew Upson, clung on for an important win. At the full-time whistle, the Irish players were inconsolable.

But Kerr was still quietly optimistic that his side could progress to the final. 'It's not clutching at straws as far as I am concerned – there's no question of that. We need to win our last game against Cyprus and we need Croatia to beat England to get through. I would not rule out either possibility.'

Cyprus had lost both their previous games to England and Croatia, and went into this one with a weakened side because of two bizarre accidents. Their first-choice goalkeeper fell off a treatment-room table while having a massage and injured his arm, and one of their midfielders needed four stitches in an eye injury after a team-mate had accidentally slammed a door in his face. Talk about the luck of the Irish! The game kicked off in Agia Napa at 8pm local time, with the other match, involving England, 10 kilometres away in Deryneia.

Captain Barry Quinn gave the Republic the lead on 18 minutes with a thumping header from a Richie Dunne cross before Keane doubled the lead with a scintillating finish. Gerard Crossley's cross-field pass found Keane, who turned and sent a perfectly executed shot into the far corner.

Defender Jason Gavin later revealed that he, Dunne and Keane had rehearsed a special goal celebration to put their beloved Tallaght on the football map. Gavin told the *Daily Mirror*, 'We decided to do our own celebration if either Robbie, myself or Richie – the third fella in the side from Tallaght – scored. Sure enough, Robbie did the business and the three of us went over to the sideline and performed our routine. It was our way of saying: "We are the Tallaght Three. We're Tallaght and we're proud."'

Moments later and an even bigger cheer could be heard inside the stadium – Croatia were beating England. Then Keane made it three late on, poking a Richie Partridge cross into the Cypriot goal. As the full-time whistle sounded in Agia Napa, the Irish celebrations were put on ice. The players and coaching staff stood by on the pitch waiting for confirmation of a Croatia victory. A phone call from an Irish journalist in Deryneia informed them that Croatia had also won 3–0 and the Republic of Ireland toasted a magical night. They were through to Sunday's final against Germany.

Afterwards, a jubilant Keane told the *Irish Examiner*, 'The lads were on a high tonight and we just wanted to get to the final. Now that we are there, it's a bonus for us. It took a combination of results on the night, but first and foremost we had to do the business and beat the host nation. We are all delighted with the result and, personally, I am well pleased because I have now scored three goals at this level. It was nerve-racking at the end waiting for the other results and I kept thinking to myself that England might get two "penos" or something like that because they usually do.'

Germany were favourites to win the final in Larnaca, but Kerr fed off that to motivate his troops ahead of the last hurdle before they could lift the trophy. 'Now that we are back in a major Euro decider, I think we are in with more than a shout. My players have had to fight for their releases from their clubs in England rather than go on pre-season tours, and it would be nice to think that we can justify that fight and sacrifice now by winning the bloody thing outright.'

Sebastian Deisler, number 10, had been singled out as the

most gifted player in the tournament and Germany were blessed with a fine crop of individuals destined for trophy-laden careers. German footballers are bred to win and the Under-18 side of 1998 had been brought up to achieve great things. But Kerr insisted his players would not be fazed by the fact that some of the opposition played for well-known *Bundesliga* clubs.

His message was that Germany should be scared of what the Irish boys were going to bring to the party. 'We will show them huge respect OK, given their reputations and traditions in world football, but I wonder has Rainer Bonhof, like me, got a Hammond Cup medal from the Leinster Senior League, which I won with CYM out in TEK's ground one night?'

On the evening of 26 July 1998, Kerr picked the following team to represent the Republic of Ireland in the UEFA Under-18 Championship final at the Zenon Stadium, Larnaca: Alex O'Reilly, Thomas Heary, Richie Dunne, Jason Gavin, Keith Doyle, Gerard Crossley, Barry Quinn, Stephen McPhail, Richie Partridge, Liam George and Robbie Keane, with Alan Quinn, Ryan Casey and Paul Donnolly as substitutes.

Alan Quinn had sustained a serious ankle injury in the Cyprus game and Kerr thought it would be wise to leave him on the bench. But, after a goalless first half, Kerr summoned Quinn to come on for Crossley and the Sheffield Wednesday midfielder made a telling contribution.

Keane dribbled past his marker, Marcel Rapp, before slipping an inviting pass into the area which Quinn drilled past German keeper Timo Hildebrand to give the Republic the lead with 18 minutes left on the clock. The Irish fans roared with delight and the players felt the Championship was within their grasp – surely nothing could go wrong. But

Robbie Keane

Germany has a long and proud tradition of being able to stage comebacks and they equalised through Andreas Gensler with just 10 seconds of stoppage time remaining.

Skipper Barry Quinn recalled, 'It was really hot and then they scored in the last minute; it felt like the world was crumbling on top of us. In extra-time, they looked stronger and, if anyone was going to score, it was them.'

With the pressure cranked up, Germany piled forward in search of the winning goal, but Ireland stood firm, with Gavin a rock-like presence at the back. The scores were level at the end of extra-time, signalling the cruellest lottery of them all – the penalty shoot-out. Germany, the undisputed spot-kick kings, had never previously lost a shoot-out, but they missed their opening two penalties, with Alex O'Reilly saving from Andreas Voss and Tobias Schaper rattling the woodwork.

The Republic of Ireland, though, showed nerves of steel and substitutes Ryan Casey and Paul Donnolly both found the net to make it 2–0. Borussia Dortmund's Christian Timm reduced the deficit to make it 2–1 before disaster struck for Keane – he missed Ireland's third penalty. Devastated, he trudged back to join his team-mates on the halfway line and, as he retraced his steps up the pitch, Keane made a mental note to remember the emotion he was feeling and to make sure he never experienced it again.

Manuel Majunke then levelled the scores before Barry Quinn edged the Irish back in front at 3–2. A successful effort from Thorsten Schramm set up a nerve-jangling climax and the responsibility for the final penalty fell to Luton Town striker Liam George. Born in Luton with a St Lucian father and an Irish mother, George stepped up and planted the ball firmly in the net to ignite the biggest Irish party since the senior side had defeated Italy in the Giants Stadium four summers previously.

A sweat-soaked Kerr told the *Irish Examiner*, 'What can I say about that. In the second-half, I thought we were superb to come back the way we did, and to go a goal up was frightening really. We were far more composed after the break, but I don't know where the lads got it from. Our passing improved; we were more composed and we started to give them trouble at the back, with Robbie Keane and Liam George coming more and more into the action. Robbie Keane pulled out the tricks for the goal, and I was more than happy with that, even after he'd missed one of the penalties in the shoot-out.'

Captain Barry Quinn – now with Oxford United – believes it was the highlight of his career. As he later said, 'The whole tournament was like a schoolboy dream – especially the final against Germany. I remember Jason Gavin saved one off the line. We hung on and we just knew that, if we got to penalties, then we were going to win.'

The midfielder from Templeogue, near Tallaght, claimed the team spirit within the Republic of Ireland squad was the key to success. 'The lads had all grown up together and knew each other. The *craic* we all had together was brilliant and that was the main thing – especially being away together for such a long time. Everyone got on well with everyone and we were all mates.'

Similarly, the Man of the Match in the final, Jason Gavin, now with Drogheda United, said, 'At the time, we probably didn't realise how big it was. The reception we got when we got home was great. There were lots of people at the airport to support us and we knew then how much the achievement meant to Ireland.'

Eight members of the squad had grown up around the

Tallaght area and Gavin believed that the familiarity between the lads from south-west Dublin ultimately led to success. He added, 'We all got on well and it does make a big difference. There were a lot of players who knew each other from a young age.'

Hero Liam George, now playing with the Atlanta Silverbacks, still remembers the celebrations. 'It was crazy. For the next three or four days, it was just frantic – I didn't stop to breathe. I haven't got words to describe how great it was. We just went out and partied and didn't stop until we got back to our clubs.'

Looking back eight years later, George – nicknamed 'Little Gullit' by the Irish fans – recalled his special partnership with Keane. 'When I first started to play for Ireland, we always played together and we always did well. We had a good partnership because we complemented each other. When you play with players of that calibre, they are going to make you better and they are going to get you chances and get you goals. I was just honoured to play with him.'

Two months later, Keane returned to international duties with the senior team. The opening match of the qualifiers for Euro 2000 meant Croatia were to visit Lansdowne Road. Croatia had finished third in the World Cup and boasted an array of unstoppable players including AC Milan's Zvonimir Boban – it was going to be a tough test for Keane and co.

Before the match, McCarthy sang the praises of his two secret weapons – Keane and Damien Duff. He believed they could both make the step up to competitive international fixtures after featuring in a handful of friendlies. 'The two of them are confident lads, gracing the leagues they are playing in, one in the Premiership and one in the First Division. Robbie is attracting a lot of attention. They have come into the side and handled it really well. They look quick, they look powerful in training and when we played the other night.'

With an average age of just 25, McCarthy's men tore into Croatia from the start and struck twice within the opening 15 minutes. A headed goal from Roy Keane followed a penalty from Denis Irwin, and Croatia's frustration translated into two red cards for the visitors. Robbie Keane looked alert and lively up front alongside Keith O'Neill and troubled the Croatian defence until he was replaced by Lee Carsley around the hour mark.

A month later, Malta were the opposition at Lansdowne Road and, in the build-up, Niall Quinn pointedly remarked that Keane could become the greatest Irish player of all time. He said, 'As soon as Robbie gets on the score-sheet, then all the Irish scoring records will come tumbling down, and then a proper record will be set for Irish goal-scorers. I played with him against Argentina and I thought, "Is he that good?" Now, having spent more time with him and watched him play a bit more, he's an absolute gem, he's lethal. Robbie is technically better than anybody else I have ever played with.

'He has a lot to learn – how to kid people, and how they are going to try and kid him, and how he is going to be marked. That can only happen over a period of time. But for raw ability I have never played with anyone else like him. For somebody like me, he is a dream to play with because, when the ball comes to me, I know I don't have to do too much with it, just get it to him. Aldo [John Aldridge] in his prime was probably the better finisher as things stand now, but I believe that is going to happen for Robbie, too, I really do. He is as close as you can get to what we in Ireland might term a "superstar".'

Robbie Keane

Keane lived up to his 'superstar' billing with two goals in a straightforward 5–0 win over Malta and he became his country's youngest-ever goal-scorer – shattering a record previously held by John Giles dating back to 1959. But, despite picking up the Man of the Match award, Keane limped off near the end of the game with a knee injury that turned out to be serious.

McCarthy said, 'He came over to me and said that the knee was sore, and that it would be best if he came off. It showed a lot of commonsense and responsibility when he could have been selfish and tried to get his hat-trick. Everybody knows what I think of Robbie. I'll let other people praise him now. But his second goal tonight epitomised him. He showed cheeky, impudent arrogance on the ball, and then wonderful ability to finish.'

Keane was delighted with his record-breaking achievement and vowed to continue to entertain the Lansdowne Road crowd with more goals – and more somersaults. 'To get one goal, let alone two, was a bonus, and becoming the youngest player to score for Ireland was even better. Obviously, I'm absolutely delighted. To be honest, the first one was not the best I've ever scored, but it hit the net and that's the main thing. And I really enjoyed the second one. Steve Staunton played the ball over the top, and I was fortunate enough to put it through a defender's legs. Then I saw a gap on the far side of the keeper and just went for it.

'Niall Quinn was always helping me up there. I'm very lucky to be playing alongside him. I really enjoyed the second goal and that was the pick of the bunch for me. I was going to play Quinny in first of all, but the defender dived in and I just slipped it through his legs. I saw the gap on the far side of the goal and I went for it. I just curled it in over the goalkeeper's dive. If I keep scoring goals like that second one tonight – that was special for me – then I will keep doing my little cartwheels for you.'

After winning his sixth senior cap in a friendly against Paraguay in February 1999, Keane was called up into the Republic of Ireland's Under-20 squad for the FIFA World Youth Championships in Nigeria in April. His inclusion infuriated his employers, Wolves, because they needed their best player for the end-of-season run-in, but Brian Kerr was adamant he wanted his first-choice players aboard the plane to Africa, so Keane went.

Keane was handed the number 10 shirt for the tournament and the squad was virtually the same that had won in Cyprus – apart from the inclusion of Damien Duff, Millwall's Richard Sadlier, Celtic's Colin Healy and Coventry's Barry Ferguson. The Republic of Ireland were put in Group C along with Mexico, Saudi Arabia and Australia, but, before the competition was under way in Ibadan, a practice match against Korea was arranged. Sadly, Keane severely bruised his right arm in a 3–3 draw against the Asian champions and was forced to wear a protective bandage. Keane was not feeling in particularly good shape at the time because the immunisation jabs he had received before the trip had affected him badly. Nevertheless, he was picked for the opening game against Mexico, but was powerless to prevent opposing captain Rafael Marquez from scoring a decisive early free-kick.

Ireland's attempts to get an equaliser were not helped by a power failure midway through the second half, which plunged the game into darkness for 15 minutes. But Kerr's team lit up the tournament in their second game – a convincing 2–0 win against Saudi Arabia – with Duff and

Robbie Keane

Stephen McPhail scoring. Australia were next, fielding the likes of Brett Emerton, Vince Grella and Marco Bresciano.

But the Republic of Ireland were in pole position to top the group ahead of the knock-out stages. Kerr said before the game, 'I am happy to be in this position because we know that a draw will do us today. Australia have no such guarantees and that's the difference.'

In the end, Keane inspired the team to an emphatic 4–0 win and Kerr was delighted with the overall display in the African heat. He said, 'It was a fabulous display by the boys, close to perfection right from the kick-off.'

Sadlier, Duff, Healy and substitute Ger Crossley all found the net, but, after finishing as runners-up in Group C, the team now faced the host nation Nigeria in Kano. Nigeria had scraped through after a poor result against Paraguay, so Kerr and his players were confident of success. But the Republic of Ireland lost the second-round match in dramatic fashion at the Sani Abacha Stadium – going down 5–3 on penalties. Richard Sadlier had put the Irish one up 10 minutes before half-time, but Nigeria snatched a late equaliser through winger Pius Ikedia. Keane did not take a penalty and could only watch as Thomas Heary's spot-kick was saved by Nigeria keeper Sam Okoye in front of 15,000 screaming fans. It was a tragic ending for the Republic of Ireland's Golden Generation.

Manager Brian Kerr summed up the feeling of the squad when he said, 'It was an emotional night for us because it means the break-up of this particular team, but we have new challenges to look forward to now. It's the last hurrah for this team – the team which won the European championships – but they all know they are winners.'

chapter four

Sky Blue Heaven

'He is a natural goal-scorer, but he also brings a lot more into the game – his vision is great. When a young player moves to a club with a big price tag, you can usually see faults in them. They will miss a certain pass or be too greedy, but you could see that Robbie had the overall package and was capable of bringing others into the game. His finishing was also deadly and you could put money on him scoring.'

Former Coventry striker Noel Whelan on Robbie Keane, 2006

When Robbie Keane's £6 million transfer to Coventry City went through on 18 August 1999, he became the most expensive teenager in British football history after City boss Gordon Strachan showed he was willing to take a gamble.

Aston Villa boss John Gregory had only been ready to offer £5.5 million and hoped that cash-strapped Wolves would reluctantly accept a bid that was below the Molineux club's valuation. Meanwhile, Manchester United's Sir Alex Ferguson famously was said to have insisted that Keane was only worth a paltry £500,000 and not even ready for regular first-team football in the Premiership. Both were proved horribly wrong.

Strachan had a gut instinct that the huge fee shelled out would prove to be money well spent. His knowledge of the player he was buying was second to none because he had first discovered him playing for Wolves, a team managed by his best friend in football, Mark McGhee – proving once again that it is not what you know, but who you know. McGhee had handed Keane his debut at Wolves, and his friendship with Strachan dated back to their time together at Ferguson's successful Aberdeen side two decades previously. In fact, Strachan had been best man at McGhee's wedding in 1979.

But McGhee insists that he never once recommended his former protege to his old friend – Strachan had seen what a phenomenal player Keane was with his own eyes. 'I think Gordon made that decision on his own. The circumstances helped because, on account of my relationship with him, Gordon came to more Wolves games than any other manager would have done.

'He was at a lot of our games as a friend and colleague. He saw a lot of Robbie Keane, so he was willing to take that chance where other managers were maybe hesitating.'

At Keane's official unveiling as a Coventry player, Strachan explained the reasoning behind his decision to pull out all the stops to sign Keane. 'Mark McGhee is my best mate in football and I used to go across to watch his team, so I know all about Robbie. I used to watch his progress with envy because I could not have him in my team. When the chairman telephoned me to say he was on the motorway on his way to make a big signing, I must admit I didn't realise there was so much money in the coffers.

'Speculation about Robbie had been going on for over a year and I was impressed with the way he handled it. There was a lot of pressure on the young man, but he still improved as a player. That showed me he is mentally strong.

Sky Blue Heaven

I see him either as a goal-scorer or a goal-creator. He can do either job. He is one of the best prospects in the game and that says a lot for Wolves' youth system. They have brought him up the right way.

'A few people may scratch their heads and wonder why he has come to us. Well, we are having a bash at it. People should say, "Good for them". Some people talk ambition, but we set out to try to do it: action not words. Any transfer is a gamble. This is a courageous move by us. We watch players for a long time, but we have done more homework on Robbie than anyone else.'

After constant comparisons with Liverpool's Michael Owen and frequent question marks over whether he could cut it in England's top flight, Robbie was delighted with the opportunity Coventry had given him – the chance to prove himself in the Premiership. At his first press conference as a Coventry player, Keane said, 'I am pleased it's settled because it has been going on for a long time. I did want to play in the Premiership with Wolves, but it was not to be. They are a big club and I am sure they will get there. Maybe the money they have got for me will enable them to do it.

'I had a long talk with Gordon Strachan before I signed and he told me about Coventry's hopes and ambitions. He told me about the new stadium and it is all very exciting. I wanted to be part of it. I also knew of Mr Strachan's reputation for improving young players. He has played football at the very highest level and all that came into it. The size of the fee does not bother me. I just want to concentrate 100 per cent on my football.'

The move was arranged by Keane's agent, Tony Stephens, who reasoned that his client would be best served by joining a team where he could continue his development rather than rot in the reserves at a more fashionable club. Likewise, Robbie was canny enough to weigh up the pros and cons, realising that Coventry was the next logical step on the ladder to the top.

Keane signed a five-year contract and was a ready-made replacement to fill the creative void left in Coventry's attack following Darren Huckerby's sale to Leeds for £5.5 million the previous week. His new club was only 36 miles away across the Midlands, which meant that Robbie wasn't forced to uproot himself completely or lose his Wolverhampton-based friends. That was important for the teenager because he considered that part of the Black Country to be his 'home from home'. After a spell in a hotel, he finally moved out of his house in Telford and chose to live in Balsall Common in Warwickshire – 14 miles from Coventry's training ground.

At Coventry, Keane again met up with another Tallaght native and close friend, Barry Quinn, the midfielder who had captained the Republic of Ireland's Golden Generation to victory the previous summer. Quinn recalled, 'He got a great move and just went on and did his stuff really. Playing with him was special. Sometimes you'd just have to stand back and look on in awe at some of the things he did in training.'

Another key figure to help Keane fit quickly into life at Highfield Road was experienced striker Noel Whelan. Despite having previously represented England at Under-21 level, Whelan was of Irish stock. Whelan joked, 'I took him under my wing. Me and Robbie got on very well during our time at Coventry. I think Gordon Strachan probably warned him to stay away from me.

'We did spend a bit of time together and Robbie is like me

– a bit of a character with a good sense of humour like most Irish boys. The fact that we got on so well, I think, showed on the pitch. It makes a big difference for a strike partnership if you have a bond both on and off the pitch.'

But Whelan's first impression of Keane was that the £6 million wunderkind didn't exactly have the physique of a world-class footballer. 'The first thing I can actually ever remember about Robbie was when I was sat in the changing room and he strolled in for his first training session at the club. He parked himself next to me to get changed and I turned around and I thought he had the least athletic physique I had ever seen on a footballer, but obviously those doubts were put to bed when I saw him out on the pitch.'

Coventry were an established top-flight club with a strong squad of seasoned professionals and ex-internationals, including the likes of Gary McAllister, Moustapha Hadji and Carlton Palmer. But even the players who had performed at the highest level against the world's best were taken aback by Keane's all-round performance in his first training session at the club's Ryton training ground.

Whelan recalled, 'Even then, when you first saw him play, you knew what a talent he was and you realised why the club paid the money they did for him. He had a very mature head on his shoulders football-wise. You could see straight away that the fact that he was a big-money signing didn't get to him at all. He had a strong personality and he just carried it off. Nothing could faze him and he did what he came to do which was to play football, and he did that very well.'

Another Coventry team-mate, Marc Edworthy, remembered that being assigned the job of marking Keane – even in a training session – was an unwelcome headache. 'He was a nightmare in training from a defender's point of view. His movement was very good and he had a great eye for goal. I knew from that point that he was going to go on to big things and, as his career has panned out, all credit to him – he has had a fantastic career so far.'

Before his arrival at Highfield Road, Coventry had started the season sluggishly and only accumulated one point from their opening three games – this came from a 1–1 draw at Wimbledon the previous week. Keane made his long-awaited Premiership bow against Derby County on 21 August 1999 when Strachan named him in the starting line-up and handed him the number 7 shirt – it proved to be a lucky omen for the 19-year-old.

Far from being nervous, Keane scored his first Premiership goal two minutes before half-time and it was a stunning effort. The Moroccan midfield pairing of Youssef Chippo and Moustapha Hadji combined to put Keane through and he embarked on a long winding run up the pitch. Keane steadied himself and shimmied past his marker, Jacob Laursen, before cheekily planting the ball between the legs of Derby keeper Mart Poom from a tight angle.

Keane doubled his tally in the second half when he raced on to Steve Froggatt's through-ball before swerving past the advancing figure of Poom and slotting the ball into an unguarded net – cue scenes of unbridled joy from Keane and complete and utter shock from an awestruck Highfield Road crowd. The fans had thought the Irish kid would be good, but it turned out he was absolutely brilliant.

Coventry's programme editor at that time, Dan Clifford, was in the press box for the game and recalls the event that has become part of Coventry City folklore. 'I remember his first game at home to Derby County and the reception he got. You could tell he was bit different from anyone else we'd signed. The only player that came close in terms of hype was probably Gary McAllister. The reception he got when he came on to the pitch was amazing and you could tell from his first few touches that he was the type of quality player that we'd never really seen before at the club and what we've seen since.

'He scored twice that day and when his first went in I don't think I've ever seen so many people in the ground befuddled by how good it was. He weaved backwards and forwards before hitting a cross-shot into the goal. The fans celebrated, but were almost shell-shocked by what they'd seen. He was a much better player than people expected. We thought we'd signed a guy who was learning the ropes, but he was already a phenomenal player.'

When Keane was replaced by the manager's son, Gavin Strachan, with five minutes left, the Irishman received an ovation from the crowd – he had arrived on the Premiership scene! Strachan told the press afterwards, 'It's unfortunate he wasn't here at the start of the season because we've made a lot of chances and had no one to finish them off. Robbie did very well today, but that's why my chairman bought him. I knew his character was strong. I've been watching this player for two years and know what he's like. He lifted the players around him – they respected his work rate and his attitude was spot on.'

Team-mate Edworthy recalls that the feeling in the dressing room after the game was that Keane had proved a point to his doubters and that a weight had been lifted from his shoulders. 'A lot of managers were looking at him and questioning whether or not he could make the big step up into the Premiership, but he responded with two goals in his opening game. He went on from that and just absolutely frightened defenders to death.'

Keane's next match was a showdown with the champions Manchester United, and the teenager's first opportunity to face his famous namesake, Cork's Roy Keane. Almost nine years older than Robbie, Roy Keane was well aware of his fellow countryman's ability and had even recommended the player to Sir Alex Ferguson in the summer.

Roy gave his verdict on Keane the Younger to the press before the game: 'Robbie is definitely one to watch, especially for us tonight. He's skilful on the ball and he does the unexpected which is very dangerous for defenders. I have had a good close-up view of him with the Irish team and in training, and he will be an excellent buy for Coventry.

'He's a very level-headed lad and is willing to learn. The two goals he got on Saturday won't have affected him at all, definitely not! Robbie has been in the spotlight for about a year now and has still produced the goods, which is a good sign.'

With Noel Whelan dropping back into midfield, Keane was chosen to play up front on his own against the likes of Gary Neville, Jaap Stam, Henning Berg and Denis Irwin – a tough task for a Premiership rookie. The European Cup-holders surged into a two goal-lead through goals from Paul Scholes and Dwight Yorke before Coventry staged a fight-back.

Australian striker, John Aloisi, came on to partner Keane in attack and pulled a goal back with 10 minutes remaining. Keane turned provider and passed to Aloisi, who buried a half-volley. With the Highfield Road crowd urging City forward, Keane almost equalised with the final kick of the game when his 20-yard strike seemed to wrong-foot United keeper Raymond Van Der Gouw, but his shot was saved.

Four days later, Keane took his Premiership goals tally to three after Youssef Chippo put him through. He turned Sunderland keeper Thomas Sorensen before finishing off the move from an acute angle. In a heated encounter at the Stadium of Light, Sunderland equalised through Kevin Phillips midway through the second half, but Keane should have plundered the winning goal in injury-time. Coventry substitute Gary McSheffrey laid the ball into Keane's path, but somehow the Dubliner managed to scoop his effort over the target with the goal at his mercy.

Afterwards, Strachan gave the press his account of the extraordinary miss from his leading marksman. 'He had a chance at the end as well which he missed and when that happens you think, "What happened there?"'

Nevertheless, Keane had already made a substantial contribution in his opening three games in England's top flight and was duly named the Carling 'Young Player of the Month' as well as the Cisco 'Young Player of the Month' for August. Cisco Systems' panel consisted of Bobby Robson and the national team managers from England, Wales, the Republic of Ireland and Northern Ireland. They all waxed lyrical about Keane's outstanding form.

The newly appointed Newcastle boss, Robson, chairman of the panel of judges, said, 'Keane scored two goals on his debut for Coventry and then went up to Sunderland and scored there. It is a major leap from the Nationwide First Division to the Premiership, but young Robbie seems to have handled it extremely well. There is no sign that he is in any way overawed and his approach has been very mature. He seems to be a level-headed lad and I cannot think of a more suitable nomination.'

On hearing the news that he had been given the award, Keane said, 'My confidence is sky high at the moment and there is a brilliant team spirit at Coventry which has helped me settle in. I feel very honoured.'

In the next Premiership game, Keane's predecessor, Darren Huckerby, came back to haunt Coventry with his new club Leeds United. In an entertaining game, Huckerby scored one of the visitors' four goals as Leeds edged a 4–3 thriller. Keane stayed on the pitch for the entire match, but couldn't change the outcome and was naturally disappointed with the result.

Keane was rested for the ensuing Worthington Cup second-round, first-leg tie at Division One strugglers Tranmere Rovers, but even without their record signing Coventry were expected to rack up a comfortable win. Instead, Strachan's side were on the receiving end of Coventry's biggest cup defeat in two decades as Tranmere ran out 5–1 victors at Prenton Park, with David Burrows, just back from suspension, sent off in a horror show.

Keane was back into the side that travelled to Tottenham in search of a much-needed Premiership win. But from the kick-off Tottenham laid siege to the Coventry goal and went three goals ahead moments after the half-time interval. At this point, Spurs were heading towards a stress-free three points until Keane silenced the home crowd with a piece of audacious skill. He shimmied past his marker, Chris Perry, and made the experienced Premiership centre-half look like a white-shirted bollard before dispatching a measured chip into the Spurs net.

The goal was eye-catching and showed off Keane's

outstanding close control and invention. In fact, the effort was so highly regarded that it was runner-up in the BBC's 'Goal of the Month' competition. Not only was Keane proving to be a hit on the pitch, but he was also a popular character at the club with the squad and staff rapidly warming to his sense of humour.

Dan Clifford recalls, 'He was, and I'm sure still is, just one of those guys who has an infectious personality. He could be very down to earth, but he also had quite a dry sense of humour. People used to love being around him because he was such a funny guy. He was good on the pranks and he seemed to get on well instantly with all the other players. He'd only been at the club a couple of days, but he was already really good friends with people.

'But I don't ever remember any of the players ever having a gripe about him or not liking him. You always get players who don't get on with others, but that was never the case with Rob.'

As Marc Edworthy said, 'Players of his calibre just tend to adapt straight away. It was as if he had been there for his entire career. As soon as he played in the first team, he performed. It was definitely his stage and basically a stepping-stone for him. He was an instant hit and just incredible really.'

A perfectionist, Keane would spend hours practising flicks and tricks after the rest of the squad had left the club's Ryton training ground. Like an actor rehearsing before a big theatrical performance, Keane left no stone unturned in his pursuit of excellence. As he admitted to the *Daily Mirror*, 'I like to work on a few tricks – you never know when they might come in useful during a game. It has been a roller-coaster ride. I have been living in England for three years now. It has all gone by very quickly, but I'm still only 19. People sometimes forget that. There are players much older than me who are still learning every day. What has happened is great, but it would be a mistake to get too carried away. I love football, I love scoring goals. My intention is to keep enjoying it.'

As Coventry sought revenge against Tranmere after their embarrassing first-leg collapse on the Wirral, Keane was forced to miss out because he was cup-tied after featuring for 17 minutes in Wolves' 1–0 Worthington Cup first-round win at Wycombe. With Gary McAllister in imperious form, Coventry won the return leg 3–1, but crashed out of the competition 6–4 on aggregate.

Coventry's squad dusted themselves down and responded well with a 1–0 home win over West Ham. Carlton Palmer had been brought in by Strachan to provide steely determination and his introduction revitalised the Coventry midfield. In the early stages, Keane was causing West Ham problems and forced two saves from the Londoners' keeper Shaka Hislop – a header followed by a side-foot shot.

Buzzing around the final third with lethal intent, Keane's work rate led to Coventry's winning goal when he was bundled to the floor by West Ham's new centre-half, Igor Stimac. From the resultant McAllister free-kick, Mustapha Hadji directed his header into the roof of the net to secure the win.

Goodison Park awaited next and, as a boyhood Liverpool fan, it was the stadium that Keane had most wanted to score at since he had cheered on the likes of Ian Rush and John Aldridge against Everton as a small boy. But the game started off badly for Coventry, with Everton's highly rated teenage striker Francis Jeffers grabbing the opening goal. Coventry managed to equalise soon after when Hadji lofted a pass through for Keane to chase. Everton keeper Paul Gerrard could only punch the ball in the direction of Gary McAllister, who lashed a volley into the net to seal a 1–1 draw.

The fixture list threw up another eagerly awaited test for Keane, with Newcastle the visitors to Highfield Road. It meant the wide-eyed Irish teenager could test himself against the greatest-ever Premiership striker – Alan Shearer.

There was a huge buzz in the dressing room before kick-off and Keane was excited about playing in such a high-profile game, but once he crossed over the white line on to the pitch he displayed rock-steady nerves. He just wanted to take care of business.

Coventry survived an early scare when Hedman produced two saves to deny Shearer and Newcastle defender Didier Domi. Up the other end of the pitch, though, Coventry showed ruthless precision. Carlton Palmer connected with McAllister's inviting free-kick to score from a header.

A rare goal, a spectacular long-range effort from Paul Williams, doubled Coventry's lead eight minutes later before Keane took centre stage. Against his international colleague, Shay Given, Keane showed devastating sleight of foot to leave his compatriot grasping at thin air, before Keane casually rolled the ball into an empty net. Ten-man Newcastle – Warren Barton had been sent off – spent the first half completely outplayed.

Meanwhile, Keane was playing with maturity and imagination – not a combination usually associated with a 19-year-old making only his eighth Premiership appearance. Domi pulled a goal back for Newcastle on 81 minutes, before Hadji completed the rout with a deflected free-kick that sailed past Given in extra-time.

Keane was finding Premiership life very much to his liking and even a goalless draw at relegation certainties Sheffield Wednesday did little to dampen his enthusiasm. His volleyed goal in Coventry's next match against Watford meant he had notched up six goals in 10 Premiership games. The 19-year-old was named Man of the Match and also had a hand in two other goals in a 4–0 win against Graham Taylor's side.

Afterwards, Gordon Strachan told the press, 'Robbie Keane is definitely one of the greatest talents in British football. He is better than I realised when I bought him and he can go right to the top. He's been phenomenal and, if you put him in any side in Europe, he'll be able to play for that team – I don't care who it is, he'd be able to play in the side.

'He's a great talent and sometimes you've got to watch what you are doing in training with him because I don't think there is much you can teach him. Sometimes there are naturals in the game and you've got to watch what you're doing. But he's got good players around him and that's what he needs.'

Keane modestly responded by telling the *Coventry Evening Telegraph*: 'I think I did all right, but it was the team who played absolutely brilliantly – it was a team game and I was just delighted to see us get three points. It is quite flattering for the manager to say what he said, but things are going well, and long may that continue.

'People were wondering whether I could make the step up from the First Division to the Premiership, but I had played nine games for the Republic of Ireland against Argentina and teams like that, so I've always believed in myself. I've always had confidence in my own ability. Obviously I want to become a bigger and better player and that is why I have come to the club, so Gordon Strachan will help make me a better player. I'm still only young and learning.'

Former Wolves midfielder Steve Froggatt also scored for Coventry against Watford and, for unusual reasons, he said he was thrilled to be reunited with Keane at Highfield Road. 'It was great to link up with him again because, more than anything else, Robbie was the biggest practical joker ever. During my time at Wolves, I had quite a few injuries, so in order to beat boredom we used to do all sorts of ridiculous things. We'd cut people's trousers up and tie people's shoelaces together.

'Invariably, when the players came in, we'd have done something. The rest of the players were always trying to get me and Robbie back for all the tricks we played. Don Goodman poured sour milk on the leather seats of my BMW because we'd cut one of his sleeves off.

'Robbie was always having a laugh and that was what endeared him to the players. The fact was he was a great player but also a great lad and good fun to be around – a real joker in the dressing room.'

Whether scoring stunning volleys or tying a team-mate's shoelaces together, Keane undertook everything with the same cheeky enthusiasm that made him universally popular at Coventry.

He was also becoming something of a celebrity in the city and, along with Whelan, switched on Coventry's Christmas lights. They soon had Lord Mayor Councillor Joan Wright singing their praises. 'They are very popular players and we are delighted they have agreed to come along. I am a season-ticket holder at Highfield Road and am looking forward to meeting them. Hopefully, after this, they will help beat Aston Villa and chalk up three more points!'

Keane duly obliged and helped cement his place in the affections of Coventry fans with a spellbinding display against arch-rivals Aston Villa at Highfield Road. Back in August, Villa boss John Gregory told the *Birmingham Mail* that he felt Keane wasn't the right signing for his club. 'I had already changed my mind about the deal. I was annoyed initially that Wolves weren't prepared to manoeuvre on the price, but the bottom line is that I felt that the whole thing wasn't right.

'I saw Wolves play four times to assess Robbie Keane. I had to be sure he would be comfortable coming straight into my first team. I could have gone back to pursue the transfer even when Coventry were in for him, but I chose not to. It was my decision – I've made my bed and now I've got to lie in it.'

The stage was set and, in an exhilarating Midlands derby, Keane was at his best, sparking the game into life and winning glowing tributes for his all-round performance. Cedric Roussel, on loan from Gent in Belgium, struck the opening goal after eight minutes, when Keane breezed past Mark Delaney and crossed for his team-mate who directed a header past Villa keeper David James.

But Villa equalised when ex-Coventry striker Dion Dublin planted his header past Hedman from a Lee Hendrie corner to set up an adrenaline-charged finish. In an ill-tempered clash, both sides foraged for the winner, but Keane made sure Coventry finished on top with a precise finish following a clever pass from Youssef Chippo.

After the high of defeating the old enemy, Coventry's form dipped and Keane and co failed to score in their next two games – a home loss against Leicester followed by a goalless draw at Southampton. The treatment room was becoming congested and the team's performances became increasingly cluttered, too, but Keane was pleased with the club's next destination – Norwich in the FA Cup third round. In the end, though, Keane's name was not on the score-sheet in a 3–1 win for Coventry – the club's first away win since April.

Anfield beckoned next and, in front of a crowd of over 44,000, Keane had the chance to fulfil a childhood dream – by scoring in front of the Kop. Another interesting sub-plot that day was just how the Irish teenager would fare against the player he was constantly compared to – Liverpool's Michael Owen.

But it was the English wunderkind who stole the show with an expertly taken goal in first-half injury-time, and Titi Camara struck a superb second to seal maximum points for the Reds. Unfortunately for Keane, the only memento he took away from his first game on the hallowed turf of his boyhood favourites was a yellow card.

Keane was aiming to prove a point in Coventry's next match – a Boxing Day meeting with Arsenal at Highfield Road. In front of the Sky Sports cameras, Keane grabbed the winning goal in a 3–2 victory still labelled 'one of the most thrilling games ever staged at Highfield Road'. After struggling to make an impact against Arsenal's legendary defence in two successive seasons with Wolves, Keane was fully up for the challenge. With 18 minutes of the game remaining and Arsenal pressing for an equaliser, Keane had both the awareness and impudence to send an ice-cool chip over the outstretched leg of Tony Adams and past David Seaman in the Arsenal goal.

Robbie Keane

It was the first time Arsenal had conceded three goals in a game for a year and even a late Davor Suker goal couldn't stop them from crashing to defeat. The goal also ended a mini-drought in Keane's career – it was his first in five games – and boss Gordon Strachan felt he had earned it. 'He's needed that because he's been doing things right, but he's not been getting the final touch.'

Robbie Keane thus entered the new millennium on a high and his confidence had visibly risen when he took the field against Chelsea days later. With prodigious energy and boundless enthusiasm, Keane served up an irresistible display as he gave Chelsea's World Cup winner Marcel Desailly a restless night. But despite Keane scoring what appeared to be the decisive goal in the closing stages, Chelsea equalised seconds later through Tore Andre Flo to snatch a point in a 2–2 draw.

After brushing aside Burnley in the fourth round of the FA Cup, Keane added to his tally in a one-sided home win over Wimbledon. There was no denying the buzz of expectation that went round the stadium every time the adventurous and unpredictable Keane picked up the ball. After he had been impeded inside the area, referee Steve Bennett pointed to the spot and Gary McAllister converted the penalty to notch up his 100th goal in English and Scottish League football. Then Keane displayed his razor-sharp reactions inside the area when, after seeing his angled shot saved by Neil Sullivan, he chipped the rebound into the net.

By now, the Irishman had forged an excellent partnership up front with Cedric Roussel, who said, 'For the future, Ireland have a fantastic player and he can become one of the world's great players. I think he is ready-made now to be a great player.'

Sky Blue Heaven

The goal against Wimbledon was Keane's tenth in a sky-blue shirt and it put Coventry in 12th spot in the Premiership table, but there was a feeling circulating that City had a genuine chance of winning the FA Cup this time around. The club had famously upset the odds in 1987 when a lavishly skilful Tottenham side were defeated 3–2 in the final at Wembley – could that feat be repeated in 2000?

After an uninspiring goalless draw at Derby, Coventry lined up to face Division One leaders Charlton in the fifth round of the FA Cup. Sadly, it all went horribly wrong for both Keane and Coventry, with Charlton edging a topsy-turvy game 3–2 at Highfield Road. Keane showed intermittent glimpses of class as he set up both of Roussel's goals, but he also became increasingly agitated at Charlton's apparent attempts to rough him up. The teenager complained to referee Dermot Gallagher and lost his temper after a tussle with a Charlton midfielder.

After setting such lofty standards in his opening five months at Coventry, an off-key performance from Keane stood out and he came under intense scrutiny from the pundits who began questioning his consistency. His skills were pretty to look at, the critics argued, but of no practical value in a fight against the likes of Charlton. Such accusations meant nothing to Keane. He understood his own ability better than any so-called expert and quietly vowed that he would prove the prophets of doom wrong in emphatic fashion.

Before Coventry's trip to Manchester United, Sir Alex Ferguson took time off from discussing team news with the national press to clarify his opinion of Robert David Keane. Back in the summer, the Scot was reported as apparently saying, 'At £6 million I would not go near him. If he was

Robbie Keane

£500,000 and could spend some time in our second team, I might have a look.'

Now Ferguson was quick to point out that he had been misquoted. 'He's nothing to prove to me. There was all that stuff in the papers saying I didn't rate the boy which is absolutely untrue and everyone knows that. What I said was that, if I spent pounds £6 million on a player, I would need to put him in my first team. And at 19 years of age, with Yorke, Cole and Sheringham, that would be very difficult.'

A spirited display at Old Trafford saw Coventry narrowly go down 3–2, with even Ferguson claiming City deserved a point – a very rare occurrence. Keane's double act with Roussel again worked wonders, with the Belgium Under-21 international scoring twice at the 'Theatre of Dreams' – the highlight of the target man's entire career.

Sunderland were next to fall under the spell of the Tallaght-born sorcerer, when he found the net after two minutes at Highfield Road. Bright and alert, Keane pounced on a loose ball after Mustapha Hadji's long-range shot had been blocked. Both Hadji and Roussel then scored in a 3–2 win.

At this point, Keane was sky high in sky blue, enjoying the life of a Premiership footballer with all its perks – including fast cars. After being sorted out with a Fiat Brava Sport while at Wolves, Keane had been saving some of his £20,000-a-week salary to splash out on something stylish. He opted to buy a Jaguar XK8. He told the *Daily Mirror* the reasoning behind his choice of car: 'Ever since I was a kid, I would dream of having a car like this and, as soon as I could afford one, I started looking around. This was my first choice.'

But the teenager insisted that he wouldn't get carried

Wolf cub! Robbie at Wolverhampton Wanderers playing Nottingham Forest in
December 1997.

Top: Robbie and his dad at home in Tallaght in May 1997.

Bottom: At training in May 1998 in Clonshaugh.

Top: At the Republic of Ireland Under-18 team hotel in July 1998 in Cyprus with Richard Dunne.

Bottom: 'We are the Tallaght Three.' Celebrating the second goal against Cyprus in July 1998 with Richard Dunne and Jason Gavin.

Top: Robbie with Damien Duff, Mark Kinsella, Gary Breen and Kenny Cunningham. The lads warming up for training in autumn 1998.

Bottom: In April 1999 with some of the locals in Nigeria.

In action at Coventry in August 1999 against Derby County. Robbie's Premiership debut and he scored twice in a 2–0 victory.

Robbie receives the Player of the Month Award for August 1999 before
Coventry's match against Leeds.

Top: Coventry won 3–2 against Arsenal in December 1999 and Robbie assisted with this 71st minute goal.

Bottom: Hermann Hreidarsson of Wimbledon proves to be no match for Robbie Keane in a Premiership match in January 2000 which Coventry won 2–0.

Top: The Italian job – Robbie in his first match at Inter, a friendly against Bari in August 2000.

Bottom: At Leeds, Robbie listens intently to instruction from gaffer David O'Leary at the match against Aston Villa in December 2000.

away with all the fame and adulation. Speaking to the *Sunday Mercury*, he said, 'I like to see my name all over the place and it's good to be talked about. Anybody would want to better themselves and I want to be the best I can be. But I haven't changed. I'm just the same person I was three years ago. A lot of people watch over me now and talk about me, but it's something I don't worry about.

'Don't get me wrong. I don't mind the attention. It's just that I was brought up in the back streets of Dublin and I think I have to remain the person I always have been. If I'm not, and I got too big for my boots, I'm sure my parents and all the people I know back home would let me know. I wouldn't like to think fame would get to me anyway. It's the type of person I am. I think I'm just a down-to-earth guy who loves to play football.'

However, towards the end of February 2000, Keane's form wasn't headline-grabbing as Coventry lost in successive games – against Middlesbrough and Tottenham. Then, to make matters worse for City, their prize asset missed the trip to Leeds because of a knee injury and the team were promptly thrashed 3–0 – a result that disgusted ex-Leeds captain Strachan.

The next game was against Aston Villa, but doing the 'double' over their neighbours would not be a straightforward job for Keane, restored to Coventry's line-up. Keane's goal would have been enough to make Gregory wish he'd taken him up and they would really be up for the rematch. Villa assistant manager Steve Harrison told the *Birmingham Post*: 'What with Robbie Keane scoring against us and in a local derby too, losing that night did us a lot of damage. It gives an added edge to the return game – it's a chance to get even.

Robbie Keane

'There's no denying the result at Coventry left John at his lowest ebb. We couldn't carry on as we were. As it happened, losing that game was the turning point for us.'

Harrison's pre-match assessment proved to be spot on as a revitalised Villa won 1–0 and Keane experienced a miserable afternoon. He was replaced by Noel Whelan at half-time after moving around uncomfortably in the opening 45 minutes. Keane missed Coventry's next match as the club's medical team tried to resolve his recurring knee problem. But the team's form improved as their four-game losing streak ended with a 1–0 win against Everton.

Strachan was determined not to rush Keane back into competitive action until he had made a complete recovery, so he was rested for the following two games. After some light training and a practice match at Ryton, Keane's knee felt sturdy enough for the teenager to be considered for the home clash against Liverpool. He told the *Birmingham Evening Mail* about his level of fitness: 'I'm back in the swing of things now and obviously I'm looking forward to the game against Liverpool.'

The 19-year-old was named amongst the substitutes, but he came on after 33 minutes to replace the injured Noel Whelan, with Coventry already a goal down. Five minutes later, Michael Owen scored his second of the match as Liverpool steamrollered the home side. Even though he was still rusty after a three-game lay-off, Keane tried to turn the game with his unique brand of freewheeling creativity.

But Liverpool were the superior side and Emile Heskey slotted the visitors' third and final goal past Steve Ogrizovic, who was celebrating his 600th appearance for Coventry.

After losing to Chelsea's constellation of stars at Stamford Bridge, Keane churned out a vintage performance in

Sky Blue Heaven

Coventry's 2–1 win at the expense of Middlesbrough. Keane scored his first goal in 10 games after combining well with Whelan as City eased their relegation fears and he celebrated with a trademark somersault. Veteran midfielder Gary McAllister singled Keane out for his Man of the Match display and suggested that his teenage team-mate was one of the most gifted performers in the Premiership. Speaking to the *Coventry Evening Telegraph*, he said, 'He is a very special player. I can't think of anyone who's been better at his age. I don't want to build him up too high, but he has a special talent. He's up there with Ryan Giggs and Michael Owen, but he is not playing at a club which has the same profile as Manchester United or Liverpool.

'The spotlight is not as severe here, but the talent is as good – people tend to forget he is still only 19. For someone of 19, he's played a lot of first-team football. He's just got to keep improving while he's here and he's got to be just left to get on with things. Robbie works most things out for himself. He doesn't need anyone to tell him what to do. He is clever.'

Over the course of the season, Keane's delightful skills had not just entertained the paying public, but they had also attracted interest from Serie A's finest – both Lazio and Inter Milan had assigned scouts to chart his progress. At first, Strachan played down the rumours by insisting his star player would be staying at Coventry no matter which club expressed an interest in signing him.

Likewise, Keane had really enjoyed working with Strachan and believed he had benefited from the Scot's coaching. 'Gordon looks after me very well. I'm a much better player than I was at Wolves and that's down to Gordon. He doesn't treat me any differently from anyone else. When I'm not doing my job, he'll shout at me, but he's fine. At the training ground you can see his enthusiasm. He just loves the game, still joins in and even now is unbelievable. He's brilliant sometimes and I think he could still play out there on a Saturday because he is magnificent in training.'

Coventry finished the season in 14th place in the Premiership, with Keane ending up the club's leading goal-scorer in the League with a respectable 12. Keane was also voted runner-up in the PFA's 'Young Player of the Year' award, behind Leeds United's Harry Kewell – capping off a groundbreaking debut season. But rumours of his imminent departure from Coventry were beginning to look increasingly substantial, with Inter Milan's name regularly linked to Keane in the tabloids.

In late July, Strachan finally admitted that Coventry were in talks with Inter concerning a proposed deal for Robbie Keane. Speaking to the *Coventry Evening Telegraph*, he said, 'Robbie to go is the last thing that I want to happen and the chairman knows my feelings. I have been here four-and-a-half years and it is the worst thing that could happen to me as a manager.

'As a club, we would survive, but as a manager I have something special here and want to keep that. Everybody here thinks Robbie is great and to be a good manager you need great players. I have got to get on with my job and keep my fingers crossed he will be playing here this season.'

But the deal was finalised after chairman Bryan Richardson cut short his golfing holiday in America to fly over to Lake Como and discuss terms on a multi-million-pound transfer – £13 million to be precise. Richardson informed the *Daily Mirror*, 'We have accepted Inter's £13 million bid. In fact, that figure drops to £12.5 million when you deduct the size of my phone bill. Joking aside, we could not say no. We bought Robbie from Wolves for £6 million less than 12 months ago, and we cannot afford to ignore that kind of profit in so short a time.

'I wonder what Manchester United manager Sir Alex Ferguson is feeling. He described Robbie as worth £500,000 and a place among the Old Trafford reserves. Robbie will have absolutely no trouble settling in Italy. Performing in front of 80,000 crowds will be right up his street. He is a player of such enormous talent that Inter could pick him at right-back and he would still do the job comfortably.'

Strachan, on the other hand, was left feeling despondent at the disappearance of his 12-goal striker. He said, 'The chairman reckons every player has his price and, in an era of increasing uncertainty about the future of transfer fees in European football, I can understand that point of view. But I shall be desperately sorry to see Robbie go because you aren't given the opportunity to work with that sort of talent very often.

'If it was down to me, I would sell the training ground and everything else to keep him. I have been at Highfield Road for the past five years, and selling Robbie will definitely be the worst thing that has happened during that period. Robbie is something very special. I believe he deserves the description "great". You have to have great players to be a good manager, but, if the club are going to sell him, I have to get on with my job. What more can I do?

'I'm just hoping Robbie doesn't like the San Siro, doesn't like the wages – and wants to come back here.'

Team-mates Steve Froggatt and Marc Edworthy later remembered what the feeling was like in the Coventry camp the day Keane swapped Highfield Road for the San Siro and

Robbie Keane

Internazionale. Froggatt said, 'Everyone was devastated. We all totally understood why Bryan Richardson sold Robbie because, when someone comes in and offers £13 million when you are a club of Coventry's size, you just don't say no.

'We had financial troubles that were well documented. From a player's perspective, Gordon Strachan had worked really hard to get Robbie in and we had the basis of what could have been a very good side, but then we lost our best player. That really took the wind out of our sails and we struggled. The loss of Robbie was instrumental in us not doing so well from there on in.'

Edworthy recalled, 'I remember when we said goodbye and wished him all the best. Funnily enough, a lot of the lads started tuning in to Channel Four to watch the Serie A coverage. He did exceptionally well over there and he is well respected in Milan. But it was a fantastic move for him and also good business for the club at the time.'

Strachan succinctly summed up Keane's season-long stint at Coventry. 'I believe he is the best young striker in the country; show me any young striker and I will tell you that Robbie is better than them. If you put him wide left, which we did a couple of times, he could do the job as well as Marc Overmars, and *he* has just been sold for £25 million. Robbie Keane is a genius and the other players were disappointed to lose him from the squad.

'I tried everything I could to keep him, but sometimes decisions have to be made above you. The chairman is accountable to the bank and is responsible for the future of the club and I understand that.'

chapter five

Baby Irish's Italian Adventure

'Robbie is a young man who dreams with his eyes open. He is only 20, but he has the maturity of a 25- or 26-year-old. Inside his young body is the character and spirit of an older man. And you can see in him, the desire to succeed that so many players lack. I believe he will become an important player for the club.'

Marcello Lippi on Robbie Keane, August 2000

Before he had even kicked a ball in Italy, the reputation of Robbie Keane had gone before him and this prompted one of football's most endearing nicknames – *Bambino Irlandese* or 'Baby Irish'. A legend was born.

After Inter's managing director Gabriele Oriali had initiated transfer proceedings with Coventry Chairman Bryan Richardson over the telephone, the end result was inevitable and the deal was concluded in the space of four days. The 20-year-old had been on the Italian club's radar screen for over nine months – Inter had planned to shell out a sizeable sum on Keane and they swiftly made Coventry an offer they couldn't refuse.

As a result, Keane and his agent, Tony Stephens, arrived in luxurious surroundings on the banks of Lake Como on Friday, 28 July 2000 to finalise the £13 million transfer to Internazionale, or Inter Milan as they are known back in Dublin. After discussions that lasted less than a day, Keane agreed to sign a five-year contract – estimated to be worth £35,000 a week – and gratefully accepted the opportunity to continue his development in Italy.

During talks, Keane called his national team manager, Mick McCarthy, for advice. McCarthy later recalled in his book *Ireland's World Cup 2002*: 'I was back in Fitzpatrick's in Manhattan on holiday when he called and my advice was to go for it. Even if Robbie only lasts a year in Italy, he will learn from the experience and his financial future will be secure. There are no downsides to the move as far as I am concerned; he cannot come back from Italy a failure. He will be a better player for Ireland because of his time on the Continent.'

Understandably, Keane was excited about the switch and started dreaming of ever more extravagant triumphs among the elite of Serie A. He was over the moon. 'This time last year I was preparing for a new season in the First Division with Wolves – now, if all goes well, I will hopefully be preparing for the qualifying rounds of the Champions League.

'The thought of playing alongside players like Seedorf, Zamorano, Ronaldo, Vieri and Blanc, and working under a coach like Marcello Lippi, fills me with excitement. The Inter president Mr Moratti is a great fan of Premiership football and I am determined to show him, by my efforts and ability on the pitch, how grateful I am for the faith he has shown in me.'

His enthusiasm was matched by the club's board and director Giuliano Terraneo who announced, 'Robbie's a great talent, he's very young. He is one of the best strikers in Europe at the moment – I think Keane could be a new Ronaldo.'

Importantly, Keane did not forget to take the time to thank the people who had helped shape the formative stages of his career. He told the press, 'I send my best wishes to all Coventry supporters and also everyone at Molineux – I really enjoyed my time in the Midlands. I am grateful to Gordon Strachan for everything he taught me last season – I know I have learned a lot from him.

'When I used to kick a ball around in the back streets of Dublin, I could never have imagined that one day I would pull on the legendary blue-and-black striped shirt of Inter Milan. It is every kid's dream come true.'

Keane was officially unveiled before the Italian media on 1 August 2000, with the press clamouring for quotes. Only days before, Keane had been a virtual unknown to the Italian press, with some newspapers running stories about how Inter's latest signing had previously worked as a shepherd in Ireland.

Soon the impish striker with the strong south-Dublin brogue set the record straight concerning his background – it had involved playing with Wolves, but never looking after sheep. He quickly broke through the language barrier and effortlessly won over the expectant journalists with his thoughtful remarks.

Fellow Dubliner Liam Brady, widely regarded as the finest natural talent to have emerged from the Irish football scene, had been an early forerunner in Serie A when he had exchanged Arsenal for Juventus in a £600,000 deal in 1980. The 24-year-old Brady had adapted seamlessly to the world of *calcio* and twice lifted a *Scudetto* with the Turin-based club, before he fell victim to the 'two-foreigner' rule and was replaced by French midfielder Michel Platini.

But Brady resisted the temptation to retreat to England and, instead, went on to enjoy spells at Sampdoria, Inter – where he stayed for two years – and Ascoli, prior to moving to West Ham United in March 1987.

Robbie Keane

Gabriele Marcotti, a football writer with the *Corriere Dello Sport*, summed up Brady's time at Inter. 'Liam Brady has a really big reputation in Italian football and a deserved one. Liam will forever be seen as the gentleman of Italian football because his behaviour – on and off the pitch – was always exemplary. In his final year at Juventus in the 1981/82 season, after Juve told him they were going to keep him, they famously said, "Sorry, Liam, we are signing Platini and Boniek," and he took it in his stride.

'Famously in the last game of that season there was a penalty kick for Juventus and, even after being told the bad news, he wanted to take it and scored. People appreciated Liam Brady not only as a great player, but also as a great individual, so that set the benchmark pretty high for Robbie Keane.'

In total, Brady clocked up 189 Serie A appearances and Keane realised that his fellow countryman had set the standard for Irish players in the Italian League. He said, 'Brady is a model for me. I never met him or saw him play. I only know he was an important Irish player – I want to become important, too.'

After being allocated Inter's number 7 shirt for the season, Keane joked that he had originally demanded the number 9 jersey – occupied by Brazilian international Ronaldo, who at that time was considered the best player in the world. He said, 'I asked for number 9, but I think some other fellow has that.'

With his abundant skills, Keane was fully equipped for the challenge of Serie A and expectations – both in northern Italy and south Dublin – were sky high. Inter boss Marcello Lippi in particular harboured great hopes for the newcomer with the priceless knack of dribbling his way out of confined spaces and changing the outcome of a game on his own. Lippi – later to steer Italy to World Cup glory in 2006 – was very impressed with his latest signing and predicted a bright future for Keane with the *Nerazzurri*. 'You can always see the difference in quality in a player when he moves from England to Serie A.

'Quality is the most important aspect of a player to us and I believe Robbie has plenty of that. We are very happy to have signed him and I have told him that he will be a very important player for us.'

Despite all the plaudits aimed in his direction, Keane quickly understood his position in the pecking order at Inter Milan. Just because he had been bought for £13 million did not necessarily mean he would be assured of a regular place in the starting line-up. Week after week, he would be competing against the likes of Ronaldo, Vieri, Hakan Suker and Ivan Zamorano for a single place in Inter's forward line.

But Keane insisted that he viewed the whole situation as a once-in-a-lifetime opportunity and genuinely believed he would be good enough to make an impact. At his inaugural press conference, Keane told English and Irish journalists, 'I'm not a worrier. I know that getting into a team like Inter, with so many world-class players, will be a tough task. But I thrive on that sort of pressure. Nothing fazes me. If I didn't think I was going to play, I wouldn't have signed.

'The club have spent an awful lot of money to bring me here. They wanted the transfer to go through quickly, so I would be registered for the Champions League. I am sure I am going to get a chance to show what I can do. When that chance comes along, it is up to me to seize it.

'I believe I can do that. I want to play a big part at Inter

Milan. Coming to a club of this size will make me twice the player. I chose Italy because Inter have followed me for a long time.'

Mick McCarthy shared his striker's belief that he would benefit from being at Inter. As he told the *Sunday Mirror*, 'I've heard people say that, because of the rotational system clubs like Inter operate, Robbie is going to find himself short of match practice and that this, in turn, will affect his international performances. But from where I stand the change will only be for the better.

'As a result of this move, I believe he will be a lot fresher when he joins the international squad. Robbie's the type of player who wants to be involved all the time and there were times last season when he was possibly less than 100 per cent fit for games.

'That was because the pressure was on him at Coventry to get goals and steer the club out of the relegation zone. It will be different at Milan where he's going to have to get used to the prospect of sitting out games. But at the end of the day, he'll be a better player for that.'

Back in Tallaght, his father, Robbie Snr, was confident his youngest son would not be overawed by his new environment. 'Robbie's very down to earth. He's not doing this for the money or the fame, he just loves football. He's full of confidence and always has been in everything. It won't bother Robbie to walk into a stadium in front of 80,000 people. He's not affected by all the hype. When he signed for Coventry, he went out the first time and scored.'

Similarly, Keane's mother Ann was overjoyed, although she admitted she had initial reservations about the move because Milan was even further away from Dublin than Coventry. 'I said to him at first, "It's too far away." We're used to being able to just fly over and back to see him, but Milan seems a long way away.

'I said to him that he wouldn't know anyone, but he just said he didn't know anybody in England at first and he had made loads of friends. It doesn't bother him at all. Last Christmas, we went to Coventry with his brother Graham and his two sisters Natasha and Amy, and this year we'll all go to Milan. We can't leave him there for Christmas on his own.

'He's taking it all in his stride. But he won't be going for any supermodels over in Milan. He's just looking for a nice Irish girl.'

With his childhood friend John Ledwith moving over from Tallaght to Milan to keep him company, Keane was determined to fit in quickly at Inter. He later told the *Daily Mail*, 'I got an apartment near the San Siro the moment I got there and my best mate from home, John, came to live with me. Then another mate, Eddie, turned up for a weekend and ended up staying three months. We had a great time.'

The 20-year-old had seen his childhood hero Ian Rush apparently struggle to assimilate into life in Italy. Rush's £3.2 million dream move quickly turned sour – the Welshman was there only between the summers of 1987 and 1988 and he later famously complained that being in Italy was like 'living in a foreign country'.

Keane wasn't going to follow that same path. His daily routine at Inter was mapped out with precision. He would wake up at seven in the morning at his apartment and eat a protein-rich breakfast before travelling to the club's top-of-the-range training base in La Pinentina in the village of Appiano Gentile – 30 miles north of Milan – to start at nine.

Then, after a two-hour training session, he would be

massaged by members of the club's extensive backroom staff before settling down to eat lunch – specifically designed by the club's dietician to suit every player individually. The club chef was on hand to prepare chicken, fish and a variety of pasta dishes – the football equivalent of putting premium-quality fuel into high-performance sports cars. But Keane still craved a taste of home – his mum's homemade mashed potatoes with brown sauce. Keane admitted his favourite dish was a rare commodity in Italy. 'They don't have too much of that kind of thing in Milan.'

After lunch, Lippi would head up a team meeting to discuss tactics, analyse footage of future opponents and ensure everybody understood their role within the framework of the squad. No detail was too small in the club's pursuit of excellence – an ultra-professional and progressive set-up catered to the requirements of a footballing elite. And Robbie Keane loved every second of it.

One person who can vouch for that is Dan Clifford, Coventry's programme editor, who had stayed in regular contact with Keane and even went over to visit his old friend in Milan. Dan recalled, 'It was a dream come true for him. He used to go on about who he was training with and what he'd seen the others do in training.

'He'd spend hours practising tricks and, if he saw another player do something, then he'd want to know how to do it himself. He just appreciated the fact that he was training with so many quality players. He was never overawed at being on the same pitch as these guys. He just thought it was unbelievable he was allowed to go training with them every day.'

When the training session came to an end, Keane sat down with his own private tutor for Italian lessons and, although he was never particularly academic at St Aidan's, he slowly got to grips with the language. He said, 'The language is coming along slowly, but I'm picking up key words.'

Communication problems involving Keane never arose, largely because of the presence of Dutch international Clarence Seedorf, who spoke English fluently, and Italian striker Christian Vieri.

Vieri – or 'Bobo' as he was known to the rest of the Inter squad – surprised Keane with his excellent grasp of English, albeit spoken with a strong Australian accent. The golden boy of Italian football sounded more like a character from *Crocodile Dundee* than a fully fledged member of the *Azzurri* squad. After living in Sydney with his family for 11 years, Vieri moved back to his native Bologna at the age of 14 and later joined Inter for a staggering £33 million a year before Keane's arrival.

Keane revealed that he felt his on-field style would complement Vieri, who played like a traditional British centre-forward. He said, 'I hope to be playing with Vieri, but everyone is waiting for Ronaldo to come back into the team.'

Keane's love affair with Italian football dated back a decade when, as a schoolboy, he had religiously followed Italia 90. Apart from following Jack Charlton's men, Keane had also adored the glamour of the Italy team that qualified for the semi-finals as well as admiring the ruthless efficiency of the eventual winners, Germany. In particular, Keane had noted the influential trio of Lothar Matthaus, Jurgen Klinsmann and Andy Brehme – all of whom played for Inter Milan.

Even before his 10th birthday, Keane was aware of the importance of Serie A – it was where the best players in the world headed and he followed the league as best he could from his home in Glenshane Grove. 'I always supported Inter. They were, and still are, one of the world's best clubs. It is fantastic to have the chance to play for them.'

Every summer, Inter spent heavily in an attempt to produce the next golden age of the *Nerazzurri* – one to rival their dominance of the early 1960s when the club lifted three successive titles. That celebrated side contained the likes of Mario Corso, Sandro Mazzola, Angelo Domenghini and Giacinto Fachetti and they ended Real Madrid's stranglehold on the European Cup with back-to-back wins in 1964 and 1965.

The chief engineer behind the 'Great Inter' phenomenon was legendary coach Helenio Herrera, who revolutionised the modern game and was also the strategist behind the introduction of the *catenaccio* ('door-bolt') system. Herrera astutely reworked the traditional Italian 5-3-2 formation in favour of a more flexible system which included an extra defender who could turn defence into attack – leading to the birth of 'the sweeper'.

The legacy of Herrera's all-conquering team still cast a huge shadow over the club in the form of massive levels of expectation. But Keane did not carry that burden. He wanted to seize centre stage, explode on to the scene like an Irish firecracker and write himself into Inter folklore with his extraordinary ability to improvise in attacking areas.

Finally, Keane made his eagerly awaited Inter debut in a pre-season competition called the Birra Moretti Trophy. In what was a three-team tournament, the *Nerazzurri* lined up against rivals Juventus and hosts Bari in two 45-minute games. Before the trip south, Keane underlined his commitment to his new employers by telling the Italian media, 'I'm not married and I don't have a girlfriend. I'm now married to Inter.'

Baby Irish's Italian Adventure

It looked like being a joyous honeymoon for both partners when, in the opening match against Bari, Keane created the winning goal after his incisive pass found Vladimir Jugovic who in turn set up Ivan Zamorano to finish in expert fashion. In the second game against Juventus, Keane was introduced as a substitute and used as a lone striker, in which role he displayed some neat touches and showed genuine hunger for the ball.

The youngster was a pleasure to watch and the Inter fans immediately warmed to both his work rate and instinctive trickery – at one point, he left three Bari defenders on their backsides as he accelerated away.

The match ended 1–1 which prompted a rather bizarre ice hockey-style penalty shoot-out. Rather than placing the ball on the spot 12 yards from the target, the outfield player started 35 yards away from goal and had seven seconds to put the ball in the net. Unfortunately, this experimental concept did not work for Robbie and he fluffed his chance – twice. On his first attempt, he took the ball past the onrushing keeper only to be unceremoniously bundled to the floor. Then, on the rerun, he side-stepped the Juventus number one before slicing his effort wide of an open goal. His Inter team-mates did not fare much better either as Juventus won the shoot-out 2–1.

But Keane redeemed himself a few days later with his first goal in Inter colours, scoring the opener in a 3–2 friendly win over amateur side Vigevano, which had Lippi praising his new recruit's *grinta* (desire to succeed). Lippi told the Italian press, 'Inter are now a complete team with Robbie. Robbie has the *grinta* to prosper at Inter. Not every player has that quality, but I can see it in Robbie.'

The silver-haired tactician also pointed out that Inter

would patiently nurture Keane's unique ability and make sure he was given every chance to succeed. 'There is no pressure on Robbie to get into the first team because he is very young, but I am sure that will not stop him from trying to play as many games as possible. The way football is played in Italy is different to England, but we believe Robbie has qualities which will make him a success in Serie A.'

Ahead of Inter's Champions League qualifier against Helsingborgs of Sweden, Keane admitted it would be difficult to land a starting berth in the side – even in the absence of the injured Ronaldo and Vieri. He said, 'I'm probably going to struggle on that front for a while, but I'm willing to give it a go.'

At the beginning of August, Keane savoured his first taste of playing in the Champions League, but Inter suffered a hugely significant loss at Helsingborgs. After topping a newspaper poll to determine who should play up front for Inter, Keane was handed his first competitive start and he lined up alongside Turkey striker Hakan Sukur in attack.

With a Man of the Match performance, Keane refused to let his sumptuous skills be submerged in the hurly-burly of a tough encounter with the Scandinavians. The 20-year-old almost gave Inter the lead just before half-time after forcing the home side's goalkeeper Sven Andersson into a save.

In an uneventful match, Inter, with Laurent Blanc at the back, seemed to be heading towards a goalless draw. But with less than 10 minutes left, a volley from Michael Hansson stunned the *Nerazzurri* and ensured that the Swedish side took a one-goal advantage into the second leg at the San Siro.

Afterwards, Lippi said, 'I felt Robbie was probably the best player for us in the first leg, even though he missed a goal chance. He has adapted to his new environment quicker than expected.'

Two weeks later, ahead of his home debut for Inter, Keane summed up what he thought the chances were of progressing to the next round of Europe's premier competition. He said, 'Every player has ambitions to play in the Champions League and one of the reasons I agreed to come to Inter was because it would provide that opportunity.

'The players were disappointed at losing to a late goal in the first leg, but the spirit is strong and everyone believes we can overturn the deficit. Personally, I'm thrilled at the prospect of finally playing at the San Siro as all our games so far have been away from home.'

But the fairytale beginning at one of the world's most famous stadiums turned into a horror show for both Keane and Inter as the favourites crashed out of the cup without even scoring a goal. After replacing Chile international Ivan Zamorano at half-time, Keane almost opened his San Siro account with one of the cheekiest goals of all time – an audacious back-heel that cannoned off the post. But, for all his wholehearted efforts, Keane was ultimately chasing a lost cause.

In a dramatic conclusion to the tie, Inter could have forced the game into extra-time when the home side won a penalty in the last minute. But Alvaro Recoba's spot-kick was saved, Inter limped out of the tournament and the vultures started circling around under-pressure boss Lippi.

Despite the massive setback, Keane had been Inter's sole guiding light in a depressing episode in their glorious history, and the club's scout Luis Suarez singled the young Irishman out for praise. 'We knew we were getting a talented player, though in football there is no such thing as a sure thing. Keane's attitude is fantastic and, if he continues to work hard, he can have a great future here.'

Although Keane was disappointed with the result against Helsingborgs, he was looking ahead optimistically to Inter's UEFA Cup campaign. 'There is still the UEFA Cup. We have a real chance in that.'

Keane's nimbleness and courage had also marked him out as a thoroughbred in the eyes of the San Siro regulars, who chanted his nickname throughout the morale-sapping defeat. The Irishman responded with a huge compliment for the home of Inter. 'The crowd and the stadium were incredible. I had seen the stadium many times on television, but to be out there on the pitch, looking up at the massive stands just took my breath away. I never dreamed that one day I'd be playing here.'

Away from duties at Inter, Keane faced one of his club colleagues, Clarence Seedorf, in a World Cup qualifier when the Republic of Ireland faced Holland at the Amsterdam ArenA. Before the match, Keane shed light on the pre-game banter he had shared with Seedorf, who also doubled up as his room-mate on away trips with Inter.

Keane told the Irish press, 'We've been winding each other up about this match, but as the day has got nearer he hasn't been saying much. Maybe he's trying to keep something from me. Just being around someone like Seedorf is a fantastic experience; he's helped me settle in no end. He's a fantastic player and I owe him a lot because he's made life a lot easier for me.'

Keane then hit Inter's first goal in a 4–3 loss to Lazio in the Italian Super Cup before his trans-European tour took him on to Poland. Facing Ruch Chorzow in the UEFA Cup, Inter initially struggled to break down the home side's defence until Seedorf steered a spectacular volley into the net 10 minutes after half-time. Substitute Alvaro Recoba extended Inter's lead, before Keane showed his predatory instincts inside the area by sweeping a loose ball into the Polish team's net from close range.

Keane then scored his third goal for Inter against Lecce in the Italian Cup. After drawing the first leg 1–1 at the San Siro, the omens did not look good for Keane and co when Lecce edged in front after 11 minutes through Cristiano Lucarelli. Inter responded with a spellbinding display and Keane confirmed his stature as a fantastic talent. Using his amazing ball control to skip past defenders from deep positions before exposing the Lecce defence with a measured pass or a devastating shot, Keane was making a difference.

After Inter defender Ivan Cordoba had scored, Lecce were the victims of a typical piece of quick-witted genius from Keane. Picking up the ball on the edge of the box from Seedorf, Keane jinked his way into the area before calmly chipping a shot over the goalkeeper's body. A final goal from Recoba sealed a satisfying win for Inter as the club booked a quarter-final place against Parma. Keane was getting into the swing of things in Italy – September had been a good month for the Irishman.

But, after Inter lost their opening match of the Serie A season against Reggina on 1 October 2000, Lippi was sacked within three days and suddenly a question mark hung over the future of Keane. He was saddened at the exit of Lippi because he believed he had improved as a player and wanted to continue his working relationship with the former Juventus coach.

But Keane also understood that in the cut-throat world of

Italian football a manager is judged on results. 'I was shocked when I heard the news first. I was told in the afternoon, but I didn't know what the situation was. I do now. I'm disappointed because Lippi's a good man, but it's not down to me, and there's not a lot I can do about the situation. What I say doesn't matter. We just have to move on and concentrate on doing well in the league.'

Keane insisted, however, that the sudden exit of Lippi would not lead to his own departure from the San Siro – he had a mission to accomplish with the *Nerazzurri*. 'I don't think it will affect the players. All you want to do is go out and play for yourself and the team. It definitely won't be unsettling for me. There was nothing said after we were beaten, but a lot of people were expecting us to win after the disappointment of being knocked out of the Champions League.'

President Moratti acted swiftly to find Lippi's replacement, with former World Cup-winner Marco Tardelli landing Inter's top job. The 46-year-old ex-Inter midfielder was famous for the way he celebrated his goal in the 1982 World Cup Final against West Germany. After driving a 20-yard shot past Harald Schumacher, Tardelli was so overcome with emotion he ran to the halfway line consumed with sheer unadulterated joy.

The straight-talking, proud Tuscan had an impressive coaching CV as well: he had previously been in charge of the Italy Under-21 side and guided them to their European Championship triumph in 2000. Tardelli was a football purist who enjoyed working with technically skilful youngsters – at first glance, Tardelli and Keane seemed to be a match made in heaven.

The new Inter coach even highlighted the importance of

Baby Irish's Italian Adventure

Keane to the club in his first encounter with the press: 'Robbie Keane is a player who really impresses me. I've seen him a lot because I was youth coach with the Italian national side and Keane was involved with Ireland. One of the things he has going for him is youth. With luck, he has many years ahead of him in the game.

'We have a lot of excellent players at Inter and every single one of them has to earn his selection. That's good training for any player because this really is the very highest level.'

Keane was encouraged by the appointment of Tardelli and his initial impression was that he would feature in the new coach's plans. 'Players are always sorry when there's a change of management at a club – it's a natural reaction. But the signs are that I could have a good relationship with the new boss and that's a real boost at this stage of my career with Milan.'

But Inter's form did not appear to improve under the new regime, with Tardelli winning just two of his opening seven league games. It soon became an empty and frustrating time for Keane. The fans blamed Tardelli; Moratti defended his new coach and claimed it was Lippi's fault; and the Inter boss accused his players of not having the right attitude.

After an upsetting home defeat against 10-man Lecce, Tardelli said, 'We are superficial and presumptuous and we lack concentration, so it is not possible to play well. Football is also mental game and this is a serious problem for Inter. Until we solve this problem Inter cannot go forward – all the players must accept responsibility.'

As Inter's fortunes nosedived, the rumours linking Keane with a move back to England began in earnest and the Irishman was also the subject of a loan bid from Reggina. He had been taken off after an ineffectual display against Lecce and afterwards Keane answered the rumours by saying, 'I can't really comment on that. I haven't heard anything myself from Inter, so I can't really say anything until I hear from the club. We lost at the weekend, so it wasn't too good, but it's going all right.'

A few days later, Keane flew back to Dublin to represent his country in a friendly against Finland at Lansdowne Road. With his credentials under intense scrutiny, the 20-year-old welcomed the trip back home along with the opportunity to spend time with his friends and family. Unfortunately, he sustained a foot injury in a 3–0 win and that subsequently ruled him out of Inter's 2–1 victory over Perugia.

Afterwards Inter director Gabriele Martino attempted to 'clarify' Keane's future at the club, but ended up sending out a mixed message to the football world: 'I don't think Inter will let him go easily. We'll see what happens when the market reopens in January.'

Keane's bad luck with injury continued and he was forced to miss the Coppa Italia quarter-final first-leg tie against Parma with a back problem. His presence was sorely missed – Inter were on the receiving end of a 6–1 battering. The Irishman was devastated at being sidelined and explained he had no intention of leaving Inter: 'When the manager told me yesterday that I would be playing up front with Ivan Zamorano, I was delighted.

'Having missed out on the past three league games, I was really looking forward to playing. But, when I started warming up this morning, I suddenly felt a really bad pain in my back and realised immediately that I would have to pull out of the team.

Baby Irish's Italian Adventure

'With all the speculation of the last few days, I was looking forward to tonight's game – I want to show by my performances that I deserve to be in the first team. I knew when I signed that Inter had six international strikers on their books and I am determined to succeed by training hard and playing well. I have settled in Italy, I am learning the language, have moved into an apartment and made a number of new friends. Everything is going really well here.'

But the English and Irish press were convinced Keane was heading back to the Premiership.

Keane hit back at the claims: 'Life is good. I've moved into a nice apartment beside the San Siro and my Italian is getting much better. I can understand far more of what is being said in the dressing room now.

'Tardelli is a good man and he knows his stuff. He had a meeting with us when he took over and he didn't say anything negative. I'm happy with the number of games I'm playing. I started against Lecce at the weekend. Squad rotation is a way of life in Italy, but people forget that I've been involved in all bar two of the games we have played.'

However, Keane's former club Wolves tried to end his apparent nightmare by offering him a way back to Molineux on a loan basis to revitalise his career – unsurprisingly Keane's adviser, Tony Stephens, declined the offer.

Inter were adamant their summer signing would not be heading back to England, with the club's technical director Gabriele Oriali stating, 'We have no intention of sending Robbie Keane back to England. He is only 20 and he has great potential. It is likely we will send him out on loan in the near future, but only to an Italian club. There is no question of him going back to the Premiership.

Robbie Keane

'Robbie is desperate to prove he is capable of making it big in Serie A. He believes that he is still ahead of schedule with Inter, in spite of being left out of the side for the last few games.'

Meanwhile, both West Ham and Chelsea had already made formal contact with Inter with the intention of bringing Keane back to the Premiership. West Ham boss Harry Redknapp lodged a £10 million bid for Keane, but, for the second time in his career, the Irishman turned down the prospect of playing his football in London's East End.

Redknapp told the English press, 'We went over to Italy and had a meet with the people from Milan and made an offer of £10 million, but we couldn't quite agree terms with them. It wasn't far away I don't think, but I don't know if they really want to sell the boy anyway, and I don't know if the boy wants to leave – I think he probably wants to stay there.

'I'd have loved to have bought him – he is a fantastic player. We'd still like to do something if ever the chance came, but whether it will I don't know. He would have been a great player for us. He is quality and you want quality players. But at the end of the day it is what the boy wants to do and I think there are lots of other clubs in for him from England.'

Moratti then revealed to the club's official website that there was considerable interest in 'Baby Irish'. 'Inter are evaluating offers from several English clubs interested in Robbie Keane. During the Christmas break, negotiations could come to a successful conclusion, naturally with the consent of the player and a sum equal to that which we signed him for six months ago from Coventry.'

Chelsea manager Claudio Ranieri had made Keane his

number-one transfer target with the intention of pairing the livewire Irishman up front with Jimmy Floyd Hasselbaink. The west London club's managing director, Colin Hutchison, admitted to the *Daily Mirror*, 'We have had discussions with Inter Milan about Robbie Keane. That's all I will say at the moment.'

But Keane was not willing to call it quits at Inter so soon after uprooting himself, as he told Channel Five: 'I've got a contract here for five years and, as far as I'm concerned, I'm staying. It's quite flattering to think that people like Chelsea and Leeds are interested in me, but I'm very happy here at the moment. I just want to get myself back fit and, hopefully, work my way back into the team. It's different from England. Milan is a wonderful city. But I didn't come here to go shopping, I came here to play football.

'I've only been here a few months, but I'm enjoying playing alongside the likes of Christian Vieri and Ivan Zamorano. That's the only way I am going to learn to become a better player.'

Every time he spoke to the press, Keane reiterated his desire to stay at Inter and establish himself as a success in Serie A, but he was savvy enough to know deep down that the curtain was set to fall on his Italian adventure.

The interest from Leeds had struck a chord with Keane. He knew a handful of the players – Gary Kelly, Ian Harte, Alan Maybury and Stephen McPhail – and the Yorkshire club's manager, David O'Leary, was one of his boyhood heroes. O'Leary had assembled a young, vibrant side capable of challenging Manchester United for the Premiership crown and competing against the best in the Champions League.

One of the game's great entertainers, Keane was also

hugely ambitious and the thought of exchanging Inter for Leeds looked like a fair swap. As a result, three days before Christmas Eve 2000, Keane agreed to join Leeds on loan until the end of the season with a view to a £12 million permanent switch in July.

Keane – still technically an Inter employee – diplomatically told the English press, 'I have mixed emotions – when I joined Inter Milan in July I thought I would be spending years in Italy. I have settled well over there and was learning the language and had made a number of friends.

'But the most important thing was that I had only been picked for half of the Serie A games and, as any footballer will tell you, playing is everything.

'Last week, Inter officials told me that there had been a lot of interest from Premiership clubs and indicated to me that they would be considering offers. They asked me which team I would join if I had a choice and I told them it would be Leeds.'

Gabriele Marcotti – a European football columnist with *The Times* – summed up Keane's association with the *Nerazzurri* by saying, 'Around the time, Inter had a lot of ambition. Their idea was to go out and buy up as much young talent as possible.

'Robbie Keane was coming in as the fifth or sixth striker and that was the kind of thing Inter did quite a lot around that time. It was always quite obvious that he was either going to come in and make a massive immediate impact or, most likely, get loaned out with a view to being taken back later.

'When Keane came, there was no question there was a lot of potential and Inter certainly liked what they saw. But they quickly concluded that he wasn't the finished article.

Baby Irish's Italian Adventure

'I think everybody liked him. He worked very hard on the pitch which people certainly appreciated, plus you could tell he was a gifted player – that obviously helps as well. Where he was unlucky was that Inter is not the right place for a player who hasn't developed. They were looking for immediate results, but, given the competition he faced, he wasn't going to be in a position to provide that.'

Six years later, Keane set the record straight regarding his brief stay at Inter and claimed he had enjoyed every minute of his Italian adventure. As he told the *Daily Mail*, 'Leaving home at 15 was tough, not going to live in Milan at 19 – I had a great time. When I got there, it was fantastic. Marcello Lippi was the manager and he was such a gentleman. He couldn't speak much English but he had this aura about him. He was always very kind to me.

'But everything changed very quickly there. Lippi was sacked and Marco Tardelli took over, and he had his own ideas on players. I played about 10 games in the six months I was there before joining Leeds, scored a couple of goals in the cup, but soon got tired of sitting on the bench. I don't like doing that. I don't agree with earning money for doing nothing.'

chapter six

To Elland and Back

'I enjoyed watching him play, but I honestly think for the money we paid we didn't get the best out of him. He was obviously a quality player and he was still young and learning. It wasn't his fault the manager didn't pick him. We just didn't see as much of him as we would have liked.'

Peter Lorimer on Robbie Keane's Leeds United career, 2006

R obbie Keane was given a fresh start in West Yorkshire and it was a chance for him to rekindle the qualities of skill, imagination and subtlety that had originally earned him the move to Inter Milan – the 20-year-old was ready to prove the doubters wrong.

The manager who had persuaded Keane to join the Elland Road revolution on loan until July was David O'Leary, a progressive and ambitious young manager who had assembled a vibrant squad capable of emulating the achievements of the famous Leeds side of the Don Revie era. Keane had found a boss who not only shared a similar background, but also was a like-minded individual.

Despite being born in Stoke Newington, London, O'Leary had grown up in Glasnevin on the north side of Dublin, before returning to England's capital to join Arsenal as an apprentice along with his near neighbours Frank Stapleton and Liam Brady.

O'Leary went on to make his League debut against Burnley in August 1975 – three months after he had turned 17 – and registered over 700 appearances for the Gunners, before moving north to sign for Leeds in the 1993/94 season. After only featuring in 10 games, an injury brought O'Leary's career to an end, but it led to his appointment on the club's coaching staff.

Learning at the shoulder of Leeds boss George Graham, he subsequently succeeded the Scot in the manager's office and quickly made a big impression, handling the press with ease and displaying top-notch man-management skills as Leeds marched on towards glory.

A classy centre-half who had been selected 68 times for his country, O'Leary's decisive penalty kick which beat Romania goalkeeper Silviu Lung to put the Republic of Ireland into the quarter-finals of Italia 90 had made a nine-year-old from Tallaght celebrate raucously in the street with neighbours.

That schoolboy was Robbie Keane, and so, a decade later, there was no need for a proper introduction between the Leeds boss and his prospective loan signing – Keane had an old collection of stickers, several with O'Leary's face on them. During the previous season, the exuberant style of O'Leary's young side – a far cry from the dour tactics employed by Graham – had taken the club to third spot in the Premiership as well as the UEFA Cup semi-finals.

But a 4–2 aggregate defeat at the hands of Turkish giants Galatasaray was marred by tragedy when two Leeds fans, Kevin Speight and Chris Loftus, were killed in Istanbul allegedly by so-called fans of the home team. The tragedy had scarred and shocked the players, but collectively they were a bunch of strong-minded and driven young professionals, committed to taking Leeds into the record books. Leeds squad looked like the bright new force in English football and Keane wanted to be a part of that.

Prior to his arrival at Elland Road, Leeds had exceeded all expectations with a groundbreaking start in the Champions League – the first time the club had competed in Europe's premier competition since 1975. After a tentative start, Leeds had already collected the scalps of Beskitas and AC Milan at home, before famously winning away at Lazio. But the club's extraordinary exertions in Europe had taken their toll on Leeds' Premiership form, with the club only able to chalk up seven League victories before the introduction of Keane.

Another factor that influenced Keane's decision in favour of joining Leeds was the playing staff's strong Irish flavour. At Inter Milan, he had sometimes been embarrassed when his English-speaking team-mates sometimes struggled to understand his strong Dublin brogue. But, at the club's Thorp Arch training complex, he bumped into several familiar faces – including Republic of Ireland team-mates, Gary Kelly, Ian Harte, Alan Maybury and Stephen McPhail.

Maybury was the player Keane had replaced on his senior international debut, a likeable Dubliner who had come up through the youth ranks at Leeds. Keane had befriended skilful midfielder McPhail on the triumphant trip to Cyprus in 1998 when Ireland's Under-18 squad were crowned champions of Europe, and he also played with him the following year in the FIFA World Youth Championships in Nigeria.

Meanwhile, Drogheda natives Gary and Ian – uncle and

nephew, despite there being only a three-year age gap between them – were cornerstones of Mick McCarthy's national team and they had been at Leeds since their early teens.

While on international duty in Dublin the previous month, Keane had sounded them out about the set-up at Leeds. He received ringing endorsements from both of them. In fact, he had deliberately met up with them when Leeds had played AC Milan the previous month. He also ended up watching a training session before the Whites' game at the San Siro in order to get a feel for what the club had to offer.

As a renowned practical joker, Keane also enjoyed the banter and funny stories that regularly emanated from the duo. Harte could often be quiet, but was capable of ridiculing a team-mate with razor-sharp put-downs, but his uncle Gary was his Achilles heel because the older family member would mimic Harte mercilessly and humiliate him – much to the amusement of onlookers. Kelly looked out for his young countryman and made sure he felt settled in Yorkshire – culminating in Keane buying a house down the road from his team-mate.

There were other dominant personalities in the dressing room, such as London-born defenders Rio Ferdinand, who had cost the club a British record transfer fee of £18 million from West Ham, and Michael Duberry.

Also on the playing staff were no-nonsense East Anglian full-back Danny Mills, local lad Alan Smith and lively Australian Harry Kewell. There were no shrinking violets in the Leeds ranks.

Leeds were a club going places and there was a buzz around the ground that had been absent since the heady days of the late 1960s and early 1970s when Irish legend

To Elland and Back

John Giles was a key part of a golden era at Elland Road. Legendary manager Don Revie had put together a formidable blend of flair, steely determination and unity of purpose; Leeds proceeded to dominate England's top flight and Europe for seven years. That side contained the likes of Giles, Billy Bremner, Jackie Charlton, Eddie Gray, Norman Hunter, Allan Clarke and Peter Lorimer – a true British football dynasty.

Despite Leeds savouring a brief Gordon Strachan-led First Division title triumph in 1992 when Howard Wilkinson was manager, the general consensus among seasoned followers of the club was that the class of 2000 was the best they had seen since the good old days – that included Lorimer.

Lorimer, the club's record goal-scorer, said, 'There was a great feeling around the city because we had reached these heights with a lot of players that had come through our Academy system. The likes of Alan Smith, Jonathan Woodgate, Harry Kewell, Ian Harte and Gary Kelly – they'd all come up through the ranks, so it was even more of a privilege to watch this happening.

'There were lots of similarities between that team and the side I'd played in and the future for Leeds looked really bright. George Graham had left Leeds, David O'Leary took over and gave the kids a chance and they responded magnificently. It was nice to see and it brought back happy memories of what had happened at the club before. Although it is nice to buy players for lots of money, it is also nice to produce your own.'

As Keane was reintroduced to the English press, O'Leary summed up his new recruit's unshakeable self-belief and strength of character: 'You like to get good players and I've got someone who I know can go on to be a very good player.

Robbie Keane

In Robbie, we're buying potential because he is not the finished article. But we are buying a player who is out of the Alan Shearer mould. He is someone who is mentally strong to handle the big stage at a big club. He has a hunger to be a great player and that is what we want.'

By now well versed in handling the demands of inaugural press conferences at new clubs, Keane outlined his objectives at Leeds and also politely drew a line under the apparent snub he had received from Inter Milan.

Keane said, 'When I was at Wolves, I always dreamed I would do well and play for the best clubs in the world, and three years on I can say I've played for Inter Milan. And now I'm going to be playing for Leeds.

'It's been a great experience for me, a rollercoaster ride from day one, but I'm enjoying every minute of it and I'm looking forward to playing again after the disappointment of things not working out in Italy. I wanted it to work there and things were going well under Mr Lippi, but we all know things change in football and, when the new manager came in, he had his own ideas.

'I've nothing against Mr Tardelli. He is a great man and a great manager, but unfortunately I just didn't figure in his plans. It was very frustrating to be sitting on the bench. As a player you want to be playing in every game, although I knew before I went that wasn't going to happen. When you're on the bench, you're thinking how much you want to play, but that's football. It happens at all clubs, including Manchester United and Leeds, and not just at Inter Milan.

'But in coming back I don't think I've got a point to prove. I went over to Italy to be a star and unfortunately it didn't work out. I'm just grateful they gave me a chance. It was an experience for me, and something I'll never forget and I've never regretted. Now I've joined another great club and, with the squad we've got, we're quite capable of reaching the Champions League this season.

'Nine clubs came in for me, but Leeds were always the one I wanted to join. They are a club who can win the Champions League and I have come here to win things. I've been watching what David O'Leary has been doing at Leeds and I've been very impressed.'

Despite moving back to the Premiership in search of a regular spot in the starting line-up, Keane began his association with Leeds as substitute for the home fixture against Aston Villa. In a David Ginola-inspired win for John Gregory's men, Keane was introduced to add some much-needed spark up front with only 23 minutes of the game remaining.

Seldom predictable, Keane seemed to be able to sense where the gaps were and the potential holes he could punch in the Villa defence – the Leeds fans took to him immediately. But an injury-time goal from defender Jonathan Woodgate proved to be nothing more than a consolation in a surprise victory for Villa which left Leeds feeling decidedly flat just two days before Christmas.

Afterwards, O'Leary congratulated Keane on a positive first appearance and acknowledged that the Elland Road regulars had already taken a shine to him. 'Robbie looked very good for his 23 minutes, considering he had only trained for 30 minutes. His movement is excellent and the crowd will like him.'

But the Leeds boss slammed his team's pedestrian attacking performance and stressed he would not be settling for any further mediocre performances. 'I didn't come here to manage a team that is 12th! We need to be up there and we are not doing it. Teams that do well are consistent, and we are not! Quality players are here, but we are under-performing. It's a learning process. Teams coming here are well organised. The onus is on us to do something about it.'

The following game on Boxing Day was a trip up to the North East to face Newcastle United in front of an expectant St James' Park. Again, Keane began the match rooted to the bench and Leeds were knocked out by two sucker punches from Newcastle's South American duo Clarence Acuna and Nolberto Solano – even though O'Leary's side had taken an early lead.

The alarm bells had started to ring in O'Leary's ears and the straight-talking Irishman publicly questioned his team's ability to finish high enough in the Premiership standings to qualify for another Champions League adventure.

After spending £35 million on players, Leeds could have done with cashing in on the bonuses available to Europe's elite. It had been a bold gamble by the club's chairman Peter Ridsdale and Leeds needed some wins. Four defeats in five League games told its own sorry tale and left one of the clubs tipped to challenge for the title sitting just six points above the relegation zone.

Behind closed doors, O'Leary vowed to ring the changes and New Year's Day 2001 proved to be the turning point. Keane was told he would start the game against Middlesbrough ahead of Alan Smith.

On his arrival at Leeds, Keane had been allocated the same squad number that he had worn at Coventry and Inter, and now he was ready to show the West Yorkshire public he was United's 'magnificent seven'.

Middlesbrough were meant to be cannon fodder for the all-conquering Whites – unfortunately, the visitors clearly hadn't ready the script. Struggling near the foot of the table, the club had enlisted the help of former England boss Terry Venables in a last-ditch bid to avoid relegation and the Teessiders were proving a tough nut to crack. Boos from the home support then reached a crescendo after Alen Boksic, the Croatian striker, exploited a defensive mistake to score in the first half.

In the heat of battle, the calm voice counts and, as his team-mates stared another devastating defeat in the face, Robbie Keane stepped up and spoke out. Referee David Elleray awarded Leeds an apparently dubious penalty after he judged that a cross from Mark Viduka had struck Middlesbrough's Irish defender Curtis Fleming on the arm. Keane grabbed the ball, did not shirk responsibility and tucked his spot-kick into the bottom left-hand corner of Mark Schwarzer's goal before celebrating with a jubilant cartwheel in front of the Kop.

But Keane's energetic impact did not prevent him being replaced by Smith 20 minutes later as Leeds were held to a draw. After collecting just four points from six games, Leeds were in the doldrums and O'Leary reflected, 'Once we gave the goal away, we lacked confidence and we know that we are not playing as well as we should be.'

Keane retained his spot in the starting line-up for the FA Cup third-round win over Barnsley, where he operated in a three-pronged attack, just behind Viduka, who scored the only goal of the game, and Smith. But O'Leary repeatedly stressed that this was not his favoured formation. He insisted that he was only picking three central strikers because of a lack of available wide players with Kewell ruled out through injury. O'Leary said, 'We don't have any width and the players who can provide it are not fit.

'I had to play 4-3-3 against Barnsley because Jason Wilcox

wasn't 100 per cent, but the three-forwards system isn't ideal as you get three players looking for the same space. I would say 4-4-2 is my ideal formation.'

To make matters worse for Keane, he limped off nursing a slight knee problem with four minutes of the contest remaining. After struggling to train in the days leading up to the following weekend's trip to Manchester City, Keane was named among the substitutes and watched from the bench as Leeds took the lead through Eirik Bakke. Even though he was only given the nod to come on with 20 minutes remaining, Keane's influence was considerable. Lee Bowyer added a second before Keane struck twice in injury-time to set a healthy revival in motion with a much-needed victory across the Pennines.

But he knew his stunning pair of goals would not necessarily guarantee a starting place in the Leeds side – even though Ridsdale had paid Inter Milan £1 million just for the privilege of bringing him in on loan. O'Leary clearly stated that he wanted strong competition for places and quality back-up. 'I want two quality players for every position. I don't care if players are annoyed by my selection decisions. They simply have to learn to live with it. We have used 27 or so different players already this season – that is the reality of competing in the Premiership and the European Champions League.'

With extra incentive to prove his mettle, Keane continued to shine, although as his own star rose so waned the fortunes of his new club, Leeds. It only took Keane two minutes to score his fourth goal for Leeds in a home match against Newcastle with a smart side-footed finish past his fellow countryman Shay Given. But Keane's general *joie de vivre* looked decidedly out of place in a Leeds side that seemed overanxious and devoid of ideas in attacking areas.

A born crowd-pleaser, Keane emerged from the club's 3–1 loss – the fifth Premiership game Leeds had lost at Elland Road that season – with his reputation intact, but he was beginning to question his own judgement. As O'Leary conducted an hour-long post-mortem in the home dressing room, Keane must have wondered what he had walked into.

The 20-year-old had jumped at the chance of joining Leeds instead of signing for Chelsea or West Ham because he believed it would lead him to the trophies he craved. Now he found himself struggling to hold down 90 minutes of game time in a side ambling aimlessly in the Premiership's No-Man's Land.

With pundits searching for someone to blame for the team's abysmal form, O'Leary suggested that it rested on the players' shoulders: 'The bottom line is that a lot of the players are not playing with confidence at home. Expectations are high here and we are struggling to live up to them.'

With Rio Ferdinand back in the defence, Leeds headed for bogey side Aston Villa and, with Keane in sparkling form, snatched a precious 2–1 win. An instinctive player, Keane possessed the single ingredient that all great footballers have at their disposal – the ability to change the tempo of a game at will with one action. It was also becoming abundantly clear to the Leeds faithful that, when on top form, Keane didn't just simply play well – he totally controlled games.

With the game locked at 1–1, Viduka's cross gave Keane a sure-fire scoring chance until he was barged over by Aston Villa's Gareth Barry. Despite the away fans shouting for Keane to take the resultant penalty, Ian Harte converted from the spot to seal a big win for Leeds.

But once again, there was the mystifying sight of Leeds

taking off their lively number 7 at Villa Park, as Alan Smith replaced Keane with 13 minutes remaining. A relieved O'Leary said, 'We have taken a lot of disappointments on the chin, and we worked so hard for this result. Even though we rode our luck a little bit, this was one occasion when we showed how determined we are not to continue letting ourselves down.

'As for the penalty, I didn't really care who took it as long as it went in. But, if Hartey had missed it, I would have had a go, saying that Robbie Keane should have taken it! In the event, I thought Ian Harte was dead right to take it.'

Keane was also delighted that the tide had turned on the club's season and that the infamous Villa jinx had finally been laid to rest. 'We all knew beforehand that Aston Villa were our bogey side, so we knew it was vital we worked very hard. I thought it was a penalty. If he hadn't touched me, I would have had a great chance of scoring, so lucky for us it was awarded.'

Even though he wasn't eligible to take part in Leeds' Champions League adventure, Keane was available for the club's FA Cup matches and he was picked to start against Liverpool at Anfield in an eagerly awaited fourth-round tie. But even though he produced a valiant display, he was guilty of squandering two straightforward chances and was replaced by Alan Smith prior to Liverpool snatching two very late goals from Nick Barmby and Emile Heskey to secure an undeserved victory.

On the pitch, troubled Leeds were misfiring and seemingly incapable of putting the ball in the net. But off the pitch, matters were far worse, with the club making headlines for all the wrong reasons. The much-publicised trial involving first-team regulars Lee Bowyer and Jonathan

Woodgate at Hull Crown Court for alleged assault on an Asian student outside a city-centre nightclub in January 2000 was about to start.

Social commentators accused the young millionaires of thinking that they were above the law and of being poor role models for their adoring young fans. Fingers were being pointed at the thriving football industry, with Middle England accusing the money-drenched national game of creating 'monsters'.

Nevertheless, the fact was that Sarfraz Najeib was brutally attacked and had been left nursing a broken leg and a fractured cheek and nose. The prosecutors claimed that Bowyer, Woodgate and two other men, Paul Clifford and Neale Caveney, chased Najeib after an altercation outside the nightclub and then knocked him unconscious beside a wall. All four denied causing grievous bodily harm and affray. As a backdrop to the club's Champions League heroics, there was a very worrying risk that both Bowyer and Woodgate – two of the brightest young prospects in English football – could be sent to prison.

For Keane, this was a shocking scenario. Aside from an isolated minor incident which happened during his final days at Wolves, the sociable Irishman had always stayed out of trouble. Sure, as a young man he enjoyed a few drinks when unwinding with his colleagues – whether it was at Molly Heffernan's in Tallaght, or at Creation nightclub in Leeds. He liked music and meeting new people, but suddenly everyone at Leeds was under the microscope and the knives were out when it came to off-duty Leeds players.

Back on the pitch, Keane was almost single-handedly keeping Leeds within touching distance of a top-three finish with some enthralling displays – including the winning goal at his former club Coventry. In his absence, Coventry were sliding towards the relegation trap-door and Keane's replacement – £6.5 million buy from Norwich Craig Bellamy – had not worked out as hoped. Not only had the fiery Welshman struggled to emulate Keane's goal-scoring feats, but some thought he also lacked his predecessor's charisma and was apparently not as popular among the club's staff and supporters.

Coventry travelled to Elland Road, having accumulated a paltry 10 points from their previous 15 games, but Gordon Strachan's men dug deep to keep Leeds out until the 69th minute. A cross from Danny Mills was sent into the crowded area and Keane – with his back to goal – unleashed a spectacular overhead kick that beat City keeper Magnus Hedman to win the game for Leeds in thrilling style.

Afterwards, a philosophical Strachan, who had pleaded with the City board not to sell Keane, said, 'If he was still with us, it would have been a different result, but that's life – special player, special goal.'

Unstoppable against Coventry, Keane continued to dazzle with a sensational display three days later at Ipswich to help Leeds record their third successive League win. Keane's tireless running and persistence led to Leeds taking the lead when Ipswich defender Mark Venus, under pressure from the effervescent Irishman, put the ball into his own net. Then, five minutes before half-time, Keane made it six goals in six games with an expert finish from close range – Leeds' loan ranger was at the height of his playing powers.

His form did not go unnoticed and he was duly handed the Carling Player of the Month accolade for January – not a bad opening month's work back in the Premiership. He was thrilled with his prize and said, 'I'm delighted with the award. It's proof that the hard work I've put in since my arrival is paying off. But I'm not there yet. The gaffer has told me that I need to improve on my overall game and I'm going to concentrate on that now.'

David O'Leary waxed lyrical about his signing, saying, 'For £1 million, he has been a great buy for the rest of the season. He could be the key to a European place. It's been a great start for Robbie at the club. He's had a massive impact in terms of scoring vital goals in games where we desperately needed points, and I am in no doubt that he has helped us turn our season around. He came at a time when we were struggling to gain positive results and, once he settled down, has helped us get our season back on track.'

O'Leary defended Keane's form at Inter and insisted the player would get his career back on track under his guidance at Elland Road. 'What disappoints Robbie is that he wanted a chance in Italy and, if he had failed, he would have held his hands up and said he was not good enough. But he believes he just wasn't given the opportunity there – but he joined Leeds because he can achieve success here.

'He is a player who can handle the mental side of being on the big stage and he wants to play in the Champions League. Hopefully, his goals will help us achieve that again next season. I know what makes Robbie tick. Everybody sees this very gifted footballer, with great skills at beating people and a wonderful eye for goal, but he's a lot more than that.

'People sometimes miss the fact that he has this incredible mental toughness. He's desperate to be a winner and, whatever happens to him in a game or in the course of his career, he will never be put off. Robbie is determined to be one of the greatest players in English football.

'Robbie believes that, if he had stayed in Italy, he would

have been one of the top players in that country. He won't be deterred by anything or lose his focus. Nobody can stop him and that's what I admire most about the lad.'

O'Leary also admitted that it had not been an easy ride for Keane joining a club saddled with problems. 'He's only 20 and he's had to cope with coming back into a club that is playing so inconsistently and indifferently. There is a bubbly atmosphere, but the younger players have had dips in form and it has been a very difficult time. Still he has scored goals. This is why I have the height of admiration for him. I have always liked him.'

Even after such a glowing appraisal, and with or without an award, Keane was not a shoo-in to start week-in, week-out at Leeds – especially with Alan Smith turning in outstanding performances in the Champions League.

O'Leary acknowledged the cruel twist of fate that meant his most in-form player would miss the forthcoming European clash against Anderlecht as well as the stop-start nature of the team's forward line. 'We always knew that Robbie would not be able to play in Europe this season, but we still felt the investment was worthwhile.

'Anyway, as is the case in these situations, one man's loss is another's gain. Robbie has become good friends with Alan Smith off the pitch, and now he will have to fight him to get his place back after the Anderlecht game.'

Keane's goal-scoring exploits had taken Leeds up to sixth place in the Premiership standings, but his purple patch dried up in the two League games preceding the clash against the Brussels-based club, with Leeds drawing against Everton and Derby.

Anderlecht were soundly beaten – both in West Yorkshire and Belgium – with Leeds putting six goals past them over the two games and Smith contributing two in a 4–1 win in the Belgian capital. As a result, the media lauded Smith for a world-class display against an Anderlecht side that had won their previous nine home matches in Europe and praised the goals that had taken Leeds into the quarter-finals with two games to spare.

But Smith was suspended for the following Premiership fixture – an away match at Tottenham – and Keane regained his starting spot in the side. Leeds won 2–1 at White Hart Lane and the Whites' previously patchy performances suddenly mushroomed into genuine title form. Unfortunately for Keane, he did not manage to get on the score-sheet, largely because Spurs skipper Sol Campbell had been assigned to man-mark him throughout the game. Nevertheless, Leeds were on a roll and in buoyant mood ahead of the visit of the old enemy Manchester United.

Keane had played in the Black Country derby in Wolves' colours against West Brom and also represented Coventry versus Aston Villa, so he understood the tribal rivalries of English football. But he was still totally unprepared for the fierce passion that a Leeds–Manchester United derby game generates – it is said that the strong mutual dislike dates back centuries to the War of the Roses in 1455.

In an adrenaline-charged classic, Keane was upended inside the area by Manchester United's keeper, Fabien Barthez, early on in the game, but Leeds were only awarded a corner. Barthez's antics were subsequently punished by referee Graham Barber when he kicked Ian Harte in the box and a penalty was given against the French custodian. Even though everyone expected Keane to take the spot-kick, Harte stepped up and saw Barthez keep his penalty out with a great reflex save.

The visitors then edged in front through Luke Chadwick, before Mark Viduka salvaged a point for Leeds after an own goal from Wes Brown – helped in by Viduka. Manchester United's boss Sir Alex Ferguson blamed the goal on an allegedly ineffectual linesman, but Leeds United felt a draw was a deserved end product after a swashbuckling performance.

Off the pitch, the day-to-day running of the team changed considerably following the appointment of former Manchester United assistant manager Brian Kidd in the new role of head coach – Leeds fans were not pleased. As a result, the club's popular number two, Eddie Gray, was eased out of the first team's training schedule and unofficially demoted from his post, while O'Leary withdrew from the training field to his manager's office.

O'Leary explained the reasoning behind the backroom alterations by insisting it would be beneficial if he occupied a new role. 'I've never had a first-team coach – so now, with Brian in place, it will give me a break and I can step away from the lads a little bit. Instead of taking two hours for each training session, I can step in for maybe 15 or 20 minutes and oversee things.'

But some of the players preferred the older system in which the manager was present throughout the whole of the training session. Keane was forced to sit out Leeds' next two European games – a narrow loss at Real Madrid and a 3–3 draw against Lazio – with the Viduka–Smith axis flourishing in his absence.

As a result, he was left on the bench for the following League match against Charlton and watched as both Viduka and Smith found the net in a 2–1 win. The double act featuring the big Australian and the feisty Yorkshireman then repeated the feat in the next match – a 2–0 triumph at Sunderland. But Smith was sent off in a heated encounter and Keane returned to the action as a late substitute for Harry Kewell.

The Wakefield-born striker was making waves in Europe and scored in a comfortable 3–0 quarter-final, first-leg win over Deportivo La Coruna. But Keane was determined to seize his chance and, when Smith was rested, he put on a compelling performance against Southampton in a 2–0 home win. After setting up Kewell's first goal of the season, he then chipped a cheeky shot over the head of Saints keeper Paul Jones to score his first goal in two months.

Keane was back on song and O'Leary was quick to congratulate his striker: 'I said at half-time that the second goal in this match would be very important and, thankfully, Robbie Keane came up with it. As soon as he scored, it was game over and we won convincingly enough in the end. We dominated the match but I do know that, at 1–0, the opposition can come up with one shot that goes into the net and you've been mugged. You've got one point when you should have had three.

'I believe that strikers should be judged over a season and, if Robbie missed a few for Ireland, then that's just the sort of thing that happens. They're going to miss a few, but he got a cracker here.'

Despite scoring a wonderful goal, Keane was dropped for the Premiership trip to Liverpool, with Smith getting the nod to start alongside Viduka. The change had an uplifting effect on the team and Liverpool were soundly beaten 2–1 and Keane had a late cameo role in an eye-catching victory.

However, Keane was handed his first XI place back for Rio Ferdinand's return to the Boleyn Ground and responded with a well-taken goal. Ferdinand added a second and, even though David Batty was sent off, Leeds outclassed West Ham. Keane and Leeds were cartwheeling towards a top-three finish and the club had also booked a place in the Champions League semi-finals – life smelled great again at Elland Road.

The Irishman then exploded like a firecracker in the home win over much-fancied Chelsea. In what had been a drab and uninspiring game, Keane came off the bench to replace Kewell and, five minutes later, beat Carlo Cudicini with an irresistible finish. Mark Viduka scored a second moments later and Leeds were starting to look invincible – winning games when they had not performed particularly well. They also had exceptional talent waiting in the wings.

Asked by the press whether or not he thought Keane warranted a role as first-choice striker, O'Leary said, 'I want him to prove a point. I want him to go out there and score, then look at me and say, "Why am I not on from the start?" He's a cheeky lad, a nice cheeky lad, and he has that knack of putting the ball in the back of the net.'

But as the season entered its final furlong, and with the finish line in sight, Leeds' luck ran out. The 3–0 aggregate defeat to Valencia in the last four of the Champions League, coupled with a huge loss in the League at Arsenal, left O'Leary's young squad decidedly crestfallen. The dream of a second season of Champions League football had faded into oblivion and the price looked as if it was going to be extremely high.

After playing in the bitter defeat at Arsenal, Keane missed the final two games of the season through injury – both heavy wins over Bradford and Leicester – as Leeds finished in fourth spot and had to settle for a UEFA Cup place. Keane had enjoyed a successful, albeit stop-start, beginning to his

Leeds career and scored nine Premiership goals from 12 starts – an impressive ratio.

As promised, Leeds stumped up the cash to turn the loan transfer into a permanent £11 million move and Keane was now officially a Whites player, signing a five-year contract. Despite missing out on a large cash windfall by failing to qualify for Europe's premier competition, Leeds chairman Peter Ridsdale insisted that the club's financial situation was rosy and they could still afford Keane. As he told the *Yorkshire Post*, 'The funds are in place and are part of a three-year deal. The money for the transfer fee of £11 million has already been covered by guarantee. This means that we are not trying to sell players in the summer merely to find the money to pay for Robbie Keane, because that deal is done and, with it being a foreign transfer, we can pay the balance over a three-and-a-half-year period.'

Ahead of the 2001/02 season, Keane felt refreshed and it showed in his pre-season performances – he scored twice in a 6–0 win at Swedish side Kungsbacka, before netting four times against Dublin City in front of his family. He told the *People* about how things had gone over the summer: 'I've come back feeling really good. I'm playing well, scoring goals and feeling sharper than ever before in my career. It was great to come home and score goals in front of my family against City. I got injured near the end of last season, so I had to face the fact that I wasn't going to be fit going into the summer. It was also going to be a bit hard for me to keep in shape because I wasn't training.

'To be honest, I didn't feel myself at all, so I went off and had a great time, relaxing in the sun and making sure I was fit enough to return.'

After scoring twice in the 6–1 thrashing of Sparta

Rotterdam, Keane was selected ahead of rival Alan Smith for the opening match of the new Premiership season as Leeds entertained Southampton. But Keane made little impact up front and the score-line was blank when both he and David Batty were replaced by Smith and Eirik Bakke. The substitutes changed the outcome of the game, with Leeds winning 2–0 and Smith grabbing the final goal.

Afterwards, David O'Leary said, 'Eirik made things happen in midfield and Smithy played superbly up front. They made a big difference and have given me a selection headache for the next match, but that's nice. We want more headaches all over the place.'

As a result, Keane was relegated to the bench for the trip to Arsenal and was not called upon in a bruising 2–1 win at Highbury, which saw Danny Mills and Lee Bowyer red-carded. With Smith sidelined as a result of the battle of Islington, Keane was ushered back into the side for the game at West Ham, but produced a performance that was worryingly off-key in a goalless draw. Despite his below-par showing, Keane kept his place for the visit of Bolton and could have won the game right at the death, but keeper Jussi Jaaskeleinen bravely saved at his feet.

An exuberant, confident character, Keane just needed a goal to get back on track and it arrived at Charlton as he summoned up a breathtaking display in front of the watching Mick McCarthy. Buzzing in the Leeds attack, Keane opened the scoring when he punished an error from Charlton defender Mark Fish to finish from close range. The only blip on an otherwise satisfying afternoon for Keane came when he was booked, allegedly for diving, by referee Mark Halsey – a controversial decision as TV replays later seemed to show.

After the disappointment of losing to Helsingborgs with

Inter, Keane was determined to enjoy a large dose of European football in the UEFA Cup – starting with a trip to Madeiran side Maritimo.

After a 1–0 loss on the Portuguese island, O'Leary said, 'I didn't know the lads could play that badly.'

But Leeds made amends in the return leg at Elland Road, with Keane scoring his first-ever goal for Leeds in European football in a 3–0 win. He raced on to David Batty's searching through-ball and one subtle touch took him away from three Maritimo players before he struck a cross-shot into the corner of the net.

That personal milestone was followed with a stylish goal in a 2–1 win at Ipswich that kept Leeds top of the Premiership and Keane also prompted the winner – his cross was turned into his own net by Town defender Mark Venus.

Keane's form was perking up encouragingly, but he showed his gift for goals best in the 6–0 Worthington Cup demolition of Leicester at Filbert Street. Blessed with uncanny anticipation, Keane notched two poacher's goals in the space of 16 minutes. He then set up team-mate Eirik Bakke with an outrageous back-heel, before completing his hat-trick eight minutes after half-time. When he was taken off minutes after scoring his third of the night, Keane received a deserved ovation from the travelling Leeds fans.

But the razzmatazz of the Leeds revival could not help O'Leary's men get three points at Anfield as Liverpool held the League leaders to a 1–1 draw. In a scrappy, disjointed game, Keane's razor-sharp edge was blunted, but the point extended Leeds' unbeaten run to eight games and kept them in top spot.

In the next round of the UEFA Cup, Keane started against French minnows Troyes and, despite not finding the net, was his usual lively self in a 4–2 home win. But O'Leary wasn't happy with the way his side conceded a costly late goal to 10-man Troyes and predicted a tough return leg across the Channel. 'I was impressed with us up to the fourth goal, but we stopped playing when they went down to 10. The tie remains very much alive.'

On a wet Sunday at Elland Road, Leeds locked horns with age-old foes Chelsea and, in an ugly encounter littered with petulant fouls, remained undefeated after a 0–0 stalemate. Keane got involved in a tangle with Chelsea full-back Graeme Le Saux, and the England defender was lucky to stay on the pitch after what appeared to be a horrendous challenge on Danny Mills went unpunished.

Leeds were becoming a resilient, battle-hardened side capable of both outplaying and outmuscling opponents and, as part of that, Keane was suddenly showing an aggressive side to his game. But this newfound uncompromising attitude to tackling duties led to Keane sparking off an incident the following weekend against Manchester United.

On the day, Keane was a dynamic presence on the pitch, tormenting Manchester United's defence and hitting an early shot into the side netting. However, Old Trafford was primed to erupt in a fixture that always carries a volatile undercurrent, and it duly did after Beckham chopped down Keane. The Irishman reacted angrily and seemed to push Beckham in the face, a red-card offence, but referee Dermot Gallagher only dished out a caution – much to the home crowd's displeasure.

Beckham also had his name taken by the official and the Red Devils went on to have the last laugh of the afternoon when Ole Gunnar Solskjaer's late goal cancelled out Mark Viduka's opener.

To Elland and Back

Afterwards, O'Leary openly criticised Keane. 'I had a right go at him because, if you raise your hands, you are leaving yourself open to the referee. If that had happened in Europe, I think he would definitely have taken a walk. It was a nothing incident, but Robbie should not have done what he did.'

But Keane got back into O'Leary's good books with a late goal that rescued Leeds' UEFA Cup campaign after it appeared as if Troyes would achieve a major upset. With Leeds trailing 3–1 on the night, extra-time was beckoning until Keane intervened and his glancing header ultimately sealed a 6–5 aggregate victory.

Against Tottenham, the energetic Irishman chased and harried the Spurs defence, but was still replaced by Smith with 17 minutes remaining. Cue a scene of sheer frustration from Keane. Ahead of the forthcoming World Cup play-off deciders against Iran, he needed a timely boost and instead he was being hauled off – even though his display had been up to scratch.

As he sat in the home dug-out, he threw off his shin-pads in a fit of rage and aimed a steely glare in the direction of O'Leary. Keane had specifically moved to Leeds to get a run of games under his belt, but now he felt as if, whatever he did, it was never going to be good enough for his manager. To make matters worse, in his absence Leeds found a late winning goal from Harry Kewell. Keane was starting to think his days were numbered at Elland Road.

After helping his country qualify for the 2002 World Cup finals, Keane returned to club duties with a very clear perspective. After a chat with Mick McCarthy, he knew that he would have to be at the top of his game to be guaranteed a place in the Irish side that summer. That meant an uninterrupted sequence of starts at club level and he would not let anything stand in the way of that – even the form of Alan Smith.

But Keane's situation deteriorated significantly with a serious miss during the club's 2–0 defeat at Sunderland followed a barren spell in front of the target – he had scored once in five starts. And things looked tougher for Robbie Keane's Leeds career when the club announced the arrival of another multi-million-pound striker, Liverpool's Robbie Fowler.

Fowler's reputation as an out-and-out goal-scorer was second to none in the English game and O'Leary was willing to pay £11 million to bring in some much-needed firepower to aid Leeds' title bid. The Liverpudlian remarked that he had not been given any assurances of a regular starting spot at Leeds and was aware of the competition for places. 'I have neither sought nor received any assurances from David O'Leary about first-team football. In Alan Smith, Robbie Keane, Mark Viduka and Michael Bridges, there are already four top-class strikers here and it would be disrespectful to them to expect any promises about first-team football.'

But new recruit Fowler started ahead of Keane in the following Premiership match against Everton – scoring twice in a 3–2 win. Keane only got a meagre two minutes on the pitch and his sense of frustration deepened when a problem with one of his ankles got progressively worse. Surgery was required which meant a two-month lay-off.

As Keane went into hospital for an operation to sort out the recurring injury on New Year's Eve 2001, O'Leary told the *Sunday Mirror*, 'Robbie's missed some games of late. He has been complaining about a pain in his ankle for a couple of weeks. He thought he could shake it off, but it's obvious now that something has to be done about it.'

But the Leeds boss insisted that his £12 million

acquisition still had a future at the club – even though he was out of his short-term plans. 'I wouldn't have signed Robbie Keane in the first place if I didn't believe he was a very good player who could do a big job for Leeds.

'And I remain convinced of that in spite of some of the things I've read and heard. The way football is these days, with huge pressure in every game, you don't just settle on 11 players at the start of the season. We're now dependent on the squad system – and that means the players on the bench are every bit as important as those on the park.

'That's why I find it hard to accept some of these armchair critics. They haven't come to terms with the fact that the really big clubs rotate players. I've four top-class strikers here in Robbie, Robbie Fowler, Mark Viduka and Alan Smith. But normally I play only two of them at any given time. At some point each of them will find himself out of the team, but it doesn't mean that I think any less of him as a player.'

As he recovered from surgery to repair damage to his ankle ligaments, Keane missed five matches, before returning to the bench for the following four games – though he only featured twice. Viduka and Fowler were O'Leary's preferred partnership up front and 21-year-old Keane felt he was wasting valuable time sitting on the bench.

With the World Cup looming on the horizon, Keane was worried that his lack of first-team activity could see him lose his place in the Republic of Ireland team, but McCarthy went on record to state that this was not the case. 'If Robbie continues to be kept out of the side by Fowler and Viduka, I won't be worried about it, just so long as he is fit. If he doesn't play in the first team, but is playing in the reserves and playing well and is OK, then that's all that matters to me because I know he can play.'

During Keane's absence, dressing-room politics had become the main topic at Leeds. It was reported that factions were becoming more and more disgruntled with the actions of O'Leary. Back in December, the Elland Road soap opera became increasingly dramatic with the verdict reached in the trial involving Jonathan Woodgate and Lee Bowyer. After a two-month trial at Hull Crown Court, Bowyer was cleared of all charges against him, while Woodgate (who was cleared of assault) was found guilty of affray and sentenced to 100 hours' community service. Neale Caveney was also cleared of assault, was found guilty of affray and received the same sentence as Woodgate. Paul Clifford was found guilty of both assault and affray and imprisoned.

O'Leary had reassured Bowyer that the club would not punish him if he was not convicted of any crime. But the manager subsequently stepped aside when Ridsdale felt obliged to fine the player four weeks' wages for being drunk on the night of the incident.

On the outside, it appeared as if Ridsdale had bowed to public pressure, and the demands of the club's shareholders, in a desperate bid to clean up the image of Leeds United.

Inside the Leeds dressing room, the players were reportedly disgusted that Bowyer had been fined like this after being told he would not be punished. Ridsdale countered, 'How do you sack somebody for being innocent? We took disciplinary action because he was drunk. He has now paid that fine. Is there a court in the land that would have accepted that I sacked him for being drunk in his own time?

'In fact, I think the reaction has caused him and his agent to reflect more than the club. The club stuck to its principles.'

To add further fuel to the fire, O'Leary had written a book

chronicling the whole sorry saga, entitled *Leeds United on Trial*, which was serialised in a national newspaper. Ridsdale said, 'It would be fair to say the timing of it has been anything other than helpful. David knows how I feel.'

After being left on the bench for the UEFA Cup tie at PSV Eindhoven, Keane was relieved to be given the nod to start the following Premiership game against Charlton – but was selected to play on the right wing. With Kewell on the opposite flank and Viduka and Fowler marauding through the middle, O'Leary's attack-oriented line-up was designed to produce goals.

But it failed miserably as Leeds struggled to break down a spirited Charlton side and the game ended 0–0 – Leeds' second successive goalless draw. Left on the bench for the return leg against PSV, Keane looked on as his Leeds dream began to go up in smoke. With just 51 seconds of the tie remaining, Dutch striker Jan Vennegoor of Hesselink plundered the only goal to send Leeds out of the UEFA Cup – before they had even reached the quarter-finals.

The year 2002 continued to be an *annus horribilis* for O'Leary and Leeds after a goalless draw at Everton – the 10th game in which they had failed to win. Keane was an unused substitute for the trip to Merseyside and heard the Leeds fans calling for the dismissal of Kidd – blaming the ex-Manchester United player for the club's woeful run of form.

In a home match against struggling Ipswich, Leeds finally got back to winning ways with Keane coming on as a substitute, but victory just papered over the cracks. Coming off the bench became alarmingly regular for Keane and he made brief appearances against Blackburn, Manchester United, Tottenham and Sunderland.

Against the Wearsiders, Keane finally ended his goal

drought for Leeds – he had only been on the pitch for 20 minutes when his shot beat Sunderland keeper Thomas Sorensen to seal a 2–0 win. It was his first Premiership goal since September and it would prove to be his final goal of the season – he totalled nine in all competitions. After clocking up starts against Aston Villa and Fulham, he was once again dropped as Fowler came back into the side. But Fowler's return was short-lived and he limped off after 21 minutes. This time Keane replaced him in the Leeds attack.

A final-day 1–0 triumph over Middlesbrough enabled Leeds to leapfrog Chelsea into fifth spot, with Alan Smith scoring the vital goal. But the club had only managed to get a UEFA Cup place, and a second season without Champions League football increased the likelihood that surplus talent might be sold – Keane fell into that category.

With that thought planted deeply in his mind, Keane met up with the Republic of Ireland squad for the 2002 World Cup, knowing that it would be the perfect stage for him to kick-start his career once more and find an escape route out of Elland Road. In the Far East, Keane told the *Irish Times*, 'You think about the World Cup, but you want to concentrate on playing for Leeds. The two are a bit connected. If you play for Leeds, you'll probably do better.

'It was a frustrating season. I want to play every game, but it's not the way it goes. The manager has his own views. We'll have to have a chat when I go back. We had a few chats last year. I'd knock on his door, but I wouldn't be one to rant and rave.'

But O'Leary would not be around to hear his views when he returned for pre-season training in July, and his absence triggered Keane's departure from Leeds.

chapter **seven**
The Saviour of Seoul

'The feeling was there and, when Quinny headed it down, it came off my stomach and fell well for me. Kahn was on fire all night and it looked like nothing would go past him. I saw Kahn coming out this time – he comes out very fast and he looks huge. So he kept coming and I just hit it. He even got a hand to that. Sometimes you need the bit of luck. It hit the post and went in.'

Robbie Keane, 2002

After the disappointment of narrowly failing to secure a place in the Euro 2000 finals, the Republic of Ireland were allocated a spot in Group Two for the 2002 World Cup qualifiers alongside Holland, Portugal, Estonia, Cyprus and Andorra.

At first glance, it seemed as if the luck of the draw had well and truly run out for Mick McCarthy's squad. Only one country was guaranteed a place in the showpiece finals in Japan and South Korea, while the nation that finished second would still have to get through via the play-offs.

From the outset, the odds were stacked against the Republic of Ireland. Holland and Portugal were recognised superpowers in European football and had both underlined their ample qualities by reaching the semi-finals of Euro 2000.

Robbie Keane

But McCarthy was quietly upbeat ahead of the qualifying campaign. The no-nonsense Yorkshireman believed that his players would thrive on being underdogs and cause a few upsets en route to the finals – his prophecy ultimately proved to be spot on.

McCarthy told the Irish press, 'Of course, it will be tough. Anybody who's watched Holland and Portugal play cannot but have been impressed by the quality in both teams. But this football is a strange game and teams playing well in championship finals in the summer don't necessarily carry that form into the new season.

'We'll see how both the Dutch and Portuguese make out after this one. People like Arsenal's Dennis Bergkamp have had to play here on the back of a long, hard season and it will be interesting to see how they recover.'

The secret weapon in the Irish masterplan to achieve World Cup qualification was the ability to ruffle a few feathers at Lansdowne Road. McCarthy could not wait to let his troops get stuck into the Dutch and Portuguese. 'Our record shows that we're capable of beating anybody in Dublin – and that includes Holland and Portugal. So, if we can nick a point in either of the two away games in autumn, we'll still be in reasonable shape for the second half of our programme. Nobody ever said it was going to be easy, least of all me. But yes, I have seen things to encourage us.'

Robbie Keane was selected for the opening qualifier as the Republic of Ireland travelled to Amsterdam to take on Holland – needless to say the pundits predicted a straightforward home win. But the Dutch were an ageing force and their summer exploits had left them scarred by injury, with five key players ruled out for the inaugural Group Two fixture. Edgar Davids, Marc Overmars, Jaap

The Saviour of Seoul

Stam, Jimmy Floyd Hasselbaink and Boudewijn Zenden were all unavailable, leaving new Holland coach Louis Van Gaal with a threadbare squad.

But changes also had to be made to McCarthy's squad as a result of some drunken horseplay on a night out in Dublin just a few days before the match. Senior defender Phil Babb and winger Mark Kennedy landed themselves in hot water with the Irish police – and rendered themselves surplus to McCarthy's requirements – when they were arrested for rolling over the bonnet of a car owned by an off-duty *Ban Garda* (policewoman).

McCarthy explained the double expulsion from the national team's set-up. 'The players have been sent home and will not be part of my squad for the game on Saturday. They know now how much they have let me down and how hurt I have been by their actions on Monday night/Tuesday morning. It was a stupid prank that got out of hand and they have paid the price for it now. It has caused a lot of heartache now for a lot of people.'

With Babb and Kennedy left behind to rue their mistakes, the rest of the squad went to Holland in an excited mood – made even better by the news that inspirational captain Roy Keane had recovered from a back problem and would be fit to play. At the Amsterdam ArenA, Robbie Keane lined up just behind target man Niall Quinn in attack as McCarthy boldly employed a 4-4-2 formation in preference to his customary 4-5-1 away line-up.

Throwing caution to the wind proved to be a tactical masterstroke from McCarthy as the Republic of Ireland attacked with real gusto. Ian Harte had narrowly fired a free-kick wide and Quinn headed against the post, before Robbie Keane sparked the game into life with an expertly crafted goal after 21 minutes. Stephen Carr and Jason McAteer combined down the right, before the latter sent a deep cross into the area and Keane steered a header past Edwin Van Der Sar.

The 5,000 Irish fans danced with joy, Keane somersaulted towards the corner flag and the Republic of Ireland were leading in the Dutch capital. With the Republic of Ireland completely dominating the match, McAteer extended the advantage after 65 minutes, with Keane involved in the build-up. His chipped pass was flicked on by Quinn and McAteer smashed the ball into the net with his left foot.

Ireland then took their foot off the gas and, predictably, Holland somehow managed to find a route back into the game, with substitute Jeffrey Talan and Giovanni van Bronckhorst scoring late goals to equalise. The game ended 2–2 and the vast majority of the squad were satisfied with the point earned. Written off as rank outsiders before kick-off, the general feeling in the Irish camp was that they had exceeded expectations and put down a marker for the rest of the qualifying campaign.

But the player with the captain's armband did not share that mindset. Roy Keane was furious that his side had surrendered a two-goal lead to the European Championship semi-finalists away from home. The Manchester United skipper felt deflated and accused the Irish of being the architects of their own downfall because they didn't have the right professional attitude to see the job through to the end.

Straight after the game, he said, 'We've got to start giving ourselves a bit more credit. We are always underestimating ourselves. We have got good players. People are always saying the Irish will have a good time, no matter what the result. Well, I get sick to death of all that stuff.

The Saviour of Seoul

'We have got to set ourselves a higher aim. We must start winning matches because we have not qualified for a tournament since 1994. The fans might be happy with a 2–2 draw in Holland, but we're professionals and, at 2–0 up, we should have shut up shop. You have to give the Dutch credit and, with van Gaal in charge, they were always going to keep coming at us. We have got to have much higher standards than that, though.'

His namesake, striker Robbie Keane, was pleased with his own contribution on the night, especially because of a somewhat rare event – he had scored with his head. 'We seemed to have the ball for two or three minutes. We were moving it back and forth across the field. Eventually Jason put in a great cross and the ball ended up in the net.

'To be honest I thought I was going to miss it. I just jumped and somehow stayed in the air. I don't score too many with my head, so I am delighted with that.'

But, deep down, Robbie was disappointed with the result, proving that a surname is not the only thing he shares with his international captain, Roy – he also has the same mindset. 'To be 2–0 up in Holland was an unbelievable situation for us and, yet, all the lads are disappointed back in the dressing room. We know we could have won this game.'

Meanwhile, Portugal soared to the top of the Group Two table with a 3–1 win in Estonia, and Luis Figo and co were next up on the Republic of Ireland's agenda – away at the Estadio da Luz in Lisbon. Prior to kick-off in the Portuguese capital, McCarthy again boldly emphasised that his team would take the game to the favourites and questioned whether Robbie Keane was giving his opposing boss, Antonio Oliveira, sleepless nights ahead of the game. 'I wonder if they are considering marking Robbie Keane man to man, Kevin Kilbane's pace down the left-hand side, Niall Quinn's aerial threat, or our considerable threat from set-pieces and corners.

'I know what Portugal are about. Give them an inch and they'll take a mile. They have the players to cause serious problems, but I'm hoping my team can perform, individually and collectively.'

But Portugal were in a buoyant mood. The side had convincingly defeated England in Euro 2000 and had not conceded a goal in eight games at Benfica's home ground – the omens looked decidedly gloomy for the Irish. Inside the intimidating surrounds of the famous Estadio da Luz, Portugal seized the initiative and pegged Ireland back, with Luis Figo and Rui Costa causing countless problems. Portugal's persistence paid off and the home side took the lead just before the hour mark through Sergio Conceicao's deflected shot.

With the game seemingly lost, Keane was booked for kicking the ball away in frustration after chasing another lost cause as he foraged for scraps up front. But then, with only 17 minutes remaining, Republic of Ireland midfielder Matt Holland unleashed a spectacular long-range effort that flew into the top corner of the Portuguese goal. Learning from the mistakes made against Holland, the Republic of Ireland closed the game down, with Keane being replaced by defender Steve Finnan to ensure there would be no further late slip-ups. Another vital away draw had been achieved!

With the hard work seemingly out of the way, the Republic of Ireland entertained Estonia four days later and, after occupying a link-up role in the 'hole' to Quinn in the previous two games, Keane was told to push forward in a bid to find goals. McCarthy said, 'But Robbie won't be asked to drop back into the middle against Estonia. He'll be playing up front. We've had two great results away from home, but now we need a win.'

After being underdogs in Amsterdam and Lisbon, Ireland were suddenly the favourites – uncharted territory for McCarthy's men. In the event, the Republic of Ireland clinically finished off a dogged Estonia side with goals from midfielder Mark Kinsella, who had made his international debut alongside Keane two years earlier, and centre-half Richie Dunne.

It was Dunne's second goal at full international level and it proved that, even though he couldn't hold down a first-team spot at Everton, he was a natural on the international stage – not bad for a big lad from Jobstown in Tallaght. Keane was delighted for his childhood neighbour Dunne, who was nicknamed 'Meatloaf' and the 'Honey Monster' because of his sturdy frame, which weighed in at 14 stone.

Their long-standing friendship had helped them both adjust quickly to the demands of top-level football, with Dunne breaking into the Everton side at 17. Not only was there always a friendly face at international get-togethers for them both, but they also would talk together on the phone about everyday life, Tallaght and football. They could relate to each other's highs and lows because they shared the same background and worked in the same unique industry.

A few months before the qualifiers, Dunne praised his old friend's progress on the international scene and gave an insight into their special off-field bond. 'Fair play to Robbie. He was still only 18 when he got his first Ireland chance and he was a success from day one. We may be rivals on the pitch, but, off it, I regard him as a friend who has done us all proud. I know that, if I get a call-up from Mick, he'll be the first to shake my hand.'

The full-time whistle at Lansdowne Road meant it was a case of mission accomplished for Keane and the Republic of Ireland. Five points had been picked up from the opening three games, the most daunting fixtures were already out of the way and suddenly the Republic of Ireland's prospects of reaching the finals in 20 months' time looked very bright indeed.

With the next game pencilled in for March, McCarthy had arranged a friendly against Finland at Lansdowne Road for November 2000. Keane was just relieved to come back home to Dublin after a confusing two months at his club, Inter Milan. Out of the first-team picture at the San Siro, Keane was thrilled to be able to play competitive football again – even if there was nothing but national pride at stake. Keane was also delighted to meet up with his old school-friend, Middlesbrough centre-back Jason Gavin, who was called into the senior squad for the first time.

Like a caged animal suddenly set free, Keane poured his heart and soul into his performance that night. He displayed the full range of his precocious skills not only to remind potential buyers of his ability, but also to jog the memory of his beloved Dublin crowd that he was still special.

In a simple 3–0 victory over Finland, Keane did not manage to get on the score-sheet, but McCarthy was satisfied with what he had seen from his protege. As he later recalled in *Ireland's World Cup 2002*, 'Robbie, full of running, enjoys little luck in front of goal, but he is trying his heart out, perhaps too much so. The goals will come again for him, but not tonight.'

The Saviour of Seoul

After another practice match against Denmark had been postponed in February 2001 because of bad weather, Keane returned to the Republic of Ireland as the most in-form player in the Premiership following his loan move to Leeds United. In bubbly mood, Keane flew out with the rest of the squad to face Cyprus in Nicosia – the island where he had won a gold medal with the Under-18s two years before.

Although a small country, Cyprus had developed a growing reputation as a nation capable of causing shocks in the football world, particularly after defeating Spain on home soil in the qualifiers for Euro 2000. But the Republic of Ireland were in magnificent form, with captain Roy Keane the star of the show in a one-sided 4–0 away win. Playing a high-tempo brand of football, skipper Keane crushed the home team's resistance with a two-goal display and Ian Harte and his uncle Gary Kelly also found the net.

Roy Keane's performance – his 50th cap – was hailed by the press as world class and, in a developing Republic of Ireland side, he was head and shoulders above everybody else in every aspect of the game. A perfectionist, Roy Keane took pride in everything he did on the pitch and his unswerving commitment to even the most mundane on-field chores meant that the rest of the squad were in constant awe of their captain.

The Manchester United midfielder felt the heavy burden of expectation from the whole nation. But as a proud Irishman he wanted to play a significant role in helping the Republic qualify for the World Cup for the second time in his international career. Outspoken and sometimes aloof, Roy Keane kept himself to himself while on national team business, but his drive and focus left an impression on his young namesake Robbie.

Robbie Keane

Four days after the Cyprus victory, the Republic of Ireland visited Barcelona to face Andorra – a tiny principality in the Pyrenees with a population of 67,000. As expected, McCarthy selected Keane to start in attack alongside David Connolly with a very clear remit – score plenty of goals. But neither forward found the net in a disjointed game that the Republic of Ireland won comfortably 3–0, with Harte, Kevin Kilbane and Holland among the goals.

Even a brand-new pair of white boots could not bring an end to Keane's international goal drought and the frustration was beginning to take its toll. Luckily, boss McCarthy was hugely supportive when he spoke to the press afterwards: 'If you measure confidence in goals and goal attempts, then you would have to say it is not happening for Robbie. But all he can do is keep working hard with his club because club form usually transmits itself to international form and I'm sure he'll score lots of goals again.

'To be fair, we've relied on him too heavily in the past. It is nice to see other players sharing the responsibility for scoring now.'

With Holland recording a draw at Portugal, it looked good for the Republic of Ireland's chances of securing a place at the World Cup. Portugal were now group leaders and expected to qualify, but the Dutch, who had already lost to the Portuguese, were only in with an outside chance of bridging the gap to seal second spot. Everything hinged on the return match between the Republic of Ireland and Holland, scheduled for September – pressure was already mounting.

Keane was rested for the return match against minnows Andorra at Lansdowne Road to prevent the striker from picking up a second yellow card, which would mean he missed the Portugal game. Named among the substitutes, Keane watched in disbelief as Andorra took an astonishing first-half lead after a headed goal from Ildefonso Lima.

The home crowd became agitated and started chanting for the introduction of Keane, but McCarthy stuck to his original game plan. It was time for the Republic of Ireland to start playing. Within five minutes of conceding, the Irish were in front with goals from Kilbane and Kinsella, and the whole country breathed a huge sigh of relief. In freezing rain, a precious win over the country ranked 145th in the world concluded with a goal from Keane's old Coventry colleague Gary Breen, and an embarrassing slip-up had been avoided.

When Portugal made the trip north to Dublin in June 2001, Keane found he had extra competition for his place in the Republic's starting line-up, with two strikers added to the squad. Glen Crowe, who had played with Keane at Wolves, was called up following prolific form in the League of Ireland, and McCarthy had also drafted in south Londoner Clinton Morrison from Crystal Palace, who qualified to represent the country through an Irish grandmother.

But even after a four-week lay-off through injury, Keane was given the nod to start and, after a challenging first season at Leeds, he was keen to rekindle his forward partnership with Niall Quinn. Dublin was infected with World Cup fever and the city was buzzing with talk of the showdown with the Portuguese.

After an exhausting and fruitless hour of football, Keane was replaced by Damien Duff and, seven minutes after the striker's withdrawal, Roy Keane scored a memorable goal. It seemed as if the Republic of Ireland were on course for a famous triumph. But Portugal equalised through Luis Figo

10 minutes later and McCarthy's troops were forced to settle for a creditable draw.

Duff's form – for both club and country – suggested that McCarthy would find it almost impossible not to pick the richly talented Ballyboden lad ahead of Keane for the next World Cup qualifier, away to Estonia.

Undaunted, Keane said ahead of the hugely important test, 'I've never lost confidence in my ability. I know it is my job to score goals and it's true I've missed a few chances for Ireland recently, but I can give a lot more to the side and maybe it will take just one lucky strike to get me going again. Hopefully, that will come tonight because it is a very big game for us. One we have to win.'

McCarthy backed his young forward, but eventually decided he would not be included in the starting line-up. 'Robbie needed that hour, though, and I think we shall see the benefit of it against Estonia. Everybody knows how highly I rate him. There's no doubt the lay-off for injury impeded him against Portugal, but you don't just lose the quality he has.

'Sure, I'd like my strikers to be 100 per cent fit all the time, but that's not been the case with Robbie and Niall Quinn. There's not much we can do about it. I expect everybody who starts tonight to give their all and stay on as long as they can, but sometimes you have to change a player, usually when you need a goal or if you are in front and come under the cosh. It will happen from time to time, and I still believe I was right to pull off Robbie and Niall when I did last Saturday.'

As a result, Keane, plagued with a troublesome ankle problem and without an international goal for nine months, was relegated to the bench for the game at the

The Saviour of Seoul

Lillekula Stadium in Tallin four days later – it was the first time he had been dropped by McCarthy in his 25-cap career. Roy Keane was also missing because of injury, but the new-look Irish side coped admirably and won 2–0 with Dunne and Holland on target, moving to the top of Group Two in the process.

His confidence jolted, Keane spent the summer break working out what had gone wrong and figuring out what he needed to do to win his place back in the Republic of Ireland side. Since he had made his senior debut in Olomouc, everything had always fallen naturally into place and there had been very few setbacks. But now Keane was facing the sternest test of his international career and he knew that the so-called experts were beginning to question his credentials.

He vowed to regain his old momentum and knew he would come out of his barren spell with stronger resolve and unbreakable self-belief. Fortunately, Keane won his spot in the starting line-up back for the August friendly against Croatia at Lansdowne Road, but that was partly because Niall Quinn was unavailable because of a back problem.

McCarthy insisted to the press before the game that he had never lost faith in Keane: 'Robbie has been the star of the show, but at the end of last season it was not happening for him. He was injured and not fully fit. I never doubted him. Robbie's rise was meteoric. He was always going to have a dip at some stage. But he was injured then and he is back to his best now.

'Robbie has been on fire in pre-season games and his career can really kick-start once again after his ankle problems last year.'

The partnership of Keane and Duff proved to be quick, mobile and dangerous, with the latter scoring his first goal at full-international level just before half-time following an astute pass from captain Roy Keane. By half-time, McCarthy had seen enough and made a bold judgement – Keane and Duff were going to start against the Dutch because the combination of the two would give Holland defender Jaap Stam nightmares.

Six minutes after the break, Duff was replaced by Clinton Morrison, while David Connolly came on for Keane to give McCarthy an opportunity to assess his other attacking options. Morrison opened his Republic of Ireland account with 14 minutes left on the clock, but it sparked off a worrying collapse. Somehow, Croatia managed to claw their way back and equalised in injury-time with a Davor Suker penalty.

Afterwards, McCarthy reflected on the chief positive to have come out of the game – the strike partnership of Keane and Duff – telling the press, 'They were fantastic, I thought it was a partnership I wouldn't want to play against, and I think the Croatian defenders would empathise with my thoughts.'

Meanwhile, Holland had comfortably defeated England in a friendly at White Hart Lane and headed into the September showdown at Lansdowne Road seemingly at the peak of their collective powers.

Ahead of the game, Keane met up with the rest of the squad at the team hotel in Citywest, Dublin, and was reunited with his regular room-mate Richard Dunne, as the Republic of Ireland prepared for their most important game in nearly a decade. There was a relaxed feel about the place, although Keane was buzzing with excitement and hell-bent on playing pranks on unsuspecting team-mates – including turning players' rooms upside down for his own amusement.

The Saviour of Seoul

With a number of key men carrying knocks, Keane took part in a light training session with the rest of the squad against the Under-21 side at John Highland Park, Baldonnel. After training, McCarthy took Keane to one side to inform him that he would start the game against Holland, but the Irish boss wanted the Dutch to think that Quinn would be preferred alongside Duff.

McCarthy believed that any psychological advantage had to be gained ahead of the game – after all, Holland were the Republic of Ireland's nemesis. A Marco Van Basten-inspired Holland side had won 1–0 in the 1988 European Championships and then broke Irish hearts with a 2–0 second-round win in the 1994 World Cup, before inflicting another morale-crushing defeat in a play-off decider to determine who would qualify for the Euro 96 finals in England.

Payback was overdue and, as the team bus headed towards Lansdowne Road, you could almost smell the adrenaline in the air. In a nervy game, Holland emerged the superior side and almost took the lead through Patrick Kluivert. The home side took the early warning on board and began to impose themselves with a series of full-blooded, but fair tackles on the Dutch.

The noise from the East Stand was deafening as the fans cheered on their green-shirted Gladiators and the match tempo cranked up even further at the old rugby ground. Then disaster struck. Gary Kelly, who had been handed a first-half yellow card, was sent off. Keane's instant reaction was that McCarthy would have to sacrifice one of the forwards in order to reinforce the team's short-staffed defence. He told the *Sunday Independent*, 'I thought, "It's either me or Duffer off here." You're never pleased to be taken off, especially in a game like that. I was enjoying it, I felt good, felt sharp. I'm not going to lie and say I wasn't disappointed, but I knew one of us had to go.

'I went and sat in the dugout. "Oh, we've got 10 men. Oh my God, we're playing Holland and they've got an extra man!"'

Keane's replacement, Steve Finnan, filled the gap at right-back and Kelly's dismissal triggered a gigantic response from the home team. Led by a colossal performance from captain Roy Keane, the Republic of Ireland grew in strength until the match reached its unforgettable climax, and Jason McAteer scored. With 22 minutes left, Finnan's searching cross found McAteer completely unmarked at the back post and he rifled his shot into the Dutch goal.

For Keane, the time between the goal and the end of the game was almost too much to take. Sitting helplessly on the bench, Keane urged his team-mates to finish the job off. 'It was the longest 20 minutes ever. When you're playing, it's different, but when you're sitting on the bench watching! I'm no good at watching games. I get too nervous.'

Holland were out of the World Cup, the Republic of Ireland were one huge step closer to a summer trip to the Far East and the whole of Dublin celebrated long into the night. Keane and his team-mates were overcome with joy and the vast majority of the squad headed into the city centre to toast their legendary feat. His father's son, Robbie Keane Jnr behaved more like Sammy Davis Jnr at Lillie's Bordello – an exclusive Dublin nightspot – as he entertained his jubilant team-mates with a selection of songs.

Niall Quinn recalled to the *Sunday Independent*, 'They were all in the Piano Bar in Lillie's and there was a singsong. All the barriers came down. Everybody was in great humour.

The Saviour of Seoul

We all had a go at something. Robbie Keane sang all the Boyzone and Westlife numbers.'

Keane's pals at Leeds, Gary Kelly and Ian Harte, teased their club-mate, suggesting that *Pop Idol* judge Louis Walsh would be looking to sign him up. But the wannabe singer from Tallaght shrugged off their banter and insisted he had already found his one true vocation – football. He said, 'I can't help it if they want me to sing. You either have it or you haven't. [But] I think I'll stick to the football.'

With Portugal and the Republic of Ireland level on 21 points going into the final round of games, McCarthy decided to rest the players who had picked up yellow cards – in case the Irish finished in second spot and faced a play-off against a team from the Middle East. As a result, Keane was rested for the home game against Cyprus, with Quinn given the nod to start up front. The big centre-forward celebrated his 35th birthday with his 21st goal for his country and, in so doing, became the nation's record goal-scorer. Harte, Connolly and the talismanic Roy Keane also found the net in an easy 4–0 win over Cyprus.

Despite finishing the group unbeaten, the Republic of Ireland finished in second place behind Portugal, who had demolished Estonia 5–0 in Lisbon. So on 11 November 2001, the Republic of Ireland faced Iran in the first leg of a play-off to resolve which country would be invited to the greatest party in football – the World Cup finals.

With Keane restored to the starting line-up and delighting the Lansdowne Road crowd with his instinctive two-footed trickery, Irish pressure on the visitors' goal resulted in a penalty just before half-time, converted by an ice-cool Harte. Keane realised that the Republic of Ireland would need a big lead to take over to Tehran and he provided his team-mates with the perfect gift to take on their travels – a priceless second goal.

Reading a flick-on from Quinn, Keane reacted with a left-footed volley that ended up in the back of Iran's net. His persistence had paid off – his drought in green had ended. After 14 months without a goal, Keane had scored and his relief was plain for everybody in the stadium to see as the Republic of Ireland settled for a 2–0 victory.

He said, 'People expect me to score and do something special every time I put on the jersey. But I'm only human, like everyone else. It just wasn't happening, but now hopefully this goal will kick-start it for me.

'Every striker wants to score goals, no matter who it is for. Yeah, I was delighted to score against Iran, but I think it was other people who were getting more frustrated than I was. Sometimes you don't get any chances. I got one and was lucky enough to take it. On another day, it could have gone over or wide.'

His goal touch reawakened, Keane was looking forward to the return match in Iran where the game was expected to be played in front of a huge crowd. He added, 'It will be a great experience. None of us has played in front of 120,000 people before, but we just want to concentrate and get on with the job in hand.

'There are plenty of young players who will never get this chance again, so we have to get out there and forget about the crowd. There's pressure one way or the other because we're 90 minutes away from the World Cup. But we've done ourselves a favour by scoring two goals at Lansdowne Road.

'We know what they're like now. Before that we only had a rough idea, but they showed they're a good side and we also showed that there's no reason why we can't get the right result over there.'

Unfortunately, because of a knee injury, Roy Keane pulled out of the squad for Tehran and suddenly the aura of invincibility surrounding the team in Dublin began to dissipate. In Roy Keane's absence, Iran believed they could overhaul the two-goal margin and end the Republic of Ireland's World Cup dream.

With Quinn also out through injury, Robbie Keane was chosen to play up front alongside David Connolly in a one-sided game that Iran dominated throughout. They finally took the lead through Yahya Golmohammadi. But, fortunately for the Irish, Iran's response arrived in stoppage time and there was not enough time left for the home side to produce an equaliser.

The Republic of Ireland had come through a very demanding test and qualified for the 2002 World Cup. A delighted McCarthy said, 'I'm immensely proud. It's difficult to articulate how I feel. When the final whistle went, it was a wonderful, wonderful feeling. It is a great achievement, sometimes dug out of adversity. They have stuck together as a group of players. I am delighted for them and for the fans as well.'

The following month, McCarthy went to Busan to watch the World Cup draw and was not displeased to see the Republic of Ireland placed in the same group as Germany, Cameroon and Saudi Arabia. In the first warm-up match before the finals, Keane scored a header in a 2–0 win over Russia at Lansdowne Road. McCarthy was pleased with Keane's renaissance in the green shirt of his country, but still felt there was room for improvement. 'I was very satisfied with the performance of Robbie Keane, but he needs to be a bit sharper and a bit fitter and he needs more first-team football.'

After practically being ignored at Leeds, Keane relished every minute of his time with the national side. It was a welcome escape from his humdrum existence at Elland Road. Nearing full fitness and regaining his razor-sharp finishing, Keane continued his rehabilitation with a spectacular goal in the next home friendly against Denmark.

As part of an innovative set-piece that had been pre-rehearsed on the training ground, Steve Staunton flicked the ball to Keane, who rifled a breathtaking shot into the roof of the Denmark goal en route to a convincing 3–0 win. Against the United States in the next practice match, Keane's purple patch in front of the target ended, though the team won 2–1, but he still picked up the Man of the Match award and convinced McCarthy he was back to his best.

As the Republic's manager recalled in *Ireland's World Cup 2002*, 'Robbie Keane is coming good at just the right time for the World Cup. He didn't score against the US, but doesn't have to, to prove his worth to me. He is fit, sharp and hungry as his Man of the Match award confirms. He is playing football with the cheek and brashness of his youth and he is enjoying it. A month before we go to the World Cup, it is good to have him back in that sort of form.'

Keane was duly named in the Republic of Ireland's 23-man squad for the 2002 World Cup along with his close friend Richie Dunne. McCarthy went for tried and tested players and, as a result, Stephen Reid and Celtic midfielder Colin Healy both narrowly missed out on a tour spot.

McCarthy predicted a bright future for Keane in the Far East. 'I would like to think that Robbie Keane will show what a fine player he is and do it on the world stage, because

Top: Robbie Keane scoring against Middlesbrough in a match at Leeds in January 2001.

Bottom: Celebrate with deadly accuracy! The famous routine after a goal against Newcastle United on 20 January, 2001.

Drama in Kashima! Robbie beats Germany's Oliver Kahn in a World Cup Group E clash on 5 June 2002 with the final kick of the game.

Beckham goes down against Robbie in the match between Manchester United and
Leeds in October 2001 that ended in a 1–1 draw.

Pure glee as Robbie celebrates his equaliser that meant his side ended 1–1 against Germany in on 5 June 2002 and a legend had been born.

Robbie shows off the shirt that marked his transfer from Leeds to Spurs in August 2002.

Claudine Palmer, also known as Miss Fingal, at the Miss Ireland Finals in Dublin in the summer of 2002. She and Robbie announced their engagement in October 2006.

Robbie training at a stadium in Portugal in May 2006.

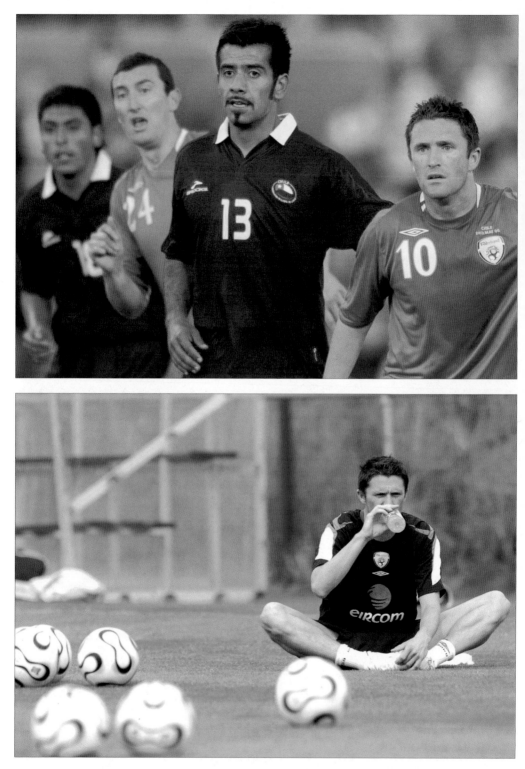

Top: Jason Byrne (second from left) and cousin Robbie (far right) playing together in May 2006 in a friendly against Chile.

Bottom: A pensive drink for the captain, lost in thought during a break in training at the end of August 2006.

I think his performances for us have been getting better and better since his ankle operation.'

Captain Roy Keane was also included, despite recovering from a serious knee injury, and Ireland's leader was poised to undergo intensive treatment to make sure he would be fit for the finals. Winger Mark Kennedy was a late withdrawal from the squad after struggling for fitness during Niall Quinn's testimonial match at Sunderland and McCarthy opted to replace him with Reid.

All set and ready to go, Robbie Keane conducted one final pre-tournament interview before heading off into the unknown. He told *FourFourTwo magazine*, 'I'm really looking forward to it. At Leeds I've tried to concentrate on my club form, but you get caught up in all the World Cup fever once you come back to Ireland and see all the Irish boys again.

'They seem to be talking about little else here; the whole country is looking forward to it. There was a tremendous amount of disappointment in missing the World Cup finals in 1998, so they're getting excited about this one. I really think we could do well in the Far East.

'This is the biggest stage in the world and it has always been my dream to play on it. Gary Kelly played in one in 1994 and he told me it is a unique experience that you have to enjoy as much as possible. As a kid growing up in the back streets of Dublin, I used to pretend I was playing in the World Cup with my mates out on the streets, and now I will be doing it for real.

'I used to pretend I was John Aldridge, or even Paul McGrath. It is a lovely feeling to know kids are now playing in the back streets of Dublin pretending to be me.'

The Republic of Ireland squad landed at Tokyo's Narita Airport on 18 May 2002 brimming with enthusiasm and ready to tackle the challenges of Group E. But Roy Keane – fully fit and focused – was far from happy with the facilities at the country's first training base at Saipan and he quickly aired his views to McCarthy.

Relations between the manager and the captain of the Republic of Ireland had never been absolutely harmonious to say the least. But another apparent incident in a later session contributed to the most talked-about episode in Irish sport – Roy Keane's initial decision to walk away from the World Cup. Conflicting agendas at the heart of the Republic of Ireland's World Cup dream were threatening to make the experience in Japan a living nightmare for Robbie Keane and co.

However, Keane had a change of heart and told McCarthy he had decided to stay and they also seemingly mended an apparent earlier dispute over the training regime. Then, in front of the entire squad, McCarthy asked Roy Keane to explain himself fully and it prompted fireworks in the form of a famous outburst from the Irish skipper – there would be no way back for the Manchester United midfielder.

With tempers exploding left, right and centre, the whole squad was forced to come to terms with not having their on-field leader on the eve of their biggest test.

Robbie Keane sat there in disbelief as the drama unravelled. He knew that it would have serious repercussions for the opening match against Cameroon. He wasn't the only one shocked by events in the team's dining area. Matt Holland told the *Daily Mirror*, 'Never have I witnessed such a foul-mouthed tirade as Keane subjected the manager, Mick McCarthy, to during that fateful team meeting on Thursday. McCarthy walked in with transcripts of interviews Keane had given earlier in the week, the gist of which is public knowledge and which concerned the supposedly amateurish preparations and training on Saipan.

'I think the manager wanted an apology from Keane, not so much for himself but for the rest of the players whom Keane had accused of "accepting second best". The rest of us just sat there. Keane refused to apologise for his comments. He launched an abusive attack on the manager. It was absolutely extraordinary to listen to and, like the rest of the squad, I was stunned.'

With Roy Keane out of the picture, Robbie Keane took centre stage and brought light relief to the camp with both goals in the team's final warm-up game – a 2–1 win against J-League side Hiroshima. After his two-goal display, he said, 'I was happy to score, but the important thing was to raise our fitness levels and we did that. Despite what has happened, our mental approach hasn't changed at all.'

The Republic of Ireland went into their first game against Cameroon in Niigata with an even greater sense of togetherness. Mark Kinsella had been given the all-clear to start in the centre of midfield in place of Roy Keane and he later endorsed the view that the team spirit was superb. Kinsella later recalled, 'The three senior lads, Quinn, Kells and Stan, took the heat off the younger lads. Obviously, both Robbie and Duffer were very young then. But the team spirit has always been good going back to the Jack Charlton era. There was never one person in particular who would lift it up.

'Gary Kelly, though, was very good at it. Harto and Robbie himself always had something to say. There was always good banter there and, taking into account what we'd been through at the start of the tournament, everyone stuck together.'

Robbie Keane

But six minutes before half-time in suffocating heat, the Republic of Ireland conceded with a goal scored by Cameroon's Patrick Mboma – a disastrous start for McCarthy's under-fire troops. Then Matt Holland replied with a stunning goal and suddenly there was life after Roy Keane as the gloom lifted and the Irish began to play with a greater sense of freedom. In fact, Robbie Keane almost snatched a late winning goal, but his shot cannoned off the post. The Irish had shown tremendous resilience when it was called for and optimism swept through the side.

The Republic of Ireland's next opponents, Germany, had overwhelmed Saudi Arabia, scoring eight goals without reply. Nevertheless, Keane had a hunch that the boys in green could match them – even without their captain. He said, 'What happened with Roy didn't bring us close together – there's no way we could be any closer. The spirit was already so strong and I don't think any team at this World Cup will have more belief and resilience than us. We've always been together as a team and we always will be.

'Personally, I'm not in awe of Germany and I don't think any of the other players are. We won't give them too much respect because we will just be concentrating on ourselves. If we play like we did in the second half, then I think we will have every chance against Germany because we have shown that no one will ever intimidate this team.'

After being humiliated by England in the qualifiers, Germany were by no means pre-tournament favourites, but Rudi Voeller's squad possessed quality. McCarthy picked Steve Staunton to receive his 100th cap for the Republic of Ireland, a huge milestone for any player. And following the Roy Keane fiasco, he was also asked to captain the side.

Keane examined the Germany squad sheet in the dressing

room at the Kashima Stadium in Ibaraki and noticed a familiar name from the UEFA Under-18 final four years previously – Sebastian Kehl.

After Keane had seen an early shot saved by Germany keeper Oliver Kahn, Voeller's team took the lead with a magnificent goal from Miroslav Klose on the 19-minute mark. Displaying tigerish determination and their legendary ruthless efficiency, Germany were unstoppable and the Republic of Ireland were comfortably contained for 70 minutes, with Kahn impressing between the posts. But McCarthy had a contingency plan designed to unsettle the German defence, which entailed bringing on his secret weapon, Niall Quinn, to play in attack with Keane and Damien Duff.

With the scoreboard clock counting down time, the Irish threw caution to the wind and kept plugging away up front, but with little to show for it. Then, in the third minute of stoppage time and, with the neutrals presuming the game was all over, something remarkable happened that would change the life of Robbie Keane forever: his genius was immortalised with an astounding goal.

In one final bold throw of the dice, Steve Finnan decided to pump a long ball deep into German territory and his floated pass found the head of Quinn in the inside-right channel. As soon as Quinn flicked a header into the area, Keane sprang to life and, leaving his marker floundering behind him, his first touch off his chest took him past the lunging challenge of Carsten Ramelow. Suddenly he found himself in on goal.

The bounce fell kindly for Keane and he hooked the ball with his right foot over the diving body of Kahn. Immediately, three-quarters of the stadium erupted with joy. And as Keane cartwheeled his way towards the corner flag, the regulars in his local pub, Molly Heffernan's in Tallaght, went bananas – Robbie Keane had done it.

Keane later revealed that he had had a premonition about the goal and how it would be scored. He told the *Irish Times*, 'Against the Germans, I knew that it was coming. I said to Quinny that I knew he was going to come on and he'd flick one on to me. It was like a film in my head.

'When I saw he was coming on, I knew that was it. When I scored, I realised that it had been in me head. Quinny couldn't have placed the header any better for me, even when I imagined him doing it. I just hope I get a few more of those feelings.'

The scenes of jubilation that followed remain a blur in Keane's memory, but he clearly recalled a hobbling Staunton joining the goal celebrations. 'The next thing, though, I just remember the lads on top of me. Quinny was first to me and I think he was trying to protect me. I fell back against the board because the boys were pushing me and, for a while, I was on the bottom and I thought I wouldn't be able to get a breath. Stan was crippled but he was still ran over to jump on.'

The last-minute goal meant that all the Republic of Ireland had to do was defeat Saudi Arabia by a two-goal margin in their final Group E game to make the second round.

Before the match in Yokohama, Keane told the assembled press that he was still coming to terms with his monumental feat against Germany. He said, 'It's great for my confidence. Obviously, I'm delighted to have scored the goal, but first and foremost it was a great result for the team. It showed the character and spirit that we have that we were able to carry on until the 92nd minute. We deserved that point in the end.

The Saviour of Seoul

'To score at the World Cup is a dream come true. You always dream of playing at the World Cup, and it's even better to score. It is one of my favourite goals already. The goal is definitely up there.'

Still buzzing from his stoppage-time goal, Keane went on, 'To be honest, I'm enjoying every minute of the tournament. Before the game against Cameroon, Niall Quinn told us that we have to enjoy moments like this – they don't come around often – and that's what I'm doing. Hopefully, we'll do well against Saudi Arabia and progress to the next stage.'

Keane also revealed what inspired the team's never-say-die attitude against Germany – the encouragement from the Irish fans. 'After Germany scored, I remembered from the moment we kicked off the Irish fans were singing straight away, it was a lift. That was when we went a goal down – when we scored it was electric.

'You can hear it on the pitch and it's great after the game when you're in front of them. They were all singing – it was a great atmosphere and something we will never forget.'

Against Saudi Arabia, it took Keane just seven minutes to make history at the International Stadium when he became the first Republic of Ireland player to score twice at the World Cup finals. Gary Kelly sent over a looping cross from the right wing and Keane connected sweetly with it to send a sweeping volley into the net. It was a goal that underlined his awesome technique and it eased any jitters lingering within the side. The Irish were heading through.

Then, after a trademark somersault, he shrugged off the congratulations from his team-mates to fire an imaginary bow-and-arrow at the TV cameras, a gesture he explained at the post-match press conference. 'I did that for a friend back in England who I spoke to on the phone before the match.'

His goal was the pick of the bunch in a 3–0 victory, with Duff and Gary Breen also getting on the score-sheet. Later Keane revealed what lay behind the audacious shot which caught everybody by surprise. 'Gary Kelly whipped it across first time and I don't think anyone was expecting it. It fell right for me and I just had to hit it, but it was his quick thinking that teed it up. I caught it well first time and, while the keeper got a touch to it, I think he saw it too late.'

But Keane's happiness at the full-time whistle was short-lived. Instead of joining the party in the dressing room, he was forced to take a drugs test – his second in successive games. 'I was called over straight after the final whistle and I didn't even get time to go into the dressing room with the rest of the lads. My name came out of the hat and I was unfortunate because it had happened two games in a row. I drank about eight bottles of water to try and produce a sample.

'It took me almost three hours to produce a sample, so I was held back for two-and-a-half hours after the Germany game. I didn't get back to the team hotel until three o'clock in the morning. It's a complete joke because people keep asking me what was it like in the dressing room and I haven't got a clue. It's ridiculous and stupid from FIFA's point of view. They've got to sort something out about the way they do these tests.'

With two goals to his name and an alarmingly full bladder, Keane reflected on a job well done for the Republic of Ireland, who had exceeded expectations by making it through to the knockout stages. He concluded, 'People will look at this as our poorest performance of the three, but I would class it as an equally good result. We have five points from a possible nine and, at the beginning, I don't think anyone really expected us to have any more.'

Next stop for the Republic of Ireland was Suwon, and Spain were now the only obstacle standing in the way of McCarthy's heroes on their way to a place in the last eight of the competition. With most of their players hailing from La Liga juggernauts Real Madrid and Barcelona, Spain were dubbed the 'dark horses' of the tournament.

In Group B, buoyed by a sequence of impressive results, Spain had regained their composure and international self-respect. Coach Jose Antonio Camacho had guided Spain to three back-to-back wins over Slovenia, Paraguay and South Africa – scoring nine goals in the process.

Never one to shirk a challenge, Keane declared that he was ready to take on the Spanish – even though he acknowledged that, on paper, it wasn't going to be easy. As he told the *Sunday Mirror*, 'This is probably the toughest game we could have got at this stage of the competition. When you consider that the likes of Argentina, France and Portugal have all gone home now, there could have been an easier game. But it is also a great challenge and a great honour to play against someone like Spain. It is the sort of game you dream about as a kid.

'And if you can't lift yourself for the challenge posed by Raul and his like, then you shouldn't really be at the World Cup finals.'

Meanwhile, Spain's players publicly admitted they were all relieved to be facing a Republic of Ireland side that did not contain Roy Keane. But striker Fernando Morientes conceded that Robbie Keane could still prove to be a potent threat: 'It is a good thing for Spain that Roy Keane is not here, but they still have good players like Robbie Keane, with excellent technique.'

In an adrenaline-charged atmosphere, Spain's class shone through as early as the eighth minute when Morientes swooped ahead of Gary Breen to place his header beyond Shay Given into the net. Ireland were understandably rattled, but memories of the comeback against Germany were still fresh and they prompted a spirited comeback. Keane led the charge and almost rustled up an equalising goal before half-time, but one of his shots curled wide, while another acrobatic effort sailed harmlessly over.

After the break, Quinn was introduced to partner Keane in attack, with the lively Duff moving out to the right flank. This tactical switch led to a breakthrough. Duff turned his marker Juanfran inside the area, but seemed to be impeded and referee Anders Frisk pointed to the spot – Ireland had a penalty. Courageously, Harte stepped up to take the spot-kick, but agonisingly the left-back's effort was saved by Spain keeper Iker Casillas and Kevin Kilbane scuffed the rebound wide.

With time rapidly running out, McCarthy brought on another striker, David Connolly, in a desperate last-ditch bid to find an equaliser. Then, with seconds remaining, Spain defender Fernando Hierro pulled Quinn's shirt and referee Frisk awarded a second penalty to the Republic of Ireland.

With Harte's confidence shot to pieces, Keane instantly picked up the ball and took responsibility for the most important kick of his career. Behind Harte, Keane was the nation's second-choice penalty-taker and, without even hesitating, he strolled up purposefully to the spot.

Memories of his shoot-out miss in the UEFA Under-18 Final may have been buried deep in his psyche, but Keane was completely nerveless. He wasn't going to let anything distract him. McCarthy, watching speechless from the bench, recalled the moment in *Ireland's World Cup 2002*: 'What a kid. Imagine the emotions going through his head as he waits for the fuss to die down. We are seconds away from a World Cup exit and he is about to take the biggest penalty of his life.'

In the event, his penalty was perfect and Casillas was left rooted to the spot as Keane's quick-fire shot slid into the far corner of the net – Tallaght's Houdini had helped the Irish escape again.

In the midst of the melodrama, Keane launched himself into his customary somersault as the emerald part of South Korea erupted into ecstasy. The striker had a strange look of calm on his face. He later told the *Independent*, 'I was just enjoying it. I'd scored in the two games before that and my confidence was high. Going into the game, I really believed we were going to win. And we should have beaten them.

'I was very confident with the penalty. I just knew I was going to score for some reason. I always feel that when I play I'm going to do something. If you don't, you've got no chance.'

The successful penalty was the last kick of normal time and, as the Republic of Ireland team prepared for the energy-sapping demands of extra-time, there was a euphoric glow about them. Football is all about confidence and momentum and, with Keane spearheading the attack, the Irish players were optimistic that Spain could be beaten. Thoughts of victory were encouraged by the sight of Spain substitute David Almeda departing injured from the pitch – leaving the Republic of Ireland's opponents with only 10 men in extra-time.

Robbie Keane

Keane pulled out all the stops in search of the crucial golden goal, but sadly his three attempts on goal couldn't provide the much-needed breakthrough. With extra-time over, referee Frisk signalled a penalty shoot-out and the Republic of Ireland squad gathered round McCarthy. The discussions, centring on which players would take part in the World Cup equivalent of spinning a roulette wheel, were brief and to the point.

Keane was the first player to stick his hand up, so he was charged with the onerous responsibility of taking the Republic of Ireland's first spot-kick. Matt Holland, David Connolly, Kevin Kilbane and Steve Finnan followed him in the line-up.

All eyes were on Keane as he placed the ball on the spot. Like an expert poker player, his body language gave nothing away as he turned and ran towards the spot. Casillas was in two minds as to whether his opponent would bluff his second penalty and direct his shot towards the same place as his original effort, or go the other way.

Keane was both courageous and single-minded as he struck a shot that flew high into the top left-hand corner of Casillas's net – the same side as his earlier attempt – and joy swept through the Irish camp.

Hierro also kept his nerve from the spot to beat Shay Given, before Holland rattled the crossbar with his penalty. With Baraja on target, Connolly needed to gain the upper hand over Casillas, but the keeper saved his strike – making it 2–1 to Spain. Luckily, Juanfran's miscued effort gave the Republic of Ireland a World Cup lifeline and Kilbane could have levelled the score, if only Casillas hadn't guessed correctly and kept his penalty out.

The tension inside the stadium in Suwon was unbearable

and, after Calderon had missed another of Spain's penalties, it was left to Limerick-born Steve Finnan to make it 2–2. He rose to the occasion to find the net. With the last remaining spot-kick, Spain's Gaizka Mendieta's mis-hit penalty crept past Given to bring the curtain down on the Republic of Ireland's incredible World Cup journey.

His team might have been knocked out of the tournament, but Keane had collected enough memories from his adventure in the Far East to last him a lifetime. Few Irishmen will forget how he did his country proud. Mark Kinsella later confirmed how popular Keane had been with the rest of the squad: 'You live and die by goals. With Robbie, we had a goal-scorer who had been on fire. He'd always create a chance for himself or finish a chance we created as a team.

'You know with your strikers that, if they are any good, then you're going to qualify and, if they're not, then you're going to struggle. With Robbie, we had a lad who could put the ball in the back of the net. He is a great finisher and a good lad off the park as well – one of the best strikers I have played with.'

The broken-hearted players decided that the only way to ease their woes would be to go out and paint Seoul an unforgettable shade of green. Out on their travels, the younger members of the squad bumped into celebrity dancer Michael Flatley at a bar called Billy Mulligan's in Itaewon. The self-styled 'King of the Dance' – an ardent fan of the team – allegedly left his credit card behind the bar to fund the players' drinks tab and was apparently left with a £20,000 bill for his troubles.

Before flying back to Dublin, Keane telephoned his parents back home in Tallaght to discuss what had happened – Robbie Snr and Anne had cancelled a holiday in Spain to watch the game at home – and he was told that his estate had gone crazy with 'Robbiemania'. Anne told the *Irish Mirror*, 'Robbie rang us after the match and he was pretty disappointed, but he sounded in good enough form. I know he went out last night and no doubt he had a few drinks. He said he's tired and really looking forward to coming home now.'

Keane flew back with the rest of the squad on 18 June 2002 to a hero's welcome at Phoenix Park, but he realised that his next priority was to sort out his future at club level. That probably meant leaving Leeds.

chapter eight

Keane Earns His Spurs

'You're always confident. I don't go to games thinking he's great and he's great. My job is to get the better of them. I love that. I can enjoy a game if I'm playing well and we're winning, but I love scoring goals. I want to score in every game. I look at any defender and think I can score against him. That's the way I am. That's the way I have to be.'

Robbie Keane talking to the Irish Times, *2002*

W hen Robbie Keane returned to pre-season training at Leeds United on 26 July 2002, a whirlwind of changes had swept through the place in his absence. The striker was on holiday when he heard that David O'Leary had been sacked as boss, and the news did not come as a complete surprise. Events preceding the announcement suggested that his manager had outstayed his welcome at the club.

The transfer rumour mill was in overdrive, but there was substance behind some of what was being said. It was soon clear that Keane was no longer wanted at Leeds either. At the beginning of July, Sunderland lodged a bid that was accepted by the hard-up board, but Keane turned the move down flat. He said he did not want to miss out on playing European football.

Keane insisted he wasn't going anywhere. 'I don't want to

speak to any other club. I'm happy at Leeds and believe I can impress the new manager with my ability and commitment.'

Two weeks after O'Leary's departure, the Elland Road board installed his successor, former Tottenham and England manager Terry Venables, in a bid to balance the books and reunite the playing staff. The new man was keen to bring in his own players and the directors wanted to cash in on Keane's World Cup success and subsequent inflated value in the marketplace.

Tottenham had publicly declared their interest in Keane, with the club's director of football David Pleat admitting the north Londoners were watching the situation with interest. He told the *Evening Standard*, 'We are keeping abreast of the Robbie Keane situation.'

But Tottenham manager Glenn Hoddle publicly dismissed the rumour, hinting at a case of crossed wires behind the scenes at White Hart Lane. Hoddle had been linked to several high-profile strikers, including the likes of Enrico Chiesa, Fernando Morientes and Eidur Gudjohnsen, but he wanted to conduct matters in private. Therefore, he rejected the idea that he wanted to sign Keane.

Referring to Pleat's earlier statement, Hoddle told the press, 'If someone wants to give you a bum steer, then so be it. If people want to know, they should ask me. I have a list of players I want and Keane is not on it.'

As the 2002/03 season kicked off, there was still a heavy cloud of uncertainty hovering over Keane's future at Elland Road, with both Sunderland and Tottenham strongly linked as suitors.

In Leeds' opening game of the campaign against Manchester City, it was a case of new regime, same routine – Keane started on the bench. But, only 10 minutes after being brought on to replace Mark Viduka, he gave potential buyers a timely reminder of his abundant quality with a classic goal. With Leeds already two in front, Keane capitalised on a flick-on from Alan Smith to send a toe-poked chip over the head of City keeper Carlo Nash.

After the game, Venables insisted Keane was not for sale and that the Irishman had a part to play in the new era at the club. 'Robbie doesn't want to leave at the moment and I don't want to let him go. That's my side of it. I've got six strikers at the club and I want all of them to stay.

'Whether I'll be allowed to do that is a different matter. It's something we will have a discussion about. We'll see what comes after that.'

However, being left on the bench for the next Premiership match at West Brom proved the last straw for Keane and the Irishman told Venables he wanted out. There was only one week to go before the summer transfer window closed. Venables told the press, 'If there's any interest, I will look at it and, if he doesn't want to be here, I would feel the same.

'If someone wants to come to me and make something possible on the club's terms, it's possible it could go through. He had a great World Cup and comes back and wants to show what he can do. I didn't really expect this after two games, but then again maybe normally he wouldn't have said it if there wasn't only a week left to the transfer deadline. But it's running out of time now and I would think, at this stage, nothing will happen.'

Then, on 30 August 2002, a day before the transfer deadline, Tottenham agreed a £7 million deal with Leeds to finalise Keane's fourth move in just three years. Tottenham boss Glenn Hoddle was thrilled with his latest signing and predicted that the newest recruit at White Hart Lane would quickly capture the Spurs fans' hearts.

In the previous season, Tottenham had been on the verge of securing a UEFA Cup place, but a lacklustre display against underdogs Blackburn in the Worthington Cup final prompted a virtual collapse in the Premiership and Spurs' ageing side were left with nothing. After such disappointment, Hoddle was keen to inject some much-needed vitality, zest and energy into his side – most notably up front where the squad was seriously understaffed – and, after scouring the European marketplace, he believed Keane was the solution.

The most gifted English footballer of his generation, Hoddle had transferred his playing skills and knowledge of the game into the coaching side, where he showed a rare and insightful understanding of tactics. After Hoddle became the youngest-ever England boss, the press who had originally championed him as the right man for the job, then turned on him and hounded him out of the job.

Accusations of poor man-management skills and oddball ideas about reincarnation and disabled people were flung at Hoddle as he resigned from the post. These allegations had followed him into his next job at Southampton and now his beloved Tottenham.

But Keane instantly struck up a great rapport with Hoddle. They could relate to each other because they shared similar backgrounds. Like Keane, Hoddle had grown up in a new town on the outskirts of a capital city – Harlow, 28 miles from London – where there were plenty of open spaces to play football, but not much else.

Hoddle sensed that Keane would be a good acquisition not only because he was a hugely talented player, but also because, with his immensely likeable personality, he would be an uplifting presence in the dressing room. The manager explained to the national press that he hoped Tottenham could offer Keane a degree of stability in his footballing life. In return, he expected to see the striker fulfil his potential at White Hart Lane.

He said, 'Robbie is 22 and nowhere near his peak and, if that pattern of moving around had continued, you would never have seen him at his peak. He needs consistency now, both inside and outside his football life. Robbie is at home now and I think he will be here for a long time.

'He has signed a long contract and I told him he needed consistency to get the best out of himself. If you keep travelling around and are not quite settled – and your feet are never under the table – then you are not going to get the best out of yourself. It is time now for Robbie to really concentrate on his football and get some consistency.'

The Spurs boss also believed Keane's friends – former Wolves team-mate Dean Richards and his SFX agency stable-mate Jamie Redknapp – would help the 22-year-old settle into London life. 'I think Robbie is going to enjoy playing here and living down here. He knows Dean Richards from his Wolves days and he also knows Jamie Redknapp well, and he has been introduced to everyone in the dressing room.'

Hoddle predicted that Keane could be a big success, an outstanding match-winner for Tottenham. 'I feel we have got Robbie at a very good time and he has got his best moments to come. He is a bubbly character, he is infectious and he loves the game. The fans will take to him because he is nice to watch.

'Robbie is a cute player who sees things and he will give

us something new. He has got an end product, which players like Dennis Bergkamp and Gianfranco Zola have, and certainly he could progress to being that quality. He is a great player now.'

But Keane's debut for Tottenham was delayed because he wasn't registered in time for the Premiership match against Southampton, the team managed by his old boss Gordon Strachan, at White Hart Lane. Outside the sun-drenched stadium, the street vendors had stocked up on Irish tricolours with the slogan: 'There's only one Keano'. The flags rapidly sold out and that very chant rang around the stadium when, just before kick-off, Keane, in a dark brown suit, strode out on to the pitch to rapturous applause and waved to his new admirers.

On the pitch, a last-minute penalty from Teddy Sheringham ensured Tottenham sealed a 2–1 victory and climbed to the top of the Premiership table. Life was good for the Lilywhites and it appeared that, with Keane on board, it was about to get even better.

Keane now felt as if his career was heading in the right direction, towards his goal of becoming a world-class player. Ahead of what was supposed to be his debut at Fulham, he told the *Evening Standard*, 'I am so excited at the chances this Spurs team are going to create for me and vice versa. I watched them against Southampton on the day I signed and the prospect of playing with those players really excites me, even though we are yet to have a full-strength side available.

'Teddy and Les [Ferdinand] are intelligent footballers. They know how to use the ball and space and I know that the style of football Glenn Hoddle is playing will suit me and them. I know Spurs fans will look to me to score goals, but I want to create chances for the players around me as well.

Keane Earns His Spurs

'More than anything, I want to play. Ever since I started playing football as a kid, I have wanted to be out on the pitch, playing the game and scoring goals. The frustration at Leeds was that I wasn't getting the chance to play.

'Glenn has offered me that chance now and I intend to repay him as soon as I can. Everything I have seen and heard from Spurs has been positive. Now I want to put it all into practice on the pitch.'

Despite the fanfare that greeted his arrival at the club, Keane did not feature in the starting line-up of the Premiership leaders for the match at Loftus Road – he was left on the bench in a surprise 3–2 defeat by Fulham. Afterwards, Hoddle was criticised by members of the press for leaving Keane out, but the Tottenham boss hit back with a detailed explanation as to why his £7 million recruit remained an unused substitute.

A frustrated Hoddle insisted, 'It just goes to show that these people have no nous or understanding of the game. Robbie had been with the Republic in Russia, and Les Ferdinand and Teddy Sheringham were fresh from a week off.

'On top of that, Robbie was ready to come on when Chris Perry sustained a bad injury and that forced us into a reshuffle. Robbie was set to come on again for Les Ferdinand, but Matthew Etherington then asked to come off because of a knee problem. It meant we had to do more reshuffling. The decision to use Robbie was out of my hands because of these circumstances.'

After this false start, Keane was given assurances that he would be in Tottenham's forward line for the following game, a derby clash against West Ham. Already the irrepressible mischief-maker was starting to make an impression at the Spurs Lodge training ground in Chigwell,

Essex, but you couldn't say he was up to his old tricks yet. Nevertheless, Dean Richards was pleased to see his friend. As he told the *Daily Mirror*, 'He has been a bit quiet so far, but I am sure it won't be long before he is showing his funny side. He is the sort of person who gets on well with people.'

It turned out that the big centre-back – who had cost Tottenham £8.1 million from Southampton – had played a modest part in the arrival of the Irish star. 'Glenn Hoddle asked me for my opinion of Robbie before we signed him from Leeds and I told him we would be getting a bargain. At £7 million, he is an absolute steal. I think we got him on the cheap – especially after the goals he got for Ireland in the World Cup. He would cost double that and more if he were an Italian striker.

'Robbie is my friend, but I am speaking as a footballer and I can say he has got everything a striker needs, including amazing confidence. He is going to make a major impact here.'

On 15 September 2002, Keane's debut was marked by good fortune, but for a change he did not open his goal-scoring account on his first outing against West Ham. In a 3–2 home win that took Tottenham to second place, a strike from midfielder Simon Davies, a Sheringham penalty and a late goal from Anthony Gardner gave Spurs maximum points in a spiteful derby against rock-bottom West Ham.

Keane's extraordinary control and quick thinking led to Tottenham's penalty on 71 minutes – the incident that decided the outcome. He expertly controlled the ball on his chest and his second touch enabled him to glide inside the area en route to a certain goal where he was tripped by his marker, Ian Pearce, who was red-carded for the offence.

Keane Earns His Spurs

Afterwards, Hoddle highlighted Keane's unmistakable quality. 'He showed some class touches and that was sublime skill. It is the sort of thing you see from players like Di Canio, Zola, and Bergkamp – and he's 22. Those lads are experienced.'

The mood was upbeat as second-placed Tottenham travelled up to Manchester United, but the squad was ravaged by injury, with a staggering 13 players unavailable for selection. In the end, a second-half penalty from Manchester United's Ruud van Nistelrooy proved to be the only goal of the game, although Keane almost scored inside the opening 45 minutes after disorientating Rio Ferdinand with a darting run into the area. Unfortunately, the small, dark-haired magician's shot was saved by United's Fabien Barthez to deny Keane a memorable debut goal for Tottenham.

Despite the result, Hoddle – a man not easily impressed by other footballers' ability – went on record to announce that Keane's trickery with a ball bordered on genius. 'He's settled in very easily and the other players love him. He's probably got the quickest feet I've seen in the penalty area. He can beat a man and gives us something we hadn't got.'

But the following match at the Lane resulted in a rude awakening for Hoddle's side, as opponents Middlesbrough looked a yard quicker, as well as being far more alert and ruthless in front of the goal. This was reflected in the shock 3–0 final score-line. It had been a team display completely lacking in urgency, courage and direction and it prompted a bitterly disappointed Hoddle to remark, 'I couldn't see a performance like this coming. The manner of the defeat was very disappointing, but it could be the kick up the backside we need.

Robbie Keane

'The transfer window has really hurt us. We have a lot of players out injured and could have done with getting someone in on loan.'

Spurs made amends, though, a few days later with a home win over Cardiff City in the second round of the League Cup. Sheringham scored in a straightforward 1–0 victory. Fast, fearless and clever, Keane linked up well with Sheringham in attack, but was guilty of squandering a couple of simple chances, and unfortunately his barren spell was becoming a major talking point in the pubs around Tottenham High Road.

But the drought did not affect Keane's unshakeable self-belief and the Dubliner told the press, 'At least I'm getting into the right positions. I would be really worried if I wasn't doing that. I'm missing chances, but it won't affect my confidence. I know the goals will come if I keep going in there and there's no doubt I'll be doing that.'

Hoddle endorsed that view: 'Missing does not worry Robbie too much. He's always prepared to shoot and, once the first one goes in here, there will be many more to follow.'

Accordingly, Hoddle persevered with his £7 million signing for the away game at Blackburn and reassured Keane that he would soon get off the mark. In Tottenham's change yellow strip and with the number 22 on his back, Keane responded with a breathtaking goal after only six minutes at Ewood Park. Picking up the ball in the inside-right position, Keane looked up, then embarked on a diagonal run up the pitch, keeping the ball close at all times.

The Spurs supporters inside the ground marvelled at his artistry as he conjured up a thrilling piece of individual virtuosity: he steamed down the left-hand side of the area before dispatching a razor-sharp finish into the Rovers net.

Keane Earns His Spurs

Keane's close friend Jamie Redknapp then scored a late winner for Tottenham in a 2–1 win, which pushed the club up to fourth place in the table.

Afterwards, Hoddle revealed his admiration for Keane. 'That goal he scored showed what he's got in the locker. It was a fabulous goal and that's what Robbie gives us. Until he came, we didn't really have strikers that can manufacture goals themselves. Now he's off and running and I'm sure there's more to come.'

After featuring for the Republic of Ireland against Switzerland, Keane returned to the Spurs Lodge in Chigwell hell-bent on keeping his goal-scoring momentum going. Now he had regained his eye for goal, he did not want to lose it – that meant pestering the coaching staff to be allowed to train. Ahead of the Bolton game, Hoddle said, 'He came back from international duty this week and looked very sharp in training. I wanted to calm him down and not give him a hard task, but he kept nagging me to do the main session and looked fantastic.'

Bolton were the next visitors to the Lane in a game that Tottenham were expected to win, but the away team defended with gritty determination in the first half, leaving the score-line blank at the interval. After the break, Tottenham edged in front through Keane when Goran Bunjevcevic's searching cross from the left wing was smartly knocked on by Simon Davies and the dazzling Dubliner side-footed his shot into the net. It was Keane's first goal for Tottenham at the Lane and he marked the occasion with a somersault by the corner flag in front of the jubilant home fans.

With a smart finish from a Gus Poyet cross, Keane later added a second goal in a 3–1 win and the Shelfside, the Park

Robbie Keane

Lane and the Paxton regulars had found themselves a new hero – a stand-out character with flair.

Spurs followers are renowned soccer purists and, having been brought up on tales of the immaculate feats of the celebrated Double-winning side of 1961, want to see entertaining play on top of watching the club achieve good results. It seemed as if Keane fitted the bill and suited the requirements of a demanding audience that had never warmed to previous boss George Graham's humdrum brand of football.

Bursting with confidence, Keane and Tottenham went to Liverpool with the belief that a positive result was on the cards, but some seemingly questionable decisions from referee Mike Riley led to an unjust 2–1 defeat. At one stage, Keane's shirt was apparently nearly yanked off his back by Liverpool defender Sami Hyppia inside the area, but Riley waved play on – much to Keane's disbelief. A late penalty from Liverpool's Michael Owen proved to be conclusive, but Tottenham were not outclassed at any point in the game and Hoddle took several pluses out of the general performance.

The good thing was that Robbie Keane was beginning to make his mark at Tottenham. Spurs coach Chris Hughton, a former Republic of Ireland international, predicted a bright future for the lad from Tallaght as someone who could emulate the achievements of the many great strikers who had worn the famous Lilywhite shirt. He told the *Sunday Mirror*, 'This is a club with a tradition for producing great goal-scorers. Robbie Keane certainly has got the ability and, with luck, can add to that list. Names like Jimmy Greaves and Gary Lineker are so revered here that nobody is really ever going to compare with them. Yet Robbie has his best years ahead of him.

Keane Earns His Spurs

'He is still too young to compare with those players, but Tottenham fans will tell you that there hasn't been as much excitement here about a new signing for quite a while. That's an indication of the special qualities he brings. He's so delighted to be here – at a club where his talent is fully appreciated. The fans love him for that and already it's possible to detect the early signs of a great partnership in the making as the fans chant his name.'

Back at the Lane, Tottenham completely outclassed Chelsea, but the infamous Premiership jinx continued with the visitors' keeper Carlo Cudicini producing a series of exceptional saves to keep the score-line goalless. Tottenham's best effort was a clever free-kick involving Keane and Redknapp. The Irishman rolled a short pass to the former England midfielder, who flicked the ball into air before unleashing a venomous volley that Cudicini palmed over for a corner.

Off the pitch, Redknapp, who had known Keane for years through their mutual association with the SFX agency, went out of his way to help the Irishman settle into the area. Soon Keane bought a luxurious property in leafy Hertfordshire, close to Redknapp's mansion in Essendon.

Turf Moor was the next destination on Tottenham's fixture list as the previous season's losing League Cup finalists faced Burnley in a third-round tie in front of the Sky Sports television cameras. To begin with, Keane was left on the bench as Tottenham's Premiership class told, with a Gus Poyet goal which handed the Lilywhites a healthy 1–0 lead at half-time.

After the interval, Keane was introduced into the game, but it had disastrous consequences for both the team and the player. In front of a baying crowd, Keane raced through

Robbie Keane

Burnley's flimsy defence on three separate occasions. But, with only keeper Marlon Beresford left to beat, the Irishman ran out of both steam and ideas. Gifted with a hat-trick of clear-cut chances, Keane was guilty of botching them all.

At the other end, Burnley sensed a giant-killing in the offing and promptly scored second-half goals through Robbie Blake and Steve Davis. Spurs were out of the Cup and Keane suffered a 45-minute nightmare of misses. Hoddle said he was perplexed by his team's exit from the competition. 'I just can't believe what has happened. Robbie may have missed three great chances and, at this level, you get punished if you don't take them. But there were other things wrong with our game and that's just unacceptable.'

Before the next game at Sunderland, Keane shrugged his shoulders philosophically and just put his Turf Moor horror show down as an off-day. He said, 'I know I should have scored, but, as we all know, football can be like that. I think I should have scored two of them, but that's the way it goes. There is no point in worrying about it too much; that is when it starts to affect you. You have to concentrate on things you can change – that's the way I look at it.'

But matters went from bad to worse for Tottenham on Wearside as struggling Sunderland struck twice in two second-half minutes to condemn Spurs to a demoralising defeat. Starved of decent service, Keane grafted alongside Sheringham in attack, but he was never any serious danger to the home side's defence as Tottenham suffered another loss.

In his inaugural north London derby, Keane and his teammates faced Premiership title favourites Arsenal at Highbury on the back of two results that had seriously depleted morale in the Spurs camp. Unsurprisingly, Arsenal flexed their muscles and Tottenham's makeshift line-up – still seriously undermanned due to the ongoing injury crisis – collapsed under the pressure.

Tottenham's plight worsened when Davies was sent off after only 27 minutes by referee Mike Riley for two fairly innocuous challenges on Patrick Vieira and Ashley Cole – the red card was later downgraded to just a caution on appeal. Without the Welshman on the pitch, Keane was ordered to drop back and fill the gap on the right-hand side of midfield and he could only watch as Arsenal ran riot.

The game that followed – Leeds at White Hart Lane – drew the spotlight on to Keane and the 22-year-old was happy to discuss what had made him leave a few months previously. He said, 'There are a lot of players just happy to be at clubs and pick their wages up. I'm just one of those players who love playing football. When I'm happiest is when I'm kicking the ball around the park on a Saturday afternoon. For me, playing football week-in and week-out is very important. Sitting on the bench is very frustrating and I don't think Leeds saw the best of me because I didn't play as many games as I'd have liked.

'I'd be doing well and then the next week I'd find myself on the bench again. Sometimes you find that hard to deal with. It was the same in Italy. But I'd never change anything I've done. It's all been great experience.'

The Irishman hoped that he would not get too hostile a reception from the Leeds fans. At any rate, he was planning to give certain familiar members of the crowd something to cheer about. 'I'm looking forward to it – it should be a good game. I've got the family coming over. But it'll be nice to see all the Leeds lads again. I've got a soft spot for them and I have a lot of friends up there, and good memories.

Robbie Keane

'I had a good relationship with the fans and, hopefully, I'll get a nice reception. I think maybe Leeds needed money and it worked out well for me as well, because first and foremost every footballer wants to play football.'

From the first kick of the game, Keane played like a man with a point to prove – he looked dangerous and lively throughout. His surging run led to Tottenham's opening goal when Leeds defender Teddy Lucic's last-ditch tackle only deflected the ball into the path of Sheringham, who finished with ease. Then four minutes before the break, Gus Poyet's through-ball picked out Keane's run and the Irishman struck a spellbinding shot cleanly with the outside of his right foot to score an outstanding goal.

It was an exhilarating effort that helped Tottenham to obtain a much-needed win, but the result spelled disaster for Venables and Leeds. It was their sixth defeat in nine Premiership games.

In his post-match press conference, Hoddle paid tribute to the player he called 'Keaney': 'He was a little bit special today. When you play your old team, it seems to be human nature that you have a spring in your step. But then from one to 11 we were excellent. It was an important victory.'

But the December chill froze Tottenham's progress and Hoddle's side could only draw 1–1 at Birmingham in what was described as a below-par showing from both sides. Keane was even replaced by substitute, Steffen Iversen, with Hoddle explaining that it was because the team had not created a chance. Tottenham's passing display looked decidedly off-colour and the overall performance did little to suggest that the class of 2003 were capable of bringing European football back to the Lane.

The following weekend, West Brom headed for the Lane

and Keane expected a hostile response from visiting fans and he was not disappointed, being duly subjected to a barrage of abuse because of his previous affiliation with Wolves. The Albion supporters gave him merciless stick with some hurtful chants, but, even though Spurs were not on song, Keane silenced the insults with a solo finish.

Latching on to a long through-ball, his first touch took him past the West Brom defence and he confidently dispatched a measured right-foot finish to beat Albion keeper Russell Hoult easily. As soon as the ball hit the net, Keane somersaulted his way towards the South Stand – housing a few thousand Albion fans – before cupping his hands over his ears. Keane had won the battle with a knockout punch and was enjoying the last laugh. His goal added to an impressive free-kick from Christian Ziege and ensured Tottenham emerged as 3–1 victors on the day, although Spurs were far from convincing.

Fortunately, the FA decided against reprimanding Keane for apparently inciting the West Brom fans with his goal celebration and Hoddle agreed that it was the right decision. As he told the *Evening Standard*, 'If that is the case, then I think it is a commonsense decision. Unfortunately, people have tried to make something out of nothing in this matter. Robbie was just celebrating his goal.'

Arsenal were the next visitors to the Lane and everyone with Lilywhite sympathies was gunning for a home win against the old enemy from Gillespie Road. With the atmosphere crackling amid much anticipation, Spurs raised the tempo and tore into the Arsenal defence with passion and urgency. The honest toil paid off when Ziege repeated his earlier feat against West Brom with a textbook free-kick that flew into the Arsenal net after 11 minutes had elapsed.

Robbie Keane

With Tottenham in the ascendancy, it seemed inevitable that Arsene Wenger's team would be on the receiving end of a heavy derby defeat. But a costly error from Spurs keeper Kasey Keller allowed the visitors back into the game. Racing out of his box to clear the ball from Thierry Henry, the American seriously misjudged his opponent's quickness and clattered the Arsenal striker. Referee Neal Barry pointed to the spot and Arsenal midfielder Robert Pires levelled the score with one of the final acts of the first half.

In the second half, Keane's pace and brilliant individual skill continued to trouble the Arsenal back-line and the Irishman was desperately unlucky to see his goal-bound effort cleared off the line by Cole. Somehow, Arsenal managed to stave off the incessant Lilywhite onslaught and the champions clung on for an undeserved point in the Haringey drizzle.

Two days before Christmas, Tottenham bounced back with a 3–2 win over Manchester City and, in a Man of the Match display, Keane laid on two of the goals. Keane carried his fine form over into the Boxing Day meeting with Charlton and was the stand-out player for Spurs with an unforgettable goal in a 2–2 draw. With Tottenham trailing to two goals scored by Charlton's Jason Euell, Keane took control of the game and, following a flick-on from substitute Iversen, rifled a powerful volley into the visitors' net. Then, with four minutes remaining, Iversen headed in his first goal of the season to salvage a point for a misfiring Spurs side.

Keane's 2002 ended on a low note when Tottenham were defeated by Alan Shearer's Newcastle 2–1 at St James' Park and the Irishman was taken off late on to be replaced by Milo Acimovic. The bad results continued into 2003 with two losses at Southampton's St Mary's Stadium in the space of four days – including an embarrassing 4–0 loss in the third round of the FA Cup.

Pressure was mounting on Hoddle and his injury-wrecked team had already been knocked out of both cup competitions before the Christmas decorations had been taken down. Tottenham's board were far from impressed. Spurs desperately needed a timely boost, a shot in the arm, to revitalise a season that was threatening to get lost in a fog of unacceptable mediocrity.

That's when Keane stepped forward and, against Everton, produced his first-ever Premiership hat-trick. A whispering campaign in the media had already begun, suggesting that, if Hoddle lost the home match against David Moyes's side, then he would face the sack. And the murmurs of discontent inside the stadium became louder when Brian McBride gave the Merseyside club the lead after just 10 minutes. But Poyet equalised and the score remained the same until Keane scored his opening goal five minutes after the half-time break.

Perfectly co-ordinated and composed, Keane's run on to a through-ball in an action sequence that almost looked choreographed as, like a slalom skier, he effortlessly side-stepped onrushing Everton keeper Espen Baardsen before finishing from a tight angle. Everton's Steve Watson levelled before Keane despatched an arrow-like, right-footed drive into the bottom corner of the net, then headed towards the part of the stadium where he knew his parents were sitting to cartwheel in front of them.

In a rollercoaster ride of a game, Everton restored parity to make it 3–3 through Tomasz Radzinski, before Keane completed his masterful display by cleverly knocking the ball past his would-be tackler, Joseph Yobo, before slotting the ball into the net.

Robbie Keane

On the back of a perfect day, Keane celebrated after the game with his parents; sadly, though, it was to be the last time his father would ever see him play.

Afterwards, Hoddle hailed Keane's performance and said, 'That has been waiting to happen. Robbie's had his chances before, but today he was clinical and scored a magnificent hat-trick of pure quality. It was a great exhibition of clinical finishing and he's showing now what he's capable of it.

'I don't think I've ever worked with a player who creates chances for others as well as finishing the chances we create for him. If we can get his ratio up, which I think will happen with time and hard work, there's no reason why he can't become a clinical finisher.'

Tottenham's revival continued with a 1–0 win at Aston Villa, where Sheringham scored the winner, before it ground to a halt at the Lane with Newcastle snatching a last-gasp triumph. Just 11 minutes into the game against the Tyneside club, Keane was clattered by Newcastle defender Titus Bramble and, although he soldiered on in pain, he had to be replaced by Gary Doherty nine minutes before half-time. The 22-year-old had injured an ankle and Hoddle said afterwards, 'We are just hoping it is not long term. We might be lucky.'

After missing a 1–1 draw at Chelsea, Keane returned to the starting line-up for the visit of struggling Sunderland, but only briefly – he was stretchered off after just 21 minutes. The Irishman had damaged the ligaments in his right knee when he accidentally booted the ground instead of the ball, but fortunately it would mend without the need for an operation.

After three weeks of rest, Keane resumed light training at Spurs Lodge, but he was still left feeling frustrated at such an unnecessary setback blighting his progress. As he told the *Daily Mirror*, 'I hate sitting in the physio's room, but it has to be done. I want to be back as soon as possible, but I don't want to break down again. I'm very confident that nothing else will happen. I didn't need an operation, just time for it to heal. It's a common injury that footballers get.'

In his absence, Tottenham managed to defeat Sunderland and draw with Fulham, but suffered losses against West Ham and Liverpool before the team's leading marksman was given the all-clear to return for the trip to Bolton. At the Reebok, Tottenham were beaten by a last-minute penalty from Bolton's Jay-Jay Okocha, and then Keane was devastated by the tragic news that, while he was playing, his dad had passed away.

Robbie Snr, who was 50, had lost his year-long battle against liver cancer and the family's youngest son heard the news moments after the game finished. Understandably distraught, he immediately flew home to Tallaght to grieve with his family. Keane issued a statement to the press to mark the sad occasion: 'He was more like my brother. My father was a massive influence on my career as well as being inspirational in every part of my life.

'He fought a very brave and long fight against cancer, but always remained in good spirits. It fills me with pride to remember that the last match he saw me play in was against Everton when I was lucky enough to score a hat-trick. I will miss him greatly and I would be very grateful if my family and I could be allowed our privacy to grieve for a wonderful man.'

To show their support for their friend and his family during such a difficult time, Republic of Ireland boss Brian Kerr, who had known Robbie Snr well for many years, and several members of the squad attended the funeral mass at St Agnes Church in Crumlin.

While the Republic of Ireland team was scheduled to fly out to Tirana to face Albania the day after the funeral, Kerr expected Keane would want to stay in Dublin and miss the game on compassionate grounds. But Keane not only joined the travelling party, he also played in the European Championships qualifier which ended in a goalless draw. As he later explained to the *Independent*, 'I just wanted to. He would have wanted me to go, my mum said that. He wouldn't want me to be sitting on my backside back home watching it.

'He knew I wanted to be involved in every game. I would have been no good to anyone just watching. They say time is a healer and, obviously, it was hard. But, when I do play, I play for him.'

Three days later, Keane was back in Premiership action and scored the most audacious goal of his entire career against Birmingham City at White Hart Lane. Only seven minutes had gone when Birmingham's debutant keeper Andy Marriott prepared to launch a kick up the pitch and casually threw the ball a few yards in front of him, completely unaware of any danger.

Lurking with intent over his left shoulder was Keane and, with the away fans imitating a pantomime audience and desperately crying, 'He's behind you', the cheeky Irishman swooped on to the loose ball and rolled a shot into the unguarded net in front of the amused Spurs supporters. With Marriott's confidence shot to pieces, Tottenham capitalised and chalked up an undeserved 2–1 victory, but afterwards everybody was talking about Keane's daring deed.

Keane Earns His Spurs

Hoddle revealed that Keane had practised the trick before in training and called his first-half effort the 'the cheekiest goal you'll ever see'. Keane felt sympathy for Marriott and, a week later, admitted, 'It's not nice for a goalkeeper to have it happen to him, but that's the way it goes sometimes.'

Next on the fixture list was a return to Keane's old club Leeds United – now managed by Peter Reid and looking on the verge of relegation to the Championship. Fired up and focused, Keane tormented his former employers with a special goal, which came straight out of the top drawer.

The Irishman courageously tackled his close friend Ian Harte on the edge of the Leeds area, before effortlessly side-stepping the challenge from Eirik Bakke, then sending a swerving right-foot shot into the net. While team-mate Gus Poyet hugged him, Keane remained emotionless – he did not want to celebrate in front of the Leeds fans as a mark of respect for the kindness the supporters had shown him during his time at the club.

Eventually, a mistake from Spurs keeper Kasey Keller led to a late penalty for Leeds, which was duly converted by Mark Viduka, and the 2–2 draw played a big part in keeping the West Yorkshire side in the division. After a toothless and uninspired team display during a 2–0 home defeat by Manchester City, Tottenham travelled to the Hawthorns to face West Brom. It was the perfect chance for Keane to heap further misery on his most raucous critics.

Back in the Black Country, Keane tormented relegation-bound Albion with a two-goal display. His first was a clinical finish after he had broken through the home side's offside trap and he followed it up with a second-half blockbuster – drilling a left-footed effort into the bottom right-hand corner.

Robbie Keane

Despite the season ending with a home defeat at the hands of Manchester United, Keane finished his debut campaign as the club's leading goal-scorer with 13, the Player of the Year award and having won over both the fans and the coaching staff – including assistant manager John Gorman. In 2006, Gorman recalled, 'For me, he was class and he looked like a foreign player to be honest – his touch was that good with both feet. He was always full of invention. I felt he was a special player and he was young, so he still had time to get better.

'He is better than just a goal-scorer, he is a team player – he makes goals and he works hard defensively as well. He was a fantastic character to have around the place – one of the best. He was always having a laugh which was great for team spirit.'

Keane was similarly impressed with the club and realised that he needed to work on his shortcomings – scoring straightforward goals. 'It is always nice to get praise, but you realise pretty quickly you are only as good as your last game. I've done pretty well at Spurs in my first season, but you always look to improve. It is my business to score goals and I usually get some pretty decent ones, but the coaches here have been on at me to get a few more tap-ins.

'Like all strikers, I love scoring and it is great when they fly in, but if I can knock in a few more from a few yards I'll be more than happy to add them to the total.'

However, the rumours suggesting that the Hoddle regime was living on borrowed time gathered momentum in the summer, with various well-informed sources in the press claiming that the Spurs boss would become the Premiership's next managerial casualty. Hoddle's much-publicised five-year plan designed to bring European Cup football back to the Lane had gone horribly wrong as Tottenham finished the season in 10th place.

In the pre-season leading up to the 2003/04 season, Hoddle added three new strikers to the squad – West Ham's Fredi Kanoute, FC Porto's Helder Postiga and Brighton's Bobby Zamora. Heading out of the Lane was Teddy Sheringham, who was allowed to join Portsmouth on a free transfer. But Keane was still the undisputed first-choice forward on Tottenham's books and started the first match of the new season alongside Portugal international Postiga at Birmingham. Spurs were far from impressive at St Andrew's and the calls for Hoddle's dismissal were starting to become louder, while Keane experienced an anonymous afternoon in a 1–0 defeat.

After spraining his ankle, Keane was absent for the next four games and he was powerless to prevent an under-fire Tottenham side from suffering heavy defeats to both Fulham and Chelsea. Even in the darkest hour of his tenure, Hoddle insisted that the club would eventually enjoy success and, after a rare win, he told the press, 'The only pressure comes from outside the club. We are together here. You could hear that the crowd was right behind the team.'

Keane returned to action as a substitute for the make-or-break home game against Hoddle's old club Southampton, but could not prevent a depressing 3–1 defeat. It proved to be the final straw for the Spurs board, and chairman Daniel Levy sacked his manager the following day. Levy stated, 'Following two seasons of disappointing results, there was a significant investment in the team during the summer to give us the best possible chance of success this season.

'Unfortunately, the start to this season has been our worst since the Premiership was formed. Coupled with the extremely poor second half to last season, the current lack of progress, or any visible sign of improvement, are unacceptable.

'It is critical that I, and the board, have absolute confidence in the manager to deliver success to the club. Regrettably, we do not. It is not a decision we have taken lightly. However, we are determined to see this club succeed and we must now move forward.'

With Tottenham second from bottom in the Premiership table, the League Cup proved to be a welcome distraction and Keane was thrilled when Tottenham were handed an away tie at his former club Coventry. Director of football David Pleat was handed the role of caretaker manager in the wake of so much upheaval behind the scenes and Keane was selected to start at Highfield Road.

Keane got a tremendous reception from the Highfield Road crowd, but he proved to be the architect of Coventry's downfall that night – setting up Kanoute's opening goal, before extending Tottenham's lead with an expert finish 10 minutes later. But, as soon as his goal went in, there was no somersault, cartwheel or even a raised arm; Keane was unemotional as he ran back to the centre-circle. Afterwards, he explained, 'I didn't want to celebrate. I wanted to show a bit of respect to the Coventry fans because I had a great time here.'

Keane was substituted with the game already won and he left the pitch to a standing ovation from the whole stadium, which he gratefully acknowledged.

A spectacular long-range goal from Rohan Ricketts sealed a 3–0 Carling Cup win for Spurs, but Keane's post-match message was that the result was dedicated to recently sacked boss Hoddle. He said, 'We owe a bit to Glenn Hoddle. We know that, at the start of the season, we did not do as well as we should have for him and ourselves. I have got a lot of time for Hoddle. I just wish we had done it a bit earlier for him.'

After the win, Tottenham then went on a five-match unbeaten run – clocking up three wins along the way – until the revival ended with a home defeat against Bolton. Keane had scored a goal against Everton during that sequence of results and he was beginning to forge an excellent understanding with new strike partner Kanoute. The French-born striker provided both height and ability to complement Keane's skills and the interplay between the two was the outstanding feature in an otherwise indifferent start to the season.

Pleat was pleased with Keane's contribution and, after the Everton win, said, 'When Robbie drops off and plays in that hole like a Zola, a Bergkamp or a Hoddle, he can be fantastic. Where the supporters once had David Ginola, they now have Robbie Keane. He is a real personality.'

Keane's next goal was the match-winner at the Lane – this time it was against Aston Villa, now managed by David O'Leary. With the game heading for a 1–1 draw, Keane outclassed his marker Ronny Johnsen with a magnificent turn and delivered a first-class finish with only minutes of the contest remaining.

O'Leary – the manager who rarely played Keane at Leeds – said after his club's defeat, 'If you give Keane time and space, he's going to punish you.'

And David Pleat put his finger on the one drawback with having Keane in your team. 'At times, Robbie is so talented that he tends to over-elaborate because he knows he can do things other players can't. So you have to live with his upside and accept any downsides. He has cleverness.'

Relieved at scoring, Keane said, 'I was certainly due a goal. I've not been scoring as regularly as last year. I got a bad injury which put me back a bit, so it was nice to get on the score-sheet, but the most important thing was to get the win. I'm sure it wasn't the most entertaining game to watch and, at half-time, David and Chris [Hughton] had a few words. It was important we bounced back, and we did.'

The three points from the win took Tottenham four vital places up the Premiership standings. But still there was no confirmation of who the next Tottenham boss would be, although the rumour mill had gone into overdrive. Keane gave his reaction to all the speculation in the *Independent*, 'I don't know who's going to replace him. I've heard 15 names so far.'

After a Premiership defeat at Blackburn and a Carling Cup win over Manchester City, Keane became reacquainted with the club that had given him his big break in the game. Wolves were the next visitors to White Hart Lane. After their long pursuit of top-flight football, the Midlands club had reached the Premiership courtesy of a win in the play-offs, and Keane was delighted for the club, especially his close friend Matt Murray.

Despite leaving Molineux four years earlier, Keane had stayed in regular touch with the goalkeeper and jokingly vowed to embarrass him during the December showdown. A few months before the fixture, Keane had joked, 'I might hide in the back of the net after an attack and sneak up behind Matt as he's about to clear the ball and score – like I did against Birmingham last season.

'The game at Tottenham is just before Christmas and, provided both Matt and me are selected, it will be the first time we have played against each other apart from in training.

Keane Earns His Spurs

'I've tremendous memories of my time at Wolves and the fans there. I know Matt will be going flat out to ruin my day. Whoever comes off worse between us will never hear the end of it. But it's the one at Molineux on the last day of the season we are both looking forward to.'

As fate would have it, Murray was ruled out of the game at the Lane with a fractured foot, and so his replacement, Michael Oakes, was the unlucky victim of a spectacular hat-trick from Keane. In a 5–2 victory, Keane dazzled. With dynamism, peerless technique and persistence, the 23-year-old rattled in a thrilling treble of goals, including a stunning second-half volley.

But once more Keane refused to celebrate any of his goals and afterwards revealed he hoped his first English club would stay in the division. 'I've got mixed emotions because Wolves is a club that means a hell of a lot to me. I have got a lot of friends there. I came over from Ireland and went there at 15 years of age and the people there made me feel very welcome. The fans have always been very good to me and the reception I got from them at the game says it all.

'I wanted to show a bit of respect. Wolves and the fans had a lot of respect for me, so I didn't want to rub it in by doing my celebration. I hope they stay up. I really hope so because they are a club that deserves to be in the Premiership with the fans they have.'

Unfortunately, Keane's memorable feat preceded a dismal sequence of results for Tottenham, with the club losing four games in a row – including a Carling Cup tie against Middlesbrough. But, as 2004 began, both Keane and Tottenham regained the winning habit. Birmingham, Leeds and Liverpool were all convincingly beaten in the month of January.

Robbie Keane

Keane's goal at Elland Road in particular showed how he had added improved upper-body strength to his natural talent as he shrugged off the attentions of Michael Duberry before hooking the ball into the net. Looking sharper and saddled with greater responsibility up front, Keane responded with goals in each of the victories and was unquestionably the team's most important player. How could Tottenham possibly want anybody else in attack? But, on transfer-deadline day, the club shelled out £7 million for West Ham striker Jermain Defoe – a small, out-and-out goal-scorer – and suddenly Keane's future at the club no longer seemed as assured.

chapter **nine**

The Entertainer

'Even in the modern game with so many cult figures, the number of players who entertain by their ability to do the unexpected is still pretty low – Robbie's one of them. Whether he's doing his customary cartwheel of joy when he scores or attempting the impossible in and around the box, he's an entertainer who the fans love. They like his approach to the game, and so do I. He's blessed with great self-belief and that's vital when you're taking on defenders, even on days when it's just not happening for you.'

Mick McCarthy talking about Robbie Keane, 2002

U p until February 2004, Robbie Keane was unquestionably Tottenham's chief attacking force, but the arrival of new signing Jermain Defoe from West Ham suddenly put that role in severe doubt.

Tottenham's director of football David Pleat had engineered the transfer that saw Bobby Zamora go to West Ham as part of the deal. The club's caretaker boss explained that the team needed a predatory striker with the priceless knack of scoring goals and he believed Defoe was the answer.

At a press conference held at White Hart Lane, Pleat said, 'Tottenham have a history of having top goal-scorers, including Jimmy Greaves, Clive Allen and Gary Lineker – players I consider to be real poachers. We have a mixture of different types of forwards now and they all have different qualities.

'But Jermain's goal record for a 21-year-old is quite exceptional. We hope he is going to have a fine and flourishing career at Spurs and his signing is in keeping with our policy of developing a young team to improve and get us into Europe. I cannot think of another British striker of his age who has done so much in such a short space of time at such a high level.'

The capture of Defoe triggered speculation that Keane was no longer needed at Tottenham and several pundits implied that a Defoe–Keane partnership would fail. But Pleat quickly dispelled those rumours, insisting Keane was still a valued asset at the club and that the change would not affect his future. He added, 'He's really enjoying his football. He's very bright-eyed and has probably been training a couple of hours round the back somewhere. He knows he has to put down roots because he's had some quick moves in his career. We're enjoying his contribution and have no intention of selling him.'

Still without a new manager, Tottenham entertained Manchester City in an FA Cup fourth-round replay at the Lane and Keane planned to mark his territory with a goal to ward off the imminent threat of new boy Defoe. But, despite taking a three-goal lead into the half-time break, Spurs completely caved in during the second half and, in one of the most remarkable turnarounds in modern football, 10-man City won 4–3 with a last-minute winner.

Keane scored on 19 minutes, but was in no mood to celebrate afterwards because Tottenham's season was already over three months before it was officially meant to finish. With Kanoute off representing Mali in the African Cup of Nations, Defoe lined up alongside Keane in a new-look forward partnership for the visit of Portsmouth – Tottenham had to win.

The pair combined superbly for Tottenham's opening goal. Keane's incisive pass found Defoe and the Spurs debutant rifled a powerful shot past Portsmouth keeper Shaka Hislop to give the home side a much-needed lead. But Tottenham's defence looked alarmingly fragile and Portsmouth soon equalised through Eyal Berkovic. Then it was Keane's turn and he restored Tottenham's advantage after spinning round on the edge of the box and instinctively sending a left-footed volley into the net.

In a helter-skelter game of football, Portsmouth levelled for the second time through Lomana Tresor Lua Lua before Keane added his second of the match. He latched on to a through-ball a couple of yards over the halfway line and set off for goal. His beautifully balanced dribbling enabled him to avoid two challenges inside the area before he finished off his run by hooking the ball over the body of Hislop.

But once again Spurs were caught out at the back when Portsmouth substitute Ivica Mornar made it 3–3 with six minutes left on the scoreboard clock. It was left to Tottenham substitute Gus Poyet to snatch the winner with seconds remaining when the Uruguayan calmed the home crowd's frayed nerves by steering the ball into the net off his knee to secure victory. It was a panicky win for a team that had still not come to terms with the shocking collapse against Manchester City that had led to such an untimely exit from the FA Cup.

But at least the goal-scoring form of Keane and Defoe meant that Tottenham did not have to rely on its brittle defence to obtain positive results. The goal spree continued with a midweek demolition of Charlton at the Valley.

Keane did not succeed in getting on to the score-sheet, but Defoe did in a 4–2 win, which took the club's tally to 11 in three games.

Far from feeling threatened by the rapid emergence of Defoe, Keane was delighted and tipped the side to finish the season strongly. He said, 'Jermain has come in and settled in straight away. It's as if he's been here for months, not just days. He's a real breath of fresh air. He's young, talented and a real handful for defenders.

'It's great that he has been able to start so well here. But he's a confident lad and nothing seems to bother him. With Fredi coming back from the African Nations' Cup, we certainly have the potential to score plenty more goals. There's stiff competition for places in attack and that can only be good. It will keep us all on our toes.'

The sequence of wins even prompted Keane to suggest Tottenham could mount a late challenge for Europe. 'At the very least, we must target a top-10 finish. But why shouldn't we be more ambitious and believe we can perhaps get into the top six? We're just five points behind Liverpool in fourth place. That's nothing. Just a couple of wins and you're in the chase for Europe.

'There are 10 clubs within seven points in the middle of the table and it could be crazy the way it changes between now and the end of the season. Any team which can put together a run of three or four wins will rocket up the table. We have got back into winning ways, but more importantly we are playing better. The confidence level is high and we now believe we can score goals every time we take the field.'

With Leicester providing the opposition at the Lane, manager Pleat promised his side would again throw to caution to the wind in the search for goals and Premiership points. 'We have got more attack-oriented, or appear to have done, if you believe the score-lines. The score-lines can lie a little bit. It might not be a poor defence, just a lazy forward line not getting back enough.'

The final outcome in N17 didn't disappoint spectators who had come expecting a flood of goals – it ended 4–4 and Keane notched his 50th Premiership goal with a low drive in the first half. A late equaliser from Defoe rescued a point for the shell-shocked home side, but it left David Pleat at a loss to explain his side's brand of defending. A puzzled Pleat said, 'I feel like a drunken man who hasn't had a drink.'

Defeats against Middlesbrough, Manchester United, Southampton, Chelsea, Everton and Bolton followed, as Tottenham's purple patch ended and their match-winning form deserted them with the club heading into the season's final furlong. To make matters worse, the next game was at home to arch-rivals Arsenal, who were on the verge of clinching the title.

In front of the Sky Sports cameras, the nation watched champions-elect Arsenal seize a two-goal lead at the Lane through early efforts from Patrick Vieira and Robert Pires. But then Spurs fought back, with captain Jamie Redknapp reducing the deficit with a second-half goal, which set up a thrilling finale. In the third minute of added-on time, referee Mark Halsey noticed that Keane had been pushed by Arsenal keeper Jens Lehmann inside the area and dramatically awarded a penalty to the home team.

The situation instantly brought back memories of the 2002 World Cup for the Irishman and the whole stadium held its breath as he stepped up to take the penalty kick. Even though Lehmann guessed correctly and dived to his left, Keane's unhurried effort pelted the roof of the

Arsenal net to save Tottenham's day and, after such a disappointing season, it gave the Spurs fans something genuine to celebrate.

But the late goal – the stuff of comic-book heroics – was overshadowed by the fact that, at the final whistle, Arsenal were crowned Premiership champions and the away side held an impromptu party on the pitch. The scenes sickened both the Spurs players and supporters and highlighted the increasing gulf between the two rival clubs – Arsenal would remain unbeaten for the entire season.

As Tottenham's season staggered to the finishing line, Blackburn were defeated at the Lane before the final game of the season arrived at Wolves – Keane's first match back at Molineux since he had left in 1999. Before the match at the ground where his career started, Keane revealed his long-lasting affection for Wolves and told the *Birmingham Post*, 'When I scored against Wolves, I deliberately decided not to do my usual celebration. I have too much respect for Wolves and their fans to rub their noses in it and I think they appreciated that.

'I have always had a fantastic relationship with them and that will never go away. I'm sorry about the hat-trick. But all sentiment has to go by the board once the whistle goes. I am a Spurs player now and my first duty is to them.

'But, if anyone didn't know I still had Wolves in my blood, they only have to look back to the two games Spurs played against West Brom last season. Their fans gave me terrible abuse because of my past, but I shut them up by scoring against them at White Hart Lane, and twice more at The Hawthorns.'

Keane's uncanny knack of scoring against his former clubs continued as he gave Tottenham the lead against his relegation-bound old club. Spurs debutant Mark Yeates threaded an accurate pass through to Keane, who steadied himself and, after seeing his initial effort blocked by Wolves keeper Paul Jones, the 23-year-old swept home the rebound. Again, his celebrations were muted out of respect for the fans who had encouraged his enterprising play and appreciated his talent when he was a rookie, too.

Four-and-a-half years younger than Keane, Yeates shared a similar background to his senior team-mate. Both hailed from Tallaght and both had tragically lost their fathers in 2003. Yeates told the *Sunday Mirror*, 'Robbie is just a great bloke, a brilliant bloke. We're from the same part of Tallaght, so it's easy to get on with him. He understands me, he looks after me and he looks out for me. Robbie's always making sure that I'm OK after everything that happened, always asking after my ma and making sure the family are OK.'

Defoe added a second to conclude the scoring and bring an end to Tottenham's worst season for a decade. The club had gone stale and was in urgent need of a tonic. Spurs finished the season in 14th place, while Keane finished top of the club's goal-scoring charts with 16.

With the club in serious turmoil, Pleat hinted that a decision concerning the next Tottenham manager was imminent, but the remit was seriously challenging – the new man would be charged with resurrecting the fortunes of a faded force in English football, a tough job for anyone. A number of appointees had already failed in the task.

Away from football, Keane returned to Dublin and spent time at his penthouse at Tassagard Greens in Citywest with his girlfriend Claudine Palmer. He had met Claudine on a night out at Lillie's Bordello two-and-a-half years previously and they were inevitably dubbed Ireland's answer to the Beckhams.

Daughter of a Malahide policeman, Claudine was a Miss Ireland contestant later that summer and she is now a model and TV presenter, although both of them prefer to shun the limelight. In a rare interview on the subject, Keane told *VIP* magazine, 'What's most attractive about Claudine is her personality. She has a great sense of her own independence and I really admire that trait in people. I'm really proud of Claudine – she is following her dreams and building a career. Obviously, I'll support her all the way. Once she is happy doing what she wants, then I'm happy.'

In June 2004, with all eyes on the Euro 2004 tournament in Portugal, Keane and Claudine holidayed on the sunshine island of Sardinia, but even then the paparazzi snapped Keane juggling a football on the beach – his way of relaxing. In the modern age where footballers are treated as celebrities, Keane has never wholeheartedly embraced his fame. In fact, the only time Keane – who has played with and against some of the biggest names in football – has been star-struck was when he met pop singer Robbie Williams at a concert. As he recalled, 'I was invited backstage to meet him before a gig and I was completely speechless when I saw him. In my book, he is the top man, but he was genuinely made up to meet me, which felt really weird.

'I quite fancied having a kick-about with him because he is supposed to be quite tasty, but he had to nip off and get ready for the show. I was really nervous, so I was mumbling rubbish when he asked me what he should eat before the gig. My mind went blank and all I could say was: "Er, pasta and chicken".'

The Entertainer

When Keane returned to north London, a decision had at last been reached concerning the vacant managerial post. Ambitious chairman Daniel Levy had chosen to install a continental-style structure, with a head coach overseeing the day-to-day matters of the squad and a sporting director to be in charge of transfer dealings and contract talks.

As a result, Pleat was ousted from his role of director of football to pave the way for Frank Arnesen from PSV Eindhoven to come in as the club's first sporting director, and forerunner of the new regime. With some of the best contacts in the game, former Denmark international Arnesen had impeccable credentials as well as a thorough knowledge of the global marketplace.

After appointing an outstanding candidate to the sporting director position, Levy then chose France boss Jacques Santini to occupy the job of head coach. Santini had a proven track record across the Channel and on the international scene and Levy believed he was the right man to lead the club forward. Speaking through a translator, Santini told the English press, 'I am delighted to get the opportunity to join Tottenham Hotspur. I am an ambitious man and it has always been a dream of mine to coach a big English club in the most exciting league in the world.

'Tottenham are a very big club, with a wonderful history and great traditions. Daniel and Frank have outlined their vision and I share their ambitions. I am determined to help the club return to its place among the elite and look forward to joining them after Euro 2004.'

But the Frenchman's inability to speak English worried many fans who questioned whether he would be able to handle the media demands and communicate properly with the players.

Robbie Keane

The final addition to the club's back-room staff came in the summer of 2004 with the introduction of Martin Jol, who arrived as assistant head coach. A gravel-voiced Dutchman, Jol was regarded as the finest up-and-coming coach in Holland, after taking *Eredivisie* minnows RKC Waalwijk into Europe. There was the added advantage that he knew the English game well – dating back to spells as a player with Coventry and West Brom.

Keane returned to pre-season training at Spurs Lodge bursting with enthusiasm. He was determined to establish himself as the club's first-choice striker under Santini. Portuguese player Helder Postiga had returned to FC Porto after a disappointing year-long stay in England, with Champions League-winner Pedro Mendes, a skilful midfielder, moving to north London as part of the deal.

In the massive shake-up which transformed Spurs from top to bottom, Keane was handed the number 10 shirt – once worn by arguably Tottenham's greatest player, Glenn Hoddle – and he passed on his old number 8 squad number to new signing Mendes. Goalkeeper Paul Robinson was another significant summer acquisition and Keane helped his old Leeds team-mate settle into life at the club.

With Jol taking the majority of training sessions, there was a fresh vitality about the club, and Keane was keen to get the season under way when disaster struck. In a pre-season friendly at Glasgow Rangers in late July, Keane was stretchered off after falling awkwardly under a challenge from defender Marvin Andrews and suffering ankle ligament damage.

After the game, new coach Santini said, 'For this to have happened in the two weeks before the start of the championship is a serious problem. The club needs Robbie

Keane for the first match against Liverpool, but now I do not know if he will be able to play.'

Keane was expected to be out of action for six weeks and it could not have happened at a worse time for the striker. He expressed his disappointment to the Irish press: 'I'm usually a quick healer so, please God, I will be back sooner than we expect. It will be very frustrating to miss the pre-season games and the start of the season.

'You go through pre-season to get your fitness up and get ready for the start of the season then something like this happens. It sets you back a bit, but I will keep myself ticking over and strong. Hopefully, I'll be back in not too long a time.'

Keane missed the opening two games of the Premiership season – a home draw against Liverpool and an away win at Newcastle – before getting the all-clear to travel with the squad to West Brom. The 24-year-old believed he had regained full mobility in his foot and said, 'The treatment I've been getting has been good. I usually come back a bit quicker than expected. It is a lot better than expected. I'm pleased with how things are going.'

In a 1–1 draw at the Hawthorns, Keane was a second-half replacement for goal-scorer Defoe and he struggled to make an impact. Nevertheless, Keane was given the nod to start the following home game against Birmingham up front alongside Defoe as Tottenham's winning start continued. But once again it was Defoe and not the Irishman who struck the match-winner and Kanoute replaced Keane late on.

As individuals, both Defoe and Keane were lethal and entertaining marksmen. But, in combination, there was a distinct lack of understanding and it became clear that

Santini would have to drop one of his top-class strikers. A worrying shortage of goals ensued, with Tottenham drawing blanks against both Norwich and Chelsea in back-to-back goalless draws. Keane's magic touch had deserted him.

Then Spurs faced a potential banana skin in the Carling Cup – an away tie at League One side Oldham. Keane was chosen by Santini to start alongside Fredi Kanoute in attack and the pairing worked. With slick one-touch interchanges, the 'special K' partnership looked dangerous from the start and Kanoute opened the scoring in the first half. In the second half, the floodgates opened at Boundary Park as Tottenham hit the home side for six – the club's biggest win in three years.

In the process, Keane capped a stand-out display with a smart finish to score his first goal of the season, but during the rout Defoe also scored with his first touch on the pitch. Afterwards, Keane admitted to the press that it would be tough for him to hang on to a starting spot with such competition for places. 'We know as individuals we have to play well to get in the side. The manager has been in charge of France, so he is used to having good players fighting for places. He knows how to make difficult choices. We can only continue scoring goals and hope it gives him a big headache, but a nice headache.

'The three of us are different types of players, but the good thing for the manager is that all the partnerships have gelled. We've tried Jermain and myself, Fredi and myself and Fredi and Jermain – and it's worked.'

Apart from the goal glut in the Cup, Spurs were finding goals hard to come by in the Premiership and, after a 1–0 home loss to Manchester United, Santini acknowledged that it was a huge concern. 'It is a question for my assistants and I why we have not scored in three games, but I have confidence in our strikers, Defoe and Robbie Keane. Robbie has had only one month in the championship because of an injury, but Jermain has scored three and we know that, when we have our best team in the field, they can get goals.'

Tottenham kept in touch with the chasing pack at the top of the table with an impressive 1–0 triumph at Everton, where Keane and Defoe linked up well. But transfer speculation surrounding Keane's future at the club hogged the back-page headlines, with Celtic and Everton both apparently interested in taking him away from the Lane in the January transfer window.

In the next game, Tottenham's collective deficiencies were horribly exposed in front of the Sky Sports cameras at Fratton Park, with struggling Portsmouth snatching three points and, once again, the club's progress was put under the microscope. The nation watched on and what they saw was a team that simply was not functioning as a unit. The pundits began to question whether that had anything to do with the experimental management structure.

With so many strong characters flexing their muscles behind the scenes, some sections of the media argued that there was not one clearly defined voice leading the team – Santini was under pressure.

Following the dismal performance at Portsmouth where Spurs squandered several clear-cut chances, the team had only managed to score five goals in nine Premiership games. Santini reasoned it was because the strikers were trying too hard: 'We are having a difficult time going forward. Against Portsmouth last Monday, we had all those chances. I think Robbie, Jermain and Fredi Kanoute are thinking: "Score, score, score," at all costs. They are all shooting with haste.'

Robbie Keane

Before the next home match against Bolton, fans and ex-players paid tribute to the manager that had originally brought glory to the Lane – Bill Nicholson – after the legendary boss had sadly passed away days before. But the only positive to emerge from defeat against Sam Allardyce's men was the goal from Keane that put the scores level. Linking up superbly with Kanoute, the 24-year-old's shot squirmed through the legs of Bolton keeper Jussi Jaaskeleinen.

After a woeful 2–1 defeat, Santini refused to attend the post-match press conference and the assembled media took that as a snub against the memory of his famous predecessor. It was a disastrous PR own goal for the Frenchman. He later issued a statement where he insisted he had not intended to insult Nicholson's memory, but the damage to his reputation had already been done. 'There is no way I would insult the memory of Bill Nicholson in that way. The club had already paid a fitting tribute to a great man before the game and, knowing how much he was cherished by all at Spurs, I felt it best to leave it to those who knew him well to pay their respects on behalf of the club.'

The celebration of Nicholson's life, and also his lengthy association with Tottenham, not only emphasised how great the club had once been, but it also highlighted the shortcomings of the current side. On the pitch, however, Tottenham took revenge on Bolton by knocking the Lancashire club out of the Carling Cup with an exhausting 4–3 victory after extra-time. But the cup exploits just served to paper over the cracks at a troubled club and a 2–0 reverse at Fulham plunged Tottenham into deeper desolation.

The team's attacking strategy was so below par that, in order to get any service, Keane had to drop back to just in front of the defence at Craven Cottage. The day before Halloween, Spurs had produced a horror show.

Five points from seven Premiership games painted the portrait of a club in crisis and Santini, accountable for results, might have felt that his position was no longer tenable, though he alone would not have been to blame. Citing personal reasons for his decision, Santini handed in his resignation the night before the visit of Charlton.

In the aftermath of the decision, Jol stepped in and picked the team, with Keane selected to play on the left-hand side of midfield, a recurring problem area for Tottenham. But the nightmare continued, with Spurs going three down five minutes after half-time. Then the home side were handed a lifeline when Charlton's two-goal striker Shaun Bartlett was sent off for deliberately handling the ball on the line. Keane stepped up and rammed his low spot-kick into the bottom corner of the net to reduce the visitors' lead and he jogged back to the centre-spot without even breaking into a smile. In a crisis, there is no time for celebration. Another goal soon followed, this time from Defoe, but it could not stop Charlton from winning and throwing Tottenham's new regime into further disarray.

Despite the result, Jol was handed the reins on a permanent basis a couple of days later and he led Tottenham into a date with Burnley in the Carling Cup. Keane netted a goal in each half to erase any memories of his last performance at Turf Moor and Defoe added a third late on.

Midfielder Michael Carrick, signed from West Ham apparently against the wishes of Santini, made his first start of the season and it was the England international's pass that instigated Keane's opener – a finish from six yards out.

Keane then struck his fifth goal of the season when he slid home Defoe's touchline cross seven minutes after the break.

Famed for his straight-talking, Jol claimed that the key ingredient behind his early success was not down to any complex tactical system – it was about getting the basics right. 'It's all about service. If they get that, then they will score goals because they are one of the best partnerships in England. With easy service, we can score easy goals.'

After ending Tottenham's goal drought, Jol was confident he could win his first Premiership match in charge – even though it was against the old enemy Arsenal at the Lane. In the most extraordinary north London derby on record, Tottenham attacked with panache, but defended like statues as Arsenal snatched a 5–4 win in an incident-packed match. Jol came to the conclusion that he would have to make some big decisions to balance a hideously lop-sided team.

As a result, Keane was relegated to the bench for the Monday-night trip to Aston Villa – sparking off rumours that the previous season's Player of the Year would be on his way out in January. But, lacking ideas going forward, Tottenham put in an uninspiring performance during a drab 1–0 loss at Villa Park. Both Keane and fellow substitute Calum Davenport were thrown on up front in a desperate bid to find an equaliser – even though the latter was a centre-half making his Spurs debut.

The defeat put Tottenham just two points above the relegation zone and left Keane questioning his future at White Hart Lane. Reinstated for the home game against Middlesbrough, relations between the Irishman and Jol became increasingly strained when he was replaced by Kanoute with 20 minutes of the game remaining. Frustrated, Keane stormed off down the tunnel and, to make

The Entertainer

matters worse, Kanoute scored Tottenham's second goal in a 2–0 win after Defoe had given the home side the lead.

Keane's misery continued when Tottenham were knocked out of the Carling Cup at the quarter-final stage by a seriously understrength Liverpool side. Before being substituted, Keane was denied twice at close range by Liverpool keeper Jerzy Dudek. With 18 months left on his contract, Keane started to weigh up his options because, at the age of 24, he did not want to experience the same situation that had blighted his stay at Leeds.

Fortunately, Keane showcased his sumptuous skills in the televised match at Blackburn and responded with the winning goal at Ewood Park. It was a goal fashioned by his Spurs team-mate Michael Brown's sheer determination and hard graft. With Spurs on the back foot, Brown broke away inside his own half and carried the ball up the pitch, before laying the ball into the path of Keane. Taking the pass in his stride, the Irishman won the match by driving a wicked, low shot into the back of the Rovers net.

To everyone's surprise, even after Keane had ended his goal drought, he was still taken off by Jol. Speaking to the press afterwards, he admitted that he wasn't entirely satisfied with his stop-start role under Jol. 'I've been taken off in the last few games and I've not been happy. You want to play in every game and for every minute you can get. But it was more important to win – that was a massive result. The three points is what matters.

'I've not been playing too well lately, so hopefully that will give me confidence. The whole team hasn't been playing particularly well, either. We would be lying if we said we don't look at the bottom of the table. But, if you look too much, you start to think you are in a crisis.'

Robbie Keane

With Defoe suspended, Keane stayed in the starting line-up for the journey to Manchester City along with Kanoute, who had been heavily criticised by Jol for a mistake he made during the cup defeat against Liverpool. Marked by his old friend Richard Dunne, Keane repeatedly punched holes in City's defence with his close control and awareness. One of his efforts was cleared off the line by Sylvain Distin, while another swerved wide of the target. Despite Keane's near misses, Tottenham still managed to grind out a workman-like win, with Kanoute scoring the only goal – a spectacular long-range thunderbolt.

But Jol's decision to recall Defoe, who had been serving a ban, to Tottenham's starting line-up at the expense of Keane for the home clash with Southampton suggested that the Dutchman had made up his mind concerning his preferred choice up front. Lean and lethal, Defoe boasted the single-minded efficiency of an archetypal goal-poacher in the final third and justified Jol's decision with a brilliant hat-trick in a trouble-free 5–1 win for Spurs.

Coming off the bench, Keane had only been on the pitch for five minutes when he scored Tottenham's final goal – ironically set up by Defoe. Showing great awareness, Defoe sent a looping pass over the top of the Southampton defence for Keane to chase on to and the Irishman sent a side-footed volley under the body of Southampton keeper Antti Niemi to notch up a much-needed goal. After finishing his customary cartwheel by the corner flag, Keane immediately turned around to show his gratitude to Defoe for providing him with such a simple chance.

With the transfer window set to reopen two weeks later, stories linking Keane with moves to Everton, Aston Villa and Celtic continued to appear in the national press. But,

The Entertainer

before the Boxing Day trip to Norwich, Jol slammed the rumours. Jol told the press, 'Keane is not going anywhere. It would be stupid to sell him and leave us with just two strikers. We are in a good financial position and no one on the board has told me I have to offload in the transfer window.

'We do not have a problem keeping players at Tottenham. If they are unhappy, they have to realise that they are here for the club and not as individuals. I'm happy that we have three strikers, but a lot of clubs have four and nobody speaks about it. I don't hear anything if Alan Smith is not playing for Manchester United.

'Having three strikers is a good combination. We have three quality players up front, but we could do with another young striker who would be happy to sit on the bench.'

It turned out to be a happy Christmas for Keane because not only was he brought back into the first XI ahead of the in-form Defoe, but he also scored with an instinctive half-volley in a 2–0 victory at Carrow Road. In the post-match press conference, Jol explained his decision: 'You have to create you own options. I could have left Keane out against Norwich because Fredi Kanoute and Defoe played very well in the last game.

'By playing Keane, I can imagine what would have been said if we had lost. But it is all about creating. I have faith in Robbie Keane, in Erik Edman; Thimothee Atouba played very good, and so did Jamie Redknapp.'

Despite scoring in successive games, Keane was once again consigned to the bench as Tottenham failed to win a club-record sixth consecutive game against Crystal Palace. In a jittery contest, Defoe gave Spurs an undeserved lead before Andrew Johnson struck a late equaliser for the visitors. It was only after Palace's goal that Keane was introduced to the fray, but in freezing conditions he could not alter the fact that Tottenham had finished 2004 looking both awkward and vulnerable.

But the New Year's Day encounter against Everton blew the cobwebs away with a 5–2 win, inspired by two-goal debutant Dean Marney. The midfielder had been called into the starting line-up at the very last minute by Jol and responded with a sparkling display – including setting up a goal for Keane. Racing down the right flank, Marney showed great awareness to pick out the figure of Keane, and the Irishman – undetected by the visitors' rearguard – swept the ball home from close range.

Spurs carried the momentum on to the trip to Manchester United and were cruelly denied a last-gasp win when an unbelievable, long-range shot from Pedro Mendes was fumbled on the line by United keeper Roy Carroll. Some thought that, looking decidedly suspicious, Carroll hurriedly clawed the ball away before referee Mark Clattenburg could blow the whistle for a goal. But video footage appeared to show the Portuguese midfielder's incredible effort had crossed the line and Spurs fans were furious.

After playing the entire game at Old Trafford, Keane kept his place for the visit of Championship strugglers Brighton – managed by his first-ever boss Mark McGhee – in an FA Cup third-round tie at the Lane. Before the game, Keane paid tribute to McGhee. 'I've got a lot of respect for him and he is a good man. He looked after me from when I made my debut to the time he left and I have great admiration for him.'

In an uninspiring cup-tie, Ledley King scored Tottenham's opening goal just before half-time, but it was soon cancelled out by a clever free-kick from Brighton's Richard Carpenter.

The Entertainer

Aside from the goals, the most noticeable aspect of the game was the total lack of understanding between Keane and Defoe. The pair weren't operating on the same wavelength. Intended lay-offs went astray and interlinking runs were hopelessly misinterpreted as the duo made heavy weather of outfoxing a very ordinary Brighton defence.

Then, with frustration visibly mounting, a moment of genius from Keane decided the outcome. In one smooth movement, Keane, with his back to goal, swivelled and sent an unstoppable shot into the Brighton net to save Tottenham's blushes seven minutes from the end.

Moments after the final whistle, Keane sought out the man who had handed him his debut and gave him a special keepsake – his unwashed matchday shirt with the message: 'To Mark. Thanks for everything.'

Though disappointed at his side's cup exit, McGhee was still pleased that Keane had scored the winner and said, 'Players like Robbie can always do that to you even when they're not having a good day.'

Second-rate Premiership results followed the Cup heroics – an awful 3–0 defeat at Palace, then a draw at West Brom – but the main talking point was alleged discussions that had taken place between Tottenham and Manchester City. Still lacking width in midfield, Tottenham's key decision-makers had targeted City winger Shaun Wright-Phillips as the answer to the problem and, according to tabloid reports, were offering Keane as part-exchange in a hugely important deal. After the transfer window closed, Jol said, 'We want to attack. If you can't have Shaun Wright-Phillips because he is worth a fortune, then you have to do it another way.'

Instead, Tottenham signed Keane's fellow countryman Andy Reid from Nottingham Forest in a deal that also saw

Robbie Keane

Michael Dawson move to White Hart Lane. Another new addition during the month of January was Egyptian target man Mido on loan from Roma, which meant more competition for places up front. A controversial character, Mido made his Spurs bow in the 3–1 home victory over Portsmouth and instantly struck up a sound understanding with Keane. In an impressive debut, Mido scored twice, while Keane added the third with a delightful finish. Chasing on to Reid's probing through-ball, Keane hit the ball first time with the outside of his right foot to send a looping chip over the head of Portsmouth keeper Konstantinos Chalkias.

A week later, Keane followed that up with a goal in the comfortable 3–1 FA Cup fourth-round replay win over West Brom. Just before the break, referee Rob Styles awarded Tottenham a penalty after Albion keeper Russell Hoult had clashed with Spurs defender Stephen Kelly and, once Hoult had been taken off with concussion, Keane converted the spot-kick past replacement keeper Tomasz Kuszczak.

But, when Jol wanted to change formation at half-time, it was Keane and not Defoe who was substituted – leaving the Irishman confused about his situation at the club. After scoring two second-half goals, Defoe was assured by Jol that he would be rewarded with a lucrative new contract because, even though he was keeping Keane out of the side, the Londoner was earning an estimated £25,000 less per week.

Although not first choices for Jol, both Keane and Kanoute proved their credentials in the next Premiership game against Fulham at the Lane. With Defoe and Mido starting up front, Tottenham had struggled to make the breakthrough against the visitors until the double introduction of Keane and Kanoute. Kanoute drilled home a magnificent free-kick five minutes after coming on, while Keane doubled Spurs' lead with an injury-time strike.

Facing another selection dilemma, Jol told the press, 'It was fantastic to bring on two substitutes and for them both to score. That is what you hope for. But the fact that we have those options on our bench is a sign the club is getting better and better. I think this is a big club, and hopefully it will be even bigger in the future.'

For the FA Cup fifth-round replay at Nottingham Forest, Keane was not only given a starting berth in the side, but he was also given the captain's armband. The 24-year-old responded with his 14th goal of the season – continuing his scoring streak in every round of the competition – and he was the Man of the Match in a 3–0 victory at the City Ground. After the game, Jol revealed that Spurs fans kept demanding to know why Keane was not a permanent fixture in the starting line-up: 'When Robbie does not play I get letters saying that I should put him in the team. The fact is we have got four great strikers, the only negative is that we have to leave two of them on the bench.'

Unfortunately, Keane was one of the two left out of the side for the defeat at Southampton and also the FA Cup quarter-final exit at Newcastle before he was brought back into the team for the League loss at Charlton. Demoted back to the role of substitute for the visit of Manchester City, Keane was determined to make a huge impact when he eventually got on the pitch and he achieved this aim with style. Bursting with energy, Keane had only been involved in the game for four minutes when he outfoxed City keeper David James, before prodding the ball into the unguarded net.

Robbie Keane

Afterwards, Jol hailed his 'super sub'. 'It was good to have the option to bring on Robbie and it is a pleasure to know I have people like him on the bench who will not sulk because they are not starting, but give you 100 per cent.

'I had to wait until late on because we had a lot of knocks and bruises after three games in six days, and I knew that if I used my substitutes too early there might have been a problem. But I took a gamble, and Robbie is one of those quality players who will deliver the goods for you.'

But Keane's relationship with Jol hit an all-time low during the game at Birmingham City when he stormed off down the tunnel after being stuck on the bench for the whole 90 minutes. First-half injuries to Noe Pamarot and Reto Ziegler meant that Spurs had already used up two substitutions when, with the score at 1–1, Jol decided to refresh the team's attack – bringing on Mido instead of Keane. With his Spurs career in tatters, Keane was fined £10,000 by the club and forced to train with the reserves – it was Jol's way of telling him that his conduct was unacceptable.

Jol said, 'It's not about Robbie, it's about the club. We made some good changes and Mido had a great chance. Maybe Robbie was angry, but it's not a problem for us, it's his problem. It was difficult enough as it was.'

In a bid to publicly smooth over the falling-out, Keane said, 'Hopefully, I will be playing and scoring goals and we will see how far we get. You have just got to get on with it. You cannot moan about it.'

Despite taking a hard-line stance against his vice-captain, Jol played down stories of a rift. 'He [Keane] was upset because he didn't come on. I would normally put him on, especially at home, but this situation was different. We have had a chat. Nothing is more important than the club and he knows that.

The Entertainer

'It is important we stay strong as a unit and that is why I don't like it when players step out of line. But we dealt with that and he looked fresh again today in training. It is not about him accepting my decision to put him on the bench. He was a bit emotional, but he never causes me a problem. It is one of those things. He is a good player so there are always clubs interested in him, but I don't think there will be any changes because of this incident.

'I think he is happy to stay at Spurs. He knows he is an important player for us. He has been involved in a lot of games for us this season, more than Fredi Kanoute, and he is productive for us.'

Keane later shed light on why he had snapped at St Andrew's, telling the *Daily Mail*, 'The manager was OK. He told me it wasn't acceptable. It was a heat of the moment thing, something that happens to everyone. If I could change it, of course I would, but that's life.

'I had my reasons at the time. I was frustrated. I wasn't playing. But it's gone. The manager said what he had to say and I had to swallow my pride and hold my hands up. It was out of character. But I take everything like a man, the criticism, the praise. It's part of the job.'

Back on the pitch, Tottenham stayed in seventh spot after Keane's goal had secured a draw at Liverpool. Kanoute's touchline cross was headed in by the Irishman from close range and the goal helped to mend the dispute with Jol. He followed that effort up with a right-footed drive in a 1–1 home draw against struggling West Brom, but these two results seriously dented Tottenham's chances of getting into Europe.

In the four remaining games of the season, Spurs lost their way and, after defeats at Arsenal and Middlesbrough, finished in ninth position. Meanwhile, Keane chalked up an impressive 17 goals for Tottenham, but the stories linking him with a move away from White Hart Lane continued in the national press.

With a year remaining on his contract, Keane thought long and hard about his future and even dropped a hint that he would be willing to quit the Premiership in order to join his beloved Celtic in Scotland. After scoring the only goal in Jackie McNamara's testimonial at Celtic Park, Keane revealed that he would consider an approach from the Glasgow club – especially with his old boss Gordon Strachan in the Celtic hot-seat.

Representing a Republic of Ireland XI, Keane said, 'I was a Celtic fan growing up – I think most of the lads in the Ireland dressing room are – and I always said that one day I would love to play here. I'm not going to sit here and say that I'm not going to join Celtic; there are other clubs who have been linked with me as well, but as far as I'm concerned it's all speculation.

'I'm happy at Spurs, but if the manager or chairman come to me and say they no longer want my services, then I'm going to have to sit down and consider my future. I've been linked with a move to almost every club this summer. At the end of the day, I have got one year left and I'm happy there. If things change, who knows.'

So, at the end of another season, Keane's future was as uncertain as ever.

chapter ten

The Perfect Ten

'It's been a great year. I would be lying if I said it wasn't. It has gone really well for me. It's definitely up there with my best ever. To be named captain of your country and to get Player of the Year as well considering I didn't play the first 12 games of the season, it's something special. It has been a year I will never forget.'

Robbie Keane on the 2005/06 season

On 4 September 2004, Robbie Keane scored his 21st goal for the Republic of Ireland in a 3–0 win over Cyprus in a World Cup qualifier and equalled the record held by Niall Quinn. Despite missing a handful of chances in the first half, Keane took responsibility for the spot-kick awarded 10 minutes after the break and comfortably stroked it home – it had taken him just 53 games to achieve the career milestone.

After the game, Keane said, 'It was a special moment to equal the record and I would like to dedicate it to my father. It would be nice to beat it against Switzerland on Wednesday. I would so like to put the record out of sight – maybe then folk will stop asking me questions about it!'

At that point, the heroics of the World Cup were a distant memory – Mick McCarthy had resigned as national team boss in November 2002 and had been replaced by Brian

Robbie Keane

Kerr, while Roy Keane had been persuaded to return from the international wilderness after a two-year absence. The whole set-up had changed, but one factor remained constant – Robbie Keane was the country's main source of goals.

But, after failing to find the net in the next two World Cup qualifiers against Switzerland and France, the Irish media began to question whether or not the pressure of being a record-breaker in waiting had taken its toll on Keane. Then, on 13 October 2004 at Lansdowne Road, Keane silenced his doubters by pulling off a historic feat – he smashed the record with both goals in a 2–0 win over the Faeroe Islands.

It had taken him just six years to become his country's all-time leading goal-scorer. His early penalty had given him the title, but he extended the gap further with another razor-sharp finish to put the Republic of Ireland top of the group. After the game against the Faeroes, Keane beamed at being crowned the goal king of Ireland. 'Breaking the record is something special for me. I can't describe the feeling. I just love scoring goals and want to continue doing what I do best in the years to come. But I know that some young lad will come along to beat my record some day.'

The nation's former record-goal-scorer Don Givens, who struck 19 goals in the famous green shirt and was the title-holder for over a decade before being surpassed by 20-goal striker Frank Stapleton in 1990, hailed Keane's achievement. 'What Robbie has achieved for us in such a short period of time has been fantastic for Irish football. To have a front player with that goal-scoring ability has been great for the national team. He isn't the type of player who is just happy to hang around the box and wait for his chances – Robbie wants to be involved all the time. He has got great ability on the ball and he has been a wonderful player for us.'

Republic of Ireland Under-21 boss Givens added, 'I was lucky enough to have the record for a good number of years, but you always know that it is going to be broken. When Robbie came on the international scene and started to score goals at such a young age, it didn't take long to work out that Robbie would be the one to break it eventually.

'I was delighted for Big Niall [Quinn] when he did it because he gave great service to the country as well. But, even when Niall broke the record, he knew that it wouldn't be too long before Robbie did it. I'm delighted somebody with Robbie's attitude and enthusiasm is the record-holder.

'I think he'll go on and improve on that, be a huge part of the Irish team for a good number of years and make it very difficult for somebody to break the record in the future.'

After adding to his international goal tally with strikes against Croatia and Israel, Keane returned to club duties with Tottenham in the summer of 2005, knowing that it was a make-or-break season for him. Keane started off pre-season in thrilling form and played a prominent role for Tottenham who lifted the Peace Cup in a tournament staged in South Korea. Looking both hungry and committed, Keane scored a flurry of goals as Spurs won the competition and the Irishman admitted he could not wait for the season to start.

Keane said, 'It is not a case of putting down a marker, just making sure I'm as fit as I can be. I'm 25 years of age now and I want to knuckle down – not that I haven't before – as we have quality strikers here who are battling to start the season.

'I'm no different to the other three lads in that. I've come back feeling pretty sharp and I did a bit of work on my own over the summer. I feel good and I hope I am showing that in games. It's only pre-season, though, and the most important thing is to carry it through into the season. I want to keep going, keep myself fit and do what I did in Korea once the season starts.

'It was a good two weeks and, when you go to places like that, it is important you come back with something. We've come back with good fitness and, what we went there for, the trophy.'

During pre-season, Tottenham head coach Martin Jol had already rung the changes and sold Fredi Kanoute to Sevilla, while he brought in a big-name midfielder, Dutch international Edgar Davids; a young winger, Aaron Lennon from Leeds; and also England international Jermaine Jenas from Newcastle.

Following spells in Italy with AC Milan, Inter Milan and Juventus, Davids had been one of the most effective midfielders in world football and, at the age of 32, was signed by Jol to lead Tottenham's young side to glory. Although he was a recognised top-class talent, Davids also had a reputation for being an abrasive character, but Keane soon introduced him to the dressing-room banter at Spurs by wearing his specially made protective glasses out on the training pitch. A glaucoma sufferer, Davids soon saw the funny side of his new team-mate running around in his shades and it broke the ice, helping to galvanise team spirit. Even at the mature age of 25, Keane was still a prolific practical joker and at the heart of the humour within the Spurs camp.

But Keane was not laughing about his first-team future at Tottenham – his path to the starting line-up was blocked by an immoveable object, Jermain Defoe. Keane watched from the bench as Tottenham began the new campaign in style with a slick 2–0 home win over Middlesbrough. The goals were scored by Defoe and Mido. Despite coming on late, Keane looked out of synch with the rest of the side and it sparked fresh rumours that this would be his final year in a Lilywhite shirt.

After the game, Jol insisted Keane was still a part of his plans. 'Robbie scored 12 goals last year and is a gifted player. Everybody would like to have Robbie in their team, but it is impossible. People should not forget he was injured for a week. He started training last Thursday and, hopefully, Robbie can be involved in the next couple of games.

'We had the same situation last year. Sometimes Defoe or Mido are not happy. Mido reads all the speculation and sometimes comes into my office and says, "What are you doing?" Then I tell him that I am happy with him and the rest of the strikers.'

Behind the scenes at the club, sporting director Frank Arnesen had been head-hunted by Chelsea and the Dane took the Russian money and ran off to Stamford Bridge. His replacement was former Arsenal scout Damien Comolli, and Tottenham's chairman Daniel Levy was determined his bold, ambitious project, designed to bring European football back to the Lane, would not stray off course.

But the beginning to Keane's season was a stop-start affair – in for the goalless draw at Blackburn and then dropped to the bench for the home draw against Liverpool. In the away game at Aston Villa, Keane was warming up on the touchline when he saw team-mate Jermain Defoe miss a penalty after the home team had taken an early lead through James Milner. The game looked a lost cause for

Spurs – until Keane single-handedly saved the match with a piece of individual brilliance.

On as a second-half replacement for Andy Reid, Keane was hovering on the edge of the area as the ball bobbled around three Villa defenders. Rising supreme above the mêlée, Keane swayed his way intricately through the area in a blur of feet and then, in the same movement, lashed a fierce shot into the roof of the Villa net. There was no somersault celebration, though – Keane marked the occasion by running joyously back to the halfway line.

Afterwards, his old boss David O'Leary focused on Keane's strike: 'Keano? He's a sugarbag. He has been chatting to my dad, who came over for the game. I told him what he did was no way to treat a Dubliner and his ex-boss. I told him he should have stayed on the bloody bench.'

When O'Leary returned to his office for a post-match drink, he got a timely reminder of why his side hadn't won. Keane was in there supping a beer and telling anyone who would listen what a great goal it had been. O'Leary later told the *Birmingham Post*, 'He's a good friend. But he nearly drove me mad that day. He scored a wonderful goal and, by the time I'd finished with the press, I got back to my room and the little sod's in there eating my food, drinking my beer and telling me what a great goal it was.'

After a disappointing exit from the Carling Cup at League Two minnows Grimsby, Keane was once again left out of the starting line-up for the home win over Fulham. Then he was named amongst the substitutes for the trip to Charlton. With the score locked at two goals apiece, Keane came off the bench and once again influenced the outcome. After swapping passes with Defoe, the Irishman swept a right-foot shot into the top corner behind Charlton keeper Stephan Andersen to clinch victory.

As the age-old adage tells us, you can't please all of the people all of the time. Jol was now desperately juggling his strikers in a bid to maintain a degree of harmony and frankly said, 'Robbie is a big part of our set-up. I've told him that we have to fight his situation together. It's our problem. If Robbie wants to play for us, he will. He can only get his best form by playing and that's why I am happy he is playing for Ireland. If you don't play 90 minutes, you tend to lose your fitness a bit.

'He's not like the old Liverpool "super-sub" David Fairclough – he should be playing! Robbie came on against Aston Villa and scored for us earlier in the season, but it is always very difficult and I have to make a decision. Jermain scored a very important goal for us against Fulham on Monday. With players like Robbie on the bench, you always have a chance. Nine out of 10 times he will score.'

Jol also admitted that he could only play one of the smaller strikers – Keane or Defoe – with target man Mido if he wanted the right blend in attack. 'If they both play with Mido, one has to be on the left,' Jol said. 'But they all come to me and say they want be in the middle. It's a nice problem to have, keeping them happy.'

Despite not scoring in Tottenham's previous five games, Keane was given the nod to start in the away game at Premiership new boys Wigan, and he reacted to the challenge with a Man of the Match display. The game was only eight minutes old when Keane punished some indecisive Wigan defending to give Tottenham the lead. Summer signing Teemu Tainio sent an angled through-ball to Keane and he burst clear of his marker Arjan De Zeeuw.

Robbie Keane

As he charged towards the Wigan goal, Keane craftily dummied advancing keeper Mike Pollitt, before rolling the ball into the net. It was a typical Keane goal – a blend of flair, imagination and know-how.

But the most eye-catching part of Keane's performance was that it was founded on selfless industry – tracking back deep into his own half to help out the defence, he even had time to set up the winning effort from Davids.

With Keane re-established as the club's first-choice striker, Jol warned Defoe that he would have to wait for his chance to return to the starting line-up. Keane's patience had paid off and Jol said, 'I don't think there's a lot to choose between them. I chose Jermain for the first 12 games but, when he didn't score for a couple of games, I thought about Robbie. He is motivated and always trains hard. Robbie had waited 12 games, came on and scored that very important goal against Charlton, but I still played Jermain. So I thought, after last week, it was time for Robbie.

'If you see Jermain in training, his finishing is unbelievable, but Robbie is very gifted. As a team, we have a good spirit and the players respect each other. Jermain has seen that Robbie didn't moan and he must be the same.'

After grabbing the headlines against Wigan for all the right reasons, Keane's name appeared in the following weekend's tabloids after a training-ground bust-up with team-mate Edgar Davids. According to eye-witness reports, a dispute between the pair erupted in the lead-up to the home game against Sunderland and ended with Keane flooring the Dutchman with a punch. Both players escaped punishment from the club and the falling-out was resolved in time for Keane to bundle home Tottenham's second goal in the 3–2 win over the Wearsiders.

The Perfect Ten

With a regular run of starts under his belt, Keane's game flourished and it coincided with an impressive sequence of results for Tottenham. Putting in great performances game after game, Keane looked the part – a fully fledged Premiership star – as Tottenham emerged as serious contenders for a Champions League place. Playing at the peak of his powers, Keane was at his instinctive best at Middlesbrough when he scored Tottenham's opener in a 3–3 draw.

When Tottenham defender Lee Young-Pyo, a summer recruit from PSV Eindhoven, sent a swirling cross in from the left wing, Keane deliberately took a step back from Boro keeper Mark Schwarzer. Then, when the big Australian shot-stopper dropped the ball at his feet, Keane reacted by side-footing it into the unprotected net.

On Boxing Day, Keane delivered a knockout blow to relegation-bound Birmingham City when he won a penalty after being grappled to the floor by defender Matthew Upson, before clinically burying the resultant spot-kick in a 2–0 victory. After captaining Spurs to a win over Newcastle on New Year's Eve, Keane took his exhilarating form into 2006 and saw the New Year in with a bang – rifling a right-footed half-volley into the net in a 2–0 win at Manchester City.

With the transfer window wide open, Jol denied suggestions that Keane would be leaving the club and, despite genuine interest from Celtic and Everton, it seemed as if the Irishman was enjoying life at the Lane.

Before the FA Cup third-round tie at Leicester City, Keane spelled out his situation to the national press: 'I wasn't ready to move at the start of the season, I was quite happy to stay here. I could probably have chucked one in and said

I wanted to go, but I stuck it out and was determined to do well because I believe this club is going places. There is a great squad here and I want to be part of that. This Tottenham team reminds me of the team when I first signed for Leeds, a young side with great potential.

'At the moment we have great potential, with a lot of good young players like Aaron Lennon and Michael Dawson. If we can continue on the road we have been going recently, then this team can really go places. Potentially, we can do what Leeds did. That was a big squad and we also have some quality players who can't even get in the 16.'

Keane also felt obliged to quash rumours concerning whether or not he would decide to leave the club in the summer – he made it abundantly clear that he was happy at Spurs. 'Speculation will never go away. I can sign a new contract, and still the next year, if I'm not playing in a few games, it will be the same thing again. Ask any player – no one wants to be on the bench.

'Every player wants to play, that's what we are in this job for and I am no different. Of course, there were times when it was frustrating, but it was up to me to work hard out on the training pitch and take my chance when I got it.

'At the moment it seems to be going well. I'm happy, I am playing, scoring goals and the team is going tremendous at the moment. I've been at Tottenham longer than any other club, so of course I feel settled. And, if I'm not playing, I'm not just going to be seeking a move. I wasn't playing a year ago and yet I am still here. I still have two-and-a-half years left on my contract, which is a long way to go, and we'll just see what happens.'

Although Keane was settled off the pitch, Tottenham suffered, an embarrassing hiccup on it – getting knocked out of the FA Cup by Championship strugglers Leicester. In what was almost a carbon copy of the disastrous collapse against Manchester City in the same competition two years before, Tottenham were in control with a two-goal lead after 41 minutes. But somehow a spirited Leicester side clawed their way back into the tie and sent Spurs out of the cup with a stoppage-time winner from Mark de Vries.

After being humiliated in both cups, Tottenham could now concentrate solely on the Premiership and Jol's men were on course to qualify for Europe for the first time since 1999 with a Champions League spot still an achievable target.

Local rivals Arsenal had experienced an unusual season – mediocre in the Premiership, but excellent in the Champions League – and Tottenham had taken full advantage to climb into fourth spot. Despite experiencing indifferent results towards the end of January, Tottenham kept in touch with the chasing pack and a much-needed home win against Charlton kept the dream alive in February.

Even though he hadn't scored in five games, Keane was leading from the front and inspiring his younger team-mates to ground-breaking deeds on the pitch. Keane got back on the goal trail at a shell-shocked Sunderland, managed by his old international boss Mick McCarthy. But his first-half strike, after enterprising build-up play involving both Carrick and Defoe, was not enough to secure maximum points at the Stadium of Light when Sunderland snatched a late equaliser.

Following a largely unbroken run of starts, Keane was on the bench for the visit of Wigan, with Jol preferring to field Defoe and Mido. The Irishman came on to replace January signing midfielder Danny Murphy, but he could not prevent

Tottenham dropping another two precious points in a frustrating 2–2 stalemate at the Lane.

With the Premiership programme cancelled for a week because of international fixtures, Keane flew to Dublin to join up with the Republic of Ireland squad as the country's national team entered a new era. Keane's former mentor Brian Kerr was ousted from his post as Ireland's boss at the end of 2005 after the boys in green failed to qualify for the 2006 World Cup.

As a result, in January 2006, the FAI chose the nation's record cap-holder Steve Staunton to take charge, with former England boss Bobby Robson employed in an advisory capacity to help the 37-year-old adjust to the demands of international team management.

Staunton knew what Keane was all about from their experiences as team-mates at the 2002 World Cup, and the former Liverpool defender's first big decision was to name the Tallaght-born striker as his captain, starting with the home friendly against Sweden.

Keane was delighted. 'You always dream you will captain your country, but I didn't think it would come at the age of 25. At Spurs I was given the role of vice-captain and, when Ledley King has been out injured or whatever, I've been captain and I've really enjoyed it. But I'm very honoured and privileged to captain my country and I'm grateful to Steve for putting his trust in me, and believing I can lead this team. I certainly believe I can do it, so it's a case of looking forward to what is a new chapter in my career, and in Irish football also.

'I'm not going to change overnight. But now I've been given extra responsibility, I will have to lead by example on the pitch, as well as off it. That is the important thing. I will always give 100 per cent because I'm so passionate about my country. Even if I wasn't captain, I'd continue to do that.'

New boss Staunton outlined the reasoning behind his decision: 'I thought long and hard. Shay is the obvious candidate, but he leads from the front anyway. I don't think he needs the armband, and I wanted somebody out on the park, an outfield player. Robbie is a world-class player, you only have to look at the clubs he has played for; besides which our lads respect him.

'If you have the respect of the other players first and foremost that is a big plus, while the fans see him as an idol. They take to him; he responds and gets them going, like Shay does at the other end. He has certainly handled the responsibility at Spurs very well, and now I've given him a little challenge with this. He is up for it and I know he will be very proud to do that job.'

The honour prompted the greatest week in Keane's career. On Tuesday, Keane became his country's captain; on Wednesday, he scored the Republic of Ireland's second goal in a 3–0 win over Sweden; and, on Friday, he sorted out his future with his club – signing a new deal to keep him at Tottenham until 2010. He said, 'It is something that has been going on for a while. I am just happy it is now signed and I can look forward to a good future with Tottenham. This is a club that is going places. I believe that and it is the reason why I signed here from Leeds in the first place.

'I am flattered and delighted the club have given me the opportunity to sign. I am happy and have a lot of good friends here – players and staff. Making the right decision was important for me and I feel I have certainly done that.'

But the most memorable seven days in the 25-year-old's life were far from over. Tottenham entertained Blackburn

Robbie Keane

Rovers at the Lane and Keane produced a spellbinding display that evoked memories of Diego Maradona's performance for Argentina against England in the 1986 World Cup.

Nine minutes of the game had gone when Keane conjured up a breathtaking exhibition of individual genius. Collecting a quickly taken throw from Mido on the right-hand side of the area, Keane hooked the ball over the head of Blackburn's Robbie Savage and waited for the ball to bounce by the touchline. As Rovers captain Andy Todd came over to snuff out the danger, Keane cheekily flicked the ball back and, in one flowing movement, struck a superb half-volley past Blackburn keeper Brad Friedel to score an unbelievable goal. It was a brilliant solo effort and showed that, on his day, Keane is the most inventive striker in the Premiership.

But, while his first goal showed mesmerising skill, his second was controversial because Keane appeared to handle the ball, before smashing the rebound from a Tottenham free-kick into the net. Despite Blackburn's protests, the goal stood and Tottenham clung on to register a vital 3–2 triumph.

After a 2–1 defeat at eventual champions Chelsea, Tottenham came away from Birmingham with a 2–0 win – Lennon and Keane doing the damage – and the club took a significant step closer to Europe. Gifted and glorious, Keane was the match-winner in Tottenham's next three-point haul – a 2–1 home win over West Brom. Picking up a cutting pass from Carrick, Keane turned and dispatched a neat chip into the roof of the West Brom net; it was his 50th Premiership goal for Tottenham. But the Irishman was not finished. On 89 minutes, Defoe was fouled inside the area. Keane seized the ball and planted his spot-kick beyond West Brom keeper Tomasz Kuszczak to notch his 13th goal of the season.

With seven games remaining, Tottenham were on the verge of finishing above Arsenal and clinching the Premiership's fourth place. Keane admitted he was thrilled at the prospect of qualifying for the Champions League. He said, 'We are desperate to achieve that, but we'll keep our feet on the ground because there's still a long way to go. It means a hell of a lot to us. Champions League football is the best you can achieve as a player.'

Despite scoring with a header, Keane ended up on the losing side as Tottenham crashed to a disappointing 3–1 defeat at Newcastle United – the battle for fourth spot seemed destined to go down to the wire.

On the back of a healthy 2–1 victory at the expense of Manchester City, Keane kept Tottenham's momentum going with an arrow-straight penalty at Everton as the accuracy of his right boot proved decisive in a 1–0 win on Merseyside. But Tottenham's European challenge would not just go down to a photo-finish – it might hinge on the outcome of Arsenal's Champions League campaign, too.

Tragically for Spurs, if the team from Islington – set to face Villareal in the semi-finals – were crowned European Champions in May, then Tottenham would lose out, even if they finished in fourth spot. Keane said, 'Of course we don't want Arsenal to win the Champions League, but we knew the rules from the start. We'll watch their game against Villarreal on Wednesday. It would be a big blow if we did finish fourth and they ended up winning it. If we weren't in this position, we would want the English team to do well, but the fact is we are.'

After a narrow 2–1 home defeat at the hands of a Wayne

Rooney-inspired Manchester United, Tottenham prepared for their biggest game for over a decade – the away trip to Arsenal. Ahead of the last-ever Highbury showdown between the clubs, Keane's pre-match verdict was sought by the national press. He said, 'You want to get into the best competition and we would be gutted if we missed out. Hopefully, come 7 May, we'll be in the Champions League, but it's going to be tough.

'Not losing this game is the most important thing today. If we play the way we've played this season, we should have a great chance of that. We're looking over our shoulders – that's only natural – but we're trying to concentrate on ourselves. But this will be the biggest game for me since I've been here.'

With the entire country watching the biggest north London derby since 1993, Keane famously gave Tottenham the lead on the 66-minute mark, albeit in controversial circumstances. Arsenal's Emmanuel Eboue had collided with team-mate Gilberto just inside the home team's half and Carrick threaded a pass to Davids on the left flank as Spurs broke away and the referee waved play on. The experienced Dutchman steadied himself and picked out Keane at the back post with a low cross that the Irishman prodded past Arsenal keeper Jens Lehmann.

On the touchline, Arsenal boss Arsene Wenger was furious and almost came to blows with Martin Jol because he felt Tottenham should have kicked the ball into touch when Eboue collided with his team-mate. The incident added extra spice to an already explosive atmosphere, with Tottenham edging closer to a momentous triumph. But Arsenal's Thierry Henry struck a late goal to level the scores and Tottenham's overwhelming sense of frustration resulted in Davids being red-carded moments afterwards. The game finished all-square, leaving Tottenham's bid for a Champions League place hanging by a thread.

However, the fact that everyone associated with Spurs was left feeling deflated after only achieving a draw at Arsenal showed just how far Tottenham had progressed under Jol. After the final whistle, Wenger was still seething and publicly accused rival boss Jol of cheating and of lying about not seeing Eboue go down injured.

The gloves were off, but the barrel-chested Dutchman refused to resort to a slanging match. He told the press. 'I don't think a manager should behave like that because he called me a liar, and I am not a liar. I told him I hadn't seen it because I was watching Edgar Davids, and you can see it on television. I said to Edgar twice, "Don't be offside," and then we scored.'

The drama intensified as Arsenal booked a place in the Champions League final where they would face Barcelona on 17 May – 10 days after Tottenham's last Premiership game.

Tottenham defeated Bolton in the final home game of the season and a special ceremony was held on the pitch where Keane was presented with the club's Player of the Year award. It was party time at the Lane as Keane, who had been replaced by Lee Barnard after picking up an ankle injury, hobbled on to the pitch to receive his trophy. The crowd responded with a huge roar in recognition of his outstanding achievements over the course of the campaign.

As he thanked the fans, Keane could hardly be heard above the massive wall of noise. Supporters were singing a chant dedicated to their favourite player. To the tune of the Beatles song 'Yellow Submarine', Spurs supporters showed their appreciation for the Irishman by singing: 'We all dream of a team of Robbie Keanes.'

Robbie Keane

But Keane's twisted ankle was causing Jol and the club's medical staff serious concern ahead of the final-day test at FA Cup finalists West Ham. Jol said, 'Normally, you would be out for two or three weeks with that injury. Robbie is a very good healer and he will do everything to be there on Sunday, but it is a problem and a blow.'

After getting the all-clear from the team's physiotherapist, Keane travelled with the rest of Tottenham's squad to the plush Marriott Hotel in Canary Wharf where the players were staying ahead of the game at Upton Park. Then on the eve of the most important game in Tottenham's recent history, disaster struck when 10 players – including Keane – went down with a mystery virus that was initially believed to be food poisoning.

Keane, Michael Dawson, Edgar Davids, Michael Carrick, Calum Davenport, Radek Cerny, Tom Huddlestone, Lee Barnard, Aaron Lennon and Teemu Tainio were all vomiting and suffering from severe diarrhoea.

Jol found out at 5am in the morning and immediately held emergency talks with chairman Daniel Levy to try and sort out the catastrophe. Levy attempted to get the game postponed, or even put back a day, in order for Tottenham to be able to field a team of fit players, but the Premier League insisted that the show must go on.

Later Jol said, 'This is nothing that I have experienced before. The police and Health & Safety people were called, but I don't suspect foul play. I thought it would have been OK to play tomorrow for everybody, but I am appreciative that the Premier League didn't want that and West Ham have a game next weekend.'

Severely depleted by illness and stricken by the mystery bug, which inspectors found was not caused by food

The Perfect Ten

poisoning or the fault of the hotel, Tottenham's patched-up team took to the pitch against a charged-up West Ham side. Even though West Ham's team were thinking about their forthcoming FA Cup Final date against Liverpool, local pride was at stake and, from the kick-off, the east London side tore into a sickly Tottenham.

Carl Fletcher's crisp drive gave the home side an early lead which was cancelled out by West Ham old boy Defoe, who was booed throughout, and his strike coincided with news from Highbury that Arsenal were 2–1 down to Wigan. The Spurs fans crammed into the away end at the Boleyn Ground started to celebrate believing that, against all the odds, the Lilywhites were going to seize fourth spot.

But Arsenal fought back to win their game 4–2 and a late goal from West Ham's Yossi Benayoun increased Tottenham's already abject misery. As a result, Tottenham narrowly missed out on fourth spot by a meagre two points and had to settle for a place in the UEFA Cup – qualifying for the competition for the first time since 1999. But there was some light at the end of the tunnel for Tottenham's beleaguered support – Arsenal lost to Barcelona in the Champions League final.

Once the season was over, Keane captained the Republic of Ireland in a friendly match against Chile and, coincidentally, played alongside his elder cousin Jason Byrne. Byrne, a target man with League of Ireland club Shelbourne, had won his first international cap against Poland in April 2004 and, although he missed the game through injury, Keane was thrilled for his relative.

After the Poland game, Keane told the *People*, 'You want to see your family doing well and Jason's my cousin. We grew up together and to get called up while playing for

Shelbourne was obviously tremendous for him. I was absolutely delighted he got capped. Hopefully, if he keeps banging in the goals for Shels, he'll get another call-up.

'I'd love to play with him for Ireland and I think a lot of people would like to see that. It would be good for both of us.'

In the build-up to the 2006/07 season, Keane was confident Tottenham would improve further and emerge as regular challengers for a Champions League place. 'We should be happy [at what happened last season] and we would have taken it before the season started. We now want to do well in the UEFA Cup. The main thing is to improve each season. We did it last time and we'll be looking to do it again. We must continue to progress and, if we keep doing the same things we have been doing, we'll be all right.'

After scoring 16 goals in 25 Premiership starts, Keane admitted that he was satisfied with his own form ahead of the new campaign. 'I've been fortunate enough in that the season went really well for me. It is good when the team is doing well because it makes your job a little bit easier.

'The thing I try to do each season is better what I have done in previous years. If I can continue that, then hopefully I will have a good season again.'

Since making his senior debut in 1997, Keane's flair and imagination have remained constant, but, as he has reached maturity, he has adjusted his individual game to suit the needs of his team. Keane's former boss at Wolves, Colin Lee, has followed the Irishman's career with interest since selling him to Coventry in 1999 and he has recognised a change in the striker's on-field behaviour. Speaking in the summer of 2006, Lee said, 'I think, having seen Robbie play last season and watched him mature over a period of time, he is now looking a very good player. He now realises how important it is to play as part of a team rather than as an individual. He has gained so much in his play.

'When he was younger, he always used to say that he was the entertainer. That was how he played his game. I always felt that, once the penny dropped, he could be a team player, too. He can more or less be compared to Joe Cole in that respect. Joe Cole has always been a fantastic individualist, but it was always essential that he turned out to be a team player as well. I think Robbie has done that now and is a complete team player, but one who has the flair and ability to be able to do something different.'

But, in Lee's opinion, one of Keane's traits has remained unchanged since 1997 – his likeable personality. 'He is a fantastic player and the good thing about Robbie is that he is a fantastic lad as well – it has never affected him and I think it is a big plus to Robbie Keane. He doesn't forget where he came from and I think that is a big plus as a player and also as a person.'

By 28 September 2006, Keane had still to get off the mark for the season, but he assured the press two days before a UEFA Cup tie against Slavia Prague that he was not worried by the statistic. As he explained, 'When I was younger, I would have worried about not scoring for a few games, but I am not having any nightmares about it now.

'I am more experienced and I know that, as a striker, the absolute worst thing you can do is get frustrated because that won't make things better. Now that I am older, I realise that all strikers go through spells like this and, once you get one, you tend to get another and they start to flow.

'The strange thing is that I feel really good and sharp and maybe it is just a case of getting an easy tap-in and going on from there. But I know now these things happen in football and I am not too worried about it.'

With the captain's armband on, Keane led Tottenham out for the first UEFA Cup tie at White Hart Lane since 1999, with the Lilywhites defending a slender one-goal first-leg lead against Slavia Prague. In a breathless game, Keane was starved of any decent service and even saw his first-half header smash into the side netting of the Slavia goal.

But he never stopped trying to spark the game into life and he was rewarded 10 minutes from time. Technical ability can only take you so far in football, the truly great players are blessed with an in-built mixture of unshakeable self-belief and persistence and Keane showed both those attributes to score the winner.

A right-wing cross was pumped into the area, the ball was chested down to Keane and he emphatically lashed a shot into the net.

Sliding head first across the rain-soaked turf, the Lane's best-loved entertainer had stolen the show and he celebrated the goal in the same way that he always plays his football – with a smile on his face.

Epilogue

There has never been a dull moment in the career of Robbie Keane and, between October and December 2006, his fortunes fluctuated from heady highs to crushing lows.

On the international front, Robbie experienced the morale-sapping nadir of captaining the Republic of Ireland to a tortuous Euro 2006 qualifier defeat at the hands of lowly Cyprus. But he redeemed himself by scoring a memorable hat-trick in the final soccer match staged at Lansdowne Road – a 5–0 demolition of San Marino.

Afterwards, Keane beamed: 'I've not hit a hat-trick for Ireland before so it was nice to do so on our last night at Lansdowne Road. I've a lot of great memories from there but it's important now that we move on to better things and that we better ourselves and hopefully tonight can be the start of that for us.'

In the Lillywhite shirt of Tottenham, Keane has become

the living embodiment of the mission statement that came from the club's Irish captain, the late Danny Blanchflower. A passionate football purist, Blanchflower had once summed up the spirit of the club when he said: 'The great fallacy is that the game is first and last about winning. It is nothing of the kind. The game is about glory, it is about doing things in style and with a flourish, about going out and beating the other lot, not waiting for them to die of boredom.'

After forging a lethal front partnership with £10.9m summer recruit Dimitar Berbatov – a Bulgarian target man signed from Bayer Leverkusen – Keane scored a breathtaking goal in Spurs' 3–1 UEFA Cup win over Club Brugge at White Hart Lane. Latching onto Berbatov's volleyed through-ball, Keane glided upfield before picking his spot with a measured shot into the net to cap off a glorious night in N17.

But Keane's finest moment of the season arrived in the historic triumph over Chelsea – ending a 16-year jinx during which Tottenham did not beat the west London club. The 26-year-old didn't actually end up on the scoresheet but he laid on the decisive goal with some mesmerisingly subtle skill that made his marker, Chelsea defender Khalid Boulahrouz, actually topple onto his backside. Picking up the ball on the halfway line, Keane shuffled his feet and proceeded to embark on a purposeful run up the left flank with Boulahrouz in close pursuit. But Keane slowed the ball down and sold more dummies than a persuasive mannequin salesman – leaving Boulahrouz off balance and out of the picture. With an accurate cross Keane expertly picked out Spurs team-mate Aaron Lennon, who smashed his winning effort into the roof of the Chelsea net.

Off the pitch, Keane made front page news back in his native Republic of Ireland when he announced his engagement to long-term girlfriend Claudine Palmer on 24 October, what would have been his late father's 54th birthday. The couple, who have been together for six years, are expected to wed back in Dublin during the summer of 2007 and Claudine told the *Irish Sun*: 'I love Robbie very much and I am really looking forward to planning the wedding – but we have yet to set a date.'

Keane also shed some further light on his second special talent, singing, and admitted that he has a karaoke machine in his Hertfordshire home. Keane told *Hotspur* magazine: 'I've got karaoke in the house. Well, I'm Irish and I was brought up with that kind of thing, singalongs. It's second nature and I don't feel self-conscious at all. I've been known to bang out a few tunes. The one I sing most is a Garth Brooks number called "If Tomorrow Never Comes".'

Robbie's final goal of 2006 certainly had Tottenham fans singing his praises, although his joy was short-lived. After coming on as a late substitute, he had only been on the pitch for three minutes when he scored the winner against Middlesbrough at White Hart Lane in December. He had been fouled by Middlesbrough defender Jonathan Woodgate and, with the visitors' preparing for a long-range free-kick, Spurs midfielder Tom Huddlestone cleverly picked out Keane with a short pass.

Taking one touch in order to gather momentum, Keane unleashed a rasping right-footed drive into the top corner of the Boro net to single-handedly win the game and the crowd's applause. But his on-field heroics ultimately proved to be costly – Keane sustained a serious knee injury that kept him sidelined for six weeks. The problem was officially diagnosed as strained medial ligaments and Keane was far from happy with the setback.

Robbie Keane

'I am absolutely devastated,' he said. 'Ask the physios, I am the worst person to be around when I'm injured, I'm not good at all. I just love playing games and this is a kick in the teeth for me. I am just gutted and have just got to work hard to get back as soon as I can.'

In an era when the money-saturated latest incarnation of the beautiful game threatens to permanently sever the once cherished bond between punter and player, the dark haired Irishman with the quick feet has kept it wholly intact with his down-to-earth approach and rapport with the fans.

As he learnt from an early age, a great entertainer never forgets the needs of his audience. So taking into account the fact he has still yet to reach his career peak, the best is probably still yet to come from the player who is idolised on the Emerald Isle and also celebrated at White Hart Lane.